DAVID WESTERMAN + NICHOLAS D. BOWMAN + KENNETH A. LACHLAN

D1004137

One-Time
Online
Access Code
Included

INTRODUCTION TO
MEDIATED
COMMUNICATION

SOCIAL MEDIA AND BEYOND

SECOND EDITION

Kendall Hunt
publishing company

Book Team

Chairman and Chief Executive Officer   Mark C. Falb
President and Chief Operating Officer   Chad M. Chandlee
Vice President, Higher Education   David L. Tart
Director of Publishing Partnerships   Paul B. Carty
Senior Developmental Coordinator   Angela Willenbring
Vice President, Operations   Timothy J. Beitzel
Permissions Editor   Carla Kipper
Cover Designer   Faith Walker

Cover images © Shutterstock.com

Kendall Hunt
publishing company

www.kendallhunt.com
Send all inquiries to:
4050 Westmark Drive
Dubuque, IA 52004-1840

We'd like to dedicate this book to a few people.

First, we'd like to dedicate this book to our advisor, Dr. Ron Tamborini. Ron, you are a shepherd who takes lost graduate students and makes them a little less lost at least. Thank you for all your hard work in helping us be a lot better than we would have been without you. Readers: if you like this book, and you see Ron on the street, shake his hand. If you don't like this book, shake his hand anyway . . . it's not his fault.

Second, we'd like to dedicate this book to our friend, the late Dr. Paul D. Skalski. Paul, you left us too early, and we miss you. We tried to keep rockin' out for you with this book. We think you would have liked it.

For our second edition of the book, we'd also like to thank both Paul Carty and Angela Willenbring with Kendall Hunt for their encouragement and support, our colleagues and students for using and enjoying the book in their classes, and for their critical-yet-thoughtful feedback on the first edition. We also owe a very special thanks to Kara McArthur for her remarkably constructive and precise review of our revision drafts—and for teaching us a few things about the English language that we were not aware of. Collectively, you've all reminded us that perhaps it's time for us to shift from "mass" and "interpersonal" to a more inclusive course focused on the growth of "mediated" communication.

Brief Contents

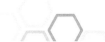

Contents

Computers and You: Technology as a Tool for Communication

Today, for under $1,000, one can purchase a portable personal computer with more computational power than could have been delivered 30 years ago by a $10,000,000 machine the size of an average living room. It is informative to consider what the current state of the automobile industry would be had similar progress been made over the past 30 years in that domain . . . each of us would be able to buy a Rolls-Royce today for roughly $2.75; it would get nearly 3,000,000 miles to the gallon and would deliver enough power to tow an aircraft carrier.

This is a quote from Stanford social psychologist Mark Lepper. If we told you that this quote was from last year, it probably would not surprise you, as computers and computing power have advanced very quickly in your lives (as well as ours). However, if we told you that this quote is from 1985 (Lepper, p. 1)—only a few years after the successful development of the Apple II home computer and the earliest IBM personal computers—it may blow your mind. To think that those simple gray boxes with green and black screens in our elementary and high schools (thinking of the authors' experiences in the late 1980s and early 1990s) might have been superior technologies was a stretch; to think of how today's tablet PCs and smartphones—capable of streaming live video, displaying rich and vibrant three-dimensional graphics, and storing enough music to fill entire record stores—compare to those technologies is astounding.

Perhaps more importantly, however, this quote highlights two things we want to discuss to establish why the book you are about to read is organized the way it is. The quote of course suggests that computers have advanced to amazing levels of processing and storage capacity in a relatively short period. So, what does this mean for how we understand them? First, it means that computers allow us to do things today that were barely dreamed of 60 years ago. The use of computers and other communication technologies in our daily lives has evolved from simply entering mathematical formulas into a large mainframe and waiting for the computer to "compute" the answer, to allowing us a personal space in which to share our innermost thoughts and feelings on a large network with others. Many of these more recent developments fall under the category of mediated communication (MC)—a central theme of our textbook that will be detailed more throughout these pages. Second, the rate of change for computers is so fast that it is difficult to keep up with it. For example, if this book had been published in 2003, it would have no coverage or discussion of social networking sites such as Twitter or Facebook, as these two sites did not yet exist, and the first edition discussed Google Glass, a technology that has now come and gone. Thus, not only is computing technology evolving to encompass more and more facets of our daily social lives, but the rate at which this evolution is happening seems to have accelerated drastically.

However, what does not seem to change as fast are people—the humans using these computers. As a species, we have pretty much the same goals as we always have had, and we use the tools around us to accomplish these goals. For us, technology in general, and CMC technologies specifically, might be understood as tools that serve a distinctly human function: to help us communicate with one another in various ways. This is why this book takes the approach that it does—an approach that communication scholars Joseph Walther and Art Ramirez refer to as a functional approach. By focusing attention on

how people use computer technology to accomplish their communication functions, we hope to help you understand CMC in a way that will not only be useful today, but will also be useful in the future. Soon, the technology may be radically different, but the people using it likely will not be, and we think this will help you appreciate both today and tomorrow. That is, studying the technologies themselves seems flawed given that technologies evolve at a rate often faster than our ability to really grasp them. However, studying the functional usage of technologies as communication tools does not seem to change, and certainly not as rapidly. After all, if we cannot satisfy a given goal with our current tools, we simply invent a new one; such has been the human story since the invention of the wheel as a means to transport ourselves and our things quickly from one location to the next.

Although there are numerous functions for which people can use technology outside of communication, as communication scholars we are going to focus attention on how technology is used to satisfy four major reasons for communication in general: informational goals, such as seeking out or sharing knowledge about our world; relational goals, such as creating and sustaining acquaintances, friendships, and even romance; persuasive goals, such as crafting or responding to purposive attempts to influence each other; and entertainment goals, such as engaging in leisure and play. Although the technology may change with each passing year, we believe that it is likely that people will continue to use these newer technologies for each of these four reasons.

We hope this book provides a great starting point for you to think about MC, as it seems that is a topic that will only continue to become more important to have a good grasp of, both for business as well as personal pursuits. We will guide you through some of what we think are important topics, and we encourage you to learn more about these and other topics related to MC by engaging your course instructor, your fellow students, and us as the authors of this text. In fact, we openly encourage you to check our textbook Web site (www.grtep.com) from time to time, as we will be posting and updating things now and then, including links to growing social media applications related to our textbook and to the general study of MC. And in true Web 2.0 fashion, we will even encourage you to participate early and often.

David Westerman

North Dakota State University

Kenneth A. Lachlan

University of Massachusetts Boston

Nicholas David Bowman

West Virginia University

References

Lepper, M. R. (1985). Microcomputers in education: Motivational and social issues. *American Psychologist, 40,* 1–18.

David Westerman

(Ph.D., Michigan State University, 2007) is an Assistant Professor in the Department of Communication at North Dakota State University. His research and teaching focuses on communication technologies and how people use them to accomplish their goals. His research has been published in such outlets as *Journal of Computer-Mediated Communication, Cyberpsychology, Behavior, and Social Networking, Computers in Human Behavior,* and *Internet and Higher Education.* Dave is currently enjoying the beautiful climate of Fargo, North Dakota with his wife Catherine. He is still anxiously awaiting the day when the Buffalo Sabres finally can hoist Lord Stanley's Cup.

Nicholas David "Nick" Bowman

(Ph.D., Michigan State University) is an Associate Professor of Communication Studies at West Virginia University, where he founded and currently serves as a Research Associate in the department's Interaction Lab (#ixlab). His research focuses on the psychological and sociological impacts of communication technologies—specifically digital media—and how these impacts have influenced the human communication process. Nick has authored or co-authored nearly four dozen original empirical studies and a dozen book chapters on the subject, with much of his work focused on video games and social media applications. He currently serves on the editorial board of several research journals, including *Media Psychology* and *New Media & Society,* is an editor for both *Journal of Media Psychology* and *Communication Research Reports,* and contributes regularly as a reviewer for the American Library Association's *CHOICE Magazine.* In 2016, he was awarded a WVU Foundation Outstanding Teacher award, and was also named a 2016 Eberly College of Arts and Sciences Outstanding Teacher.

Nick is a native of St. Louis, where he split his time between the bohemian bustle of University City and the creeks and hollers of suburban-rural Jefferson County. After graduating from the University of Missouri-St. Louis (B.A., '03; M.A., '04) he worked as a newspaper reporter and in government relations before leaving the state to pursue his doctorate. He currently lives in the heart of Morgantown, West Virginia with his partner—in research, in the lab, and in life—Jaime. Both are avid travelers and collectors of history and popular culture artifacts, and when they're not in the office (physically or digitally), they can usually be found on the road, searching the country (here or abroad) for remnants of entertainment culture past and present to add to their expanding collection of comic books, video games, and movie posters.

Ken Lachlan

(Ph.D., Michigan State University) is an Associate Professor in the Department of Communication at the University of Connecticut. Prior to his academic career, he worked in public radio and television promotions for several years. His research interests include the psychological effects of mass media, health and risk communication, media violence, and new media technologies. Recent publications have appeared in *Journal of Broadcasting and Electronic Media, Media Psychology,* and *Journal of Applied*

Communication Research, to name a few. Ken has also served as a consultant statistician for various companies and government agencies. He holds a dual B.A. in Communication and Sociology from Wake Forest, an M.A. in Mass Communication from Bowling Green State University, and a Ph.D. in Communication from Michigan State. An avid jogger and diehard hockey fan, Ken lives in Boston with his wife and their cat.

CHAPTER 1

What Is (Mediated) Communication?

So, a guy walks into a bar . . .

This is a phrase that many of you have likely heard, as it is the beginning of many jokes (both good and awful). It is also a situation that is not terribly uncommon. However, you may be thinking: Why is a book about mediated communication (MC) starting out with the opening from a bad joke? Is that a sign of things to come for the rest of this book? Hopefully you will not find the rest of this book to be a bad joke. However, if we expand upon this common situation and consider what happens when a guy (or anyone really—we don't want to suggest that only men frequent bars and taverns) walks into a bar, we can come to see that it is also a place that is ripe for beginning the study of communication (again, both good and awful). In order to get to that point, we must first begin by talking a little bit about what communication is.

Before beginning this chapter, consider the following questions:

- What is communication?
- What differentiates mass communication and interpersonal communication?
- What is computer-mediated communication?
- Why is it important to consider messages, senders, and receivers?
- What is narrowcasting?

What Is Communication?

Communication
There are many definitions of communication. McCroskey and Richmond (1996) defined it as the process by which we stimulate meaning in the minds of others using both verbal and nonverbal messages.

Audience-centered process Making sure to consider your receivers' goals, attitudes, knowledge, and so on when attempting to influence them through communication.

There are many definitions of communication. For example, on one side of things, communication is somewhat narrowly defined as any action or actions that a person consciously uses to affect another's behaviors (Miller, 1966). This suggests that communication is a deliberate and intentional process—we communicate to share information with others when and only when we want to, and when we want to get something out of another person. Another extreme argues that we "cannot not communicate" (Watzlawick, Beavin, & Jackson, 1967) and suggests that communication is an unintentional and unavoidable process—we communicate as a natural part of being human. However, we like the definition offered by James McCroskey and Virginia Richmond (1996), who suggest that communication is "the process by which one person stimulates meaning in the mind(s) of another person (or persons) through verbal and non-verbal messages." (p.3)

Taking a closer look at this definition by McCroskey and Richmond can help us understand more about communication. First, it is a process. The Merriam-Webster dictionary defines a process as "a series of actions that produce something or that lead to a particular result." Seen in this way—and as partly suggested in the Miller definition previously—communication is an intentional and goal-driven process. Of course, it is also ongoing, constantly changing, and made up of several component parts. For example, consider what might happen if you unintentionally yawned on a first date with somebody. Your yawn might be interpreted by your partner as a suggestion that you are uninterested in the date (even though the act of yawning itself is a physiological response your body has in order to increase the amount of oxygen in your bloodstream and even help regulate the temperature of your brain), and they might communicate back their disapproval or concern for your disinterest. This feedback from your partner would then set into motion a process by which, assuming you were interested in the date, you would use a series of verbal and nonverbal assurances that you were enjoying yourself.

Second, the goal of communication is to get some meaning across to another person or persons. This also suggests that effective communication is best thought of as an audience-centered process; that is, one needs to think about how best to get a desired meaning across to the target. Considering our first date example (and assuming that you wanted the date to continue after your yawn), you would need to think of the different ways in which you could communicate to your partner that you were enjoying yourself even though you might have appeared disinterested. For example, you might explain the yawn away as a result of a long day in class or at work, or you might choose to talk about something unrelated to your yawning to try to change the subject to something more interesting to your partner.

Third, communication can be done through both verbal and nonverbal messages. Considering our first date example once more,

You might explain your yawning as a long day at work, but others might see it as a lack of interest in having a conversation.

you might reassure your partner by reaching out to give them a hug or to touch their shoulder or neck (nonverbal messages) or you might simply tell them plainly "I'm really having a great time with you tonight!" or "Please don't read anything into my yawning, I'm so glad that we went out today." To this, we would also like to add that written messages can be used to stimulate meaning in another person. For example, both handwritten memos and typed postings on another person's Facebook wall can be used to stimulate meaning in another person, so we would remind you that written communication is important for communication as well. Revisiting our first date example one last time, you might send your partner a series of snaps through Snapchat the next morning thanking them for date (and perhaps, planning another one).

As noted previously, communication is a process, and as a process, it is composed of many components. The next section of this chapter will break down our understanding of communication into several components that can be more clearly analyzed. It begins with a discussion of a more traditional means of understanding communication processes and goes on to address the ways in which advances in communication technologies have challenged these conventions.

Components of Communication

As a process, communication transactions have many components. In general, we might say that a source encodes a message and sends it through a channel to a receiver, who then decodes it. The receiver provides feedback. Noise can limit the effectiveness of a message in stimulating the desired meaning in another person's mind (see MC in Action: The Shannon-Weaver Model of Communication).

Thinking about the guy who walks into the bar example from the beginning of the chapter can help illustrate each component in this model. A source is the place from which communication originates. This is the person or entity that a message comes from and who attempts to stimulate meaning in someone else's mind. In our example, the communication source is the guy who walks into the bar.

Encoding is the process that a source goes through when determining what message to send. A source has some desired meaning he or she wants to get across to someone else, but there are many possible messages to choose from. Different symbols may result in different meanings inferred by the receiver. Thus, the source must determine how they will turn a desired meaning in their own mind into a message that they hope will stimulate the desired meaning in another person's mind. For example, the guy who walks into a bar may notice an attractive person at the bar, and they want this person to know that they are interested in them. They now must consider how to prepare a message that conveys "attractiveness" and "interest" to another person; encoding is this process of preparation.

A message is simply the symbols that a person uses to try to create a particular meaning. Let us assume that the guy who walks into a bar wants to show the attractive other person that he is a creative and clever person and that he is interested. He might ask the other person, "Hey. Are you from Tennessee? Cause you're only the only 10 I see." Thus, the language in his message—the actual English words themselves—would be the message (although it might not end up as the best message, as it might communicate a lack of creativity and cleverness and might be perceived to be offensive).

Source The person/place/thing from which communication originates.

Encoding A process of choosing the symbols to use to attempt to get a meaning across to another person; turning meaning into symbols.

Message The actual symbols used in an attempt to share meaning.

Channel What a source uses to send a message through.

Receiver The target of a message; whose mind the source wants to stimulate meaning in.

Decoding A sort of reverse process to encoding; turning symbols back into meaning.

Feedback Messages sent back to a source about the original message sent.

Noise Something that impedes successful transmission of a message. This can be literal noise, but can be other things as well.

MC IN ACTION

THE SHANNON-WEAVER MODEL OF COMMUNICATION

Perhaps one of the most widely used models of communication is the Shannon–Weaver model, first proposed in 1948. Claude Shannon was working for Bell Labs—a company involved in the earliest telephone systems—when he conceived of a mathematical model for representing communication through technology, introducing the earliest concepts of encoding and decoding messages so that they could be sent efficiently through a medium while reducing noise in the transmission that could disrupt the process (in this case, the electronic signals representing the human voice transmitted through a telephone). Warren Weaver later added the notion of feedback—that is, information communicated from the receiver to the sender—to this model (see Shannon & Weaver, 1949). Although originally designed for telephone communication, this model has been applied to other forms of communication as well and is often referred to as the "mother of all models" for its application to understanding communication, education, psychology, and even electronic engineering.

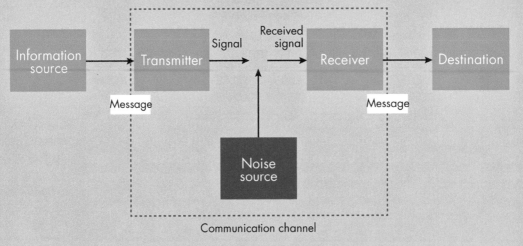

From: "A Mathematical Theory of Communication" by C. E. Shannon. *The Bell System Technical Journal*, Vol. 27, pp 379–423, July, 1948. Copyright© 1948 John Wiley and Sons, Inc. Reprinted by permission.

The channel is what is used to get the message from the sender to the receiver; given the subject of this textbook, we might also refer to this as the medium. For our example, the guy walking into the bar and giving his "Tennessee . . . 10 I see" comment is using verbal communication, so we might call the channel face-to-face. Of course, our guy could have chosen to write these words on a bar napkin or sent them as a text message, with each channel requiring a different type of encoding (pronouncing English words compared to legibly scribbling on a tissue or sending a text-conversation to a cell phone) and each channel having a potentially different impact on how the message is received. To speak of media in more detail, we might consider that, in many situations, the source will have multiple options to choose from and may try to use multiple channels to convey the same

MC IN ACTION

Is Communication Easy?

Many people might suggest that communication is easy, both as an area of study and as an everyday practice. However, think about it . . . if it is so easy, why are so many people seemingly so bad at it? And why do people who have known each other for a long time, such as married couples, often seem to have problems communicating? Consider the nature of encoding and decoding. One person has a meaning they would like to stimulate, and they have to choose the right symbols to try to stimulate that exact meaning in another person's mind. This is not easy and it takes a lot of effort and practice. In fact, when considering all of the things that could potentially be misrepresented in communication—from a facial expression to the tone of one's voice to using a word with multiple meanings for different people to even the slightest leaning to one side or another—we might start to wonder how communication is ever successful!

message. For example, a person may follow up an e-mail to their boss with a phone call to see if she has received the e-mail yet. Receivers may even attempt to make choices about which channel they would like to get a message through when they know someone is likely to try to send them one (either to the benefit or detriment of the source of the message).

Receivers are those who are the intended targets of a message. They are the ones to whom a source attempts to get a meaning across. In our example, this would be the attractive person standing at the bar (intended receiver). However, it is important to consider that there can be other receivers who get the message and who are not the intended target. This would be anyone else who overhears the cheesy pickup line (unintended receivers) and for whom the entire scenario might be seen as either hilarious or romantic (depending on the receiver). The increased possibility of unintended receivers becomes potentially more important to consider in today's social media age.

Decoding is the opposite process of encoding. When the receiver gets the symbols sent by the source through the chosen channel, they must try to understand what was meant by the symbols chosen. Of course, the meaning that a receiver decodes from the symbols may not be the same one intended by the source (see MC in Action: Is Communication Easy?). For example, if the attractive target thinks that this cheesy pickup line is just an attempt by the source to impress or entertain his friends, the receiver will likely decode a meaning that is very different from the one intended by the source.

Feedback comprises messages sent back to the sender by the receiver about the original message. For example, if the attractive person at the bar from our story slaps our guy across the face, this should tell him something about the pickup line he attempted. Likely, it communicates that the message was not processed as intended, or if it was, the receiver does not share the same sentiment as the sender!

Finally, noise is anything that gets in the way of successful message transmission. Successful transmission would exist when the meaning attempted by the

sender is the exact same meaning that the receiver gets. This can be literal noise (in our example, the bar is crowded and loud so the receiver does not even hear the cheesy pickup line), but it can also be plenty of other things that get in the way. For example, psychological noise can exist as well. If the receiver of the pickup line has had a rough day and is just not in the mood to listen to stupid pickup lines from anybody, this would likely lead to a different meaning being taken from the message than the one intended. Indeed, a central concern for Shannon and Weaver was reducing noise in telephone transmission lines so that signals would not be disrupted.

Mass Mediated Communication

Before going on to discuss the concept of MC in more depth, let us first dive into two major areas of communication that are often considered distinct from each other in the field of communication: mass mediated communication and interpersonal communication.

When most people talk about mass mediated communication, they are usually referring to newspapers, radio and television stations, and so on. Thus, they focus on the channels, or media, typically associated with this type of communication. Although each of these channels would fall into a working definition of mass mediated communication, we borrow from Chaffee and Metzger (2001), who offer three characteristics of "mass" communication: it uses mass production, there is a lack of individual (audience) control, and it is finite in its available channels.

Mass production means that the products made—in this case, the messages—are made for large and often anonymous audiences, with the goal being to attract as big of an audience as possible. Similar to an assembly line, mass messages are produced in a "one size fits all" manner to appeal to as many people as possible in a standardized way. Some have referred to this phenomenon as appealing to the lowest common denominator, usually as a criticism of this type of programming. For example, most modern U.S. newspapers are written to a fourth or sixth-grade reading level to ensure that the largest possible audience can read the news without barriers, but writing stories at a lower reading level also means that they are sometimes oversimplified and might not present in-depth coverage of societal events. Just as is demonstrated in our definition of communication, the choice of encoding can alter how a message is received.

When we talk about a lack of individual control, we are suggesting that you as an individual audience member or media user have very limited control over the content provided and over how you consume it. The content itself is created by large, anonymous companies and organizations with very little input from audience members before creation (Nielsen ratings and the like may be seen as audience input after creation and broadcast to help set advertising rates and inform future creation of content). Also, if you want to consume mass communication, you have to do it on the schedule created by the content creators. For example, for most of television's history, if you wanted to watch a particular television show, you needed to be in front of a television at a particular time. For the most part, traditional mass media audiences were at the mercy of the media production company and those running the channel in terms of when, where, and how a media product was consumed.

Mass communication is also finite in its available channels. In crafting messages for mass consumption, there are only a few channels that are actually able to reach large audiences. Highway billboards, major metropolitan newspapers, and radio and television signals are among the channels most easily accessed by large populations. Mass communication works with limited bandwidth. Bandwidth is the amount of capacity a channel has to carry a signal/information. Be it the plywood surface of a highway billboard, a particular television or radio frequency, or the amount of space on a newspaper page, each channel is physically limited in the amount of content it has, and (usually) having more content is more expensive. Therefore, only a limited amount of content can be produced and broadcast through mass mediated channels.

Mass communication Communication from a singular and impersonal source to a large and anonymous audience.

Bandwidth The amount of capacity a channel has to carry a signal/information.

Interpersonal Communication

In general, interpersonal communication differs from mass mediated communication in at least two ways. First, we can consider the intended audience size. Although mass mediated communication considers messages meant for large audiences, interpersonal communication considers messages that are exchanged between much smaller numbers of people, such as friends, romantic couples, or a small work group. Second, we can consider the nature of the relationship that typically exists between the source and receiver(s) of a message. With mass mediated communication, messages come from large and largely anonymous organizations, and it is unlikely that the source really knows any of the receivers of the message beyond a general "understanding" of the audience, such as their age, sex, and geographic location. However, sources and receivers of interpersonal communication are likely to have some understanding of each other—they very possibly already have a relationship together—and this understanding and relationship gives them far more information from which to craft meaningful messages for each other. Although this book really does not focus on the dynamics of interpersonal communication (there are entire Communication Studies courses devoted to the topic, and we would suggest that you consult your school's course catalog for such courses), the discussion of interpersonal communication is important here, because you can already suspect that a great deal of interpersonal communication tends to take place through mediated technologies. Perhaps most importantly, while you might assume that this is a new phenomenon (with smartphones and social media), understand that people have used media to communicate with each other for a very long time—from smoke signals to written love letters! (see MC in Action: From Bill to Bernadean: 70 Years Later).

Interpersonal communication Communication between a small number of people (usually, two individuals) who share some sort of relationship.

Interpersonal communication considers messages that are exchanged between smaller numbers of people, usually two.

© Stuart Jenner/Shutterstock.com

MC IN ACTION

FROM BILL TO BERNADEAN: 70 YEARS LATER

"My darling, lovable, alluring, Bernadean."

During the heart of World War II, U.S. Army veteran Bill Moore was serving in the Third United States Army (under the command of noted General George S. Patton) while they worked to liberate and secure France and Germany in the final months of the war. During a furlough, Bill met a young woman named "Bernadean" and when he was deployed, the young soldier sent her love letters from the battlefront—just as so many others did. However, one of those letters sent in the early months of 1945 never made it to Bernadean, for unknown reasons.

The missing letter didn't hurt their relationships too much—Bill and Bernadean married shortly after the war and lived together until 2010, when she passed away. Yet in 2015, Bill received a Valentine's Day surprise: the long-lost letter. Earlier in 2015, a woman found the letter in a record sleeve that she purchased, and through a series of connections was able to find Bill's daughter, who eventually got it back to Bill.

For Bill, reading that letter was a reminder that his feelings for his beloved Bernadean had changed very little, from the 20-year-old WWII soldier to the 70 years of memories with his wife.

Read more about Bill and Bernadean's story, courtesy of Yahoo! News: https://gma.yahoo.com/mysterious-wwii-love-letter-found-old-record-heads-211324601--abc-news-sex.html. You can also view video of Bill's reaction to the letter as he reads it courtesy of ABC News at: http://abcnews.go.com/US/emotional-moment-wwii-vet-reads-long-lost-love/story?id=29526157.

Do you still have love letters from when you were younger, or letters from your parents or grandparents? If you read those letters today, how do they make you feel? Share your thoughts with us on Facebook at https://www.facebook.com/groups/234255823447372/ or on Twitter, using the #MediaAsTools hashtag.

Changes in Technology Highlight Changes in Lines of Delineation

Mediated communication Communication that relies on a technology channel in order to send a message between two entities.

Chaffee and Metzger (2001) pointed out that new communication technologies decrease the importance of the three characteristics of mass communication. In fact, they go so far as to suggest a shift in nomenclature (labeling) from "mass communication" to "mediated communication" that focuses attention on the idea that, although communication via technology is still mediated, it is no longer necessarily "mass." In this way, we can understand that mediated communication differs from non-mediated communication in one very clear way: one requires technology for a message to get from the source to the receiver (mediated) and the other does not (non-mediated).

Of course, this is nothing brand new. Media technologies have a long history of "demassifying" communication; that is, working against the three characteristics that Chaffee and Metzger point out. For example, cable television introduced

a much greater availability of television channels—cable customers often have hundreds of channels compared to the half-dozen or so broadcast channels one can get through an antenna—and with these new channels, content producers were able to create content for more specific and smaller audiences (a practice known as narrowcasting). In this way, cable television became less finite in available channels and also less "one size fits all" in terms of content. Considering the notion of audience control, we can look at the advent of the VCR as an invention that shifted this. By recording television and storing it to watch later, VCRs gave media audiences much greater control over when and how they watched a program by allowing you to watch a show not at the time it was broadcast, but also fast-forwarding or rewinding through recordings (such as skipping commercials). Thus, trending away from these traditional mass communication characteristics is not new. However, newer technologies allow this to occur to a much greater degree and even allow a great deal more interpersonal communication as well.

Narrowcasting Transmitting information to smaller, less anonymous, and more well-defined audiences.

In this change from what Chaffee and Metzger (2001) call "mass" to "media" communication, six differences between the two are highlighted:

1. **Channels** As mentioned previously, mass communication is typified by a finite availability of channels, and newer technologies have allowed for many channels. For example, the Internet allows for a near infinite number of possible channels that are readily available for consumption by anyone with a network connection.

2. **Audience** Under the notion of mass media, the audience is often considered as one large and anonymous "mass" (hence the term mass communication). However, newer technologies allow message producers to identify smaller and more focused audiences that allow them to tailor content to satisfy a variety of niche markets. Moreover, as bandwidth—an important consideration in the cost of producing messages—becomes cheaper and cheaper (and in some cases free), producers can be profitable without having to attract an enormous audience, allowing for even greater narrowcasting. Even more recently, social media has helped create circumstances in which media audiences are producing as much, if not more, content than the media producers themselves! Examples of this include YouTube videos and CNN.com's popular iReport section (which features stories, photos, and videos from CNN readers).

3. **Control** Mass communication puts control of message distribution and consumption squarely in the hands of the sender—usually a media company or organization—but newer technologies move that control into the hands of the audiences, or users. Because there is such an increase in the number of available channels and because those channels can be accessed (nearly) anywhere and anytime, the individual audience members have much greater choice in what, and how, to consume.

4. **Transmission** Mass communication messages are often transmitted in a very regimented and particular way. Messages go from source to receiver(s) only (a one-way flow of communication), and they are transmitted in a time-specific manner. This means that if an individual wanted to watch a television show, that show would be beamed from a station (for instance, ABC) to the individual's television at a particular time (8:00 PM). So, if an

individual were to get home at 8:05 PM and spend a few minutes stumbling through the television channels, they would miss a good part of the show's opening scenes. However, newer technologies have allowed transmission to be more interactive (two-way) and, in terms of timing, to be more at the convenience of the audience. Referring to television as an example, many broadcast and cable stations now stream many of their more popular shows on Web sites or make them available for download, allowing audience members to both choose the particular program of the show they want to watch and control when that program is watched.

5. **Typification** Another way to think about the differences between "mass" and "media" is to consider the channels that best typify each, particularly as we see a continued evolution in communication technologies. As referenced briefly earlier, we often associate "mass" communication with newspapers and television, while we often associate "media" communication as being Internet-based, such as Web pages and social media applications. Indeed, these different types embody some of the other elements of "mass" and "media" on this list.

6. **Learning** The sixth and final difference that Chaffee and Metzger (2001) addressed when distinguishing "mass" from "media" has to do with how each encourages learning. With mass communication, the learning process is often done through modeling and observation. When somebody watches a television program—such as a segment on hand-washing on Sesame Street—they watch the segment, remember the lesson, and attempt to re-enact what was just learned (more on this in Chapter 6). However, learning through newer media technologies is more of an experiential process, particularly as new media are often more interactive. Instead of learning simply by watching others and imitating, newer media allow the opportunity to learn by experiencing things directly (or at least, more directly). This can be seen in video game systems such as the Nintendo Wii and the Sony PlayStation Move—both technologies require the user to physically interact with on-screen content; of course, even a Web site that has a child click a mouse to move objects from one screen to the next also has a layer of interactivity beyond what could be accomplished in a flat book. Even more promise for experiential learning will exist as augmented and virtual reality systems become more popular, systems that blend the virtual and actual worlds, such as Google's Glass project or MicroSoft's Hololens device— Bowman, Banks, and Westerman (2016) call this augmented sociality (see MC in Action: Google and Project Glass).

Augmented sociality Using technologies to access information from digital and social media programs, and working that information into face-to-face conversations.

Digitization Converting information into binary code to be decoded upon request by a computer processor.

Binary code The language of computing technology; this is the storing of information in electrical circuits using a series of "1" and "0" commands to represent "on" or "off."

Changes in Mediated Communication

There are other characteristics of new media that add to these changes for communication. The first is digitization. Digitization is simply the storage of information as 1s and 0s—a language known as binary code. Because information is now stored in this way, very interesting things became possible, as pointed out by Bryant and Thompson (2002) and discussed in greater detail in Chapter 12.

MC IN ACTION

GOOGLE AND PROJECT GLASS

"To label Mountain View, California-based Google Inc. as a technology innovator is a bit of an understatement. Currently one of the most profitable technology companies of the twenty-first century, Google (NYSE: GOOG), and in particular the company's X Lab, has earned a reputation for launching Internet-based technologies that make use of their search algorithms for any number of applications. A recent invention that is turning heads (pun intended) is Project Glass—an initiative to develop and distribute a wearable Web browser and streaming camera platform in an average-looking pair of eyeglasses. These glasses are capable of displaying information directly on the inside of both lenses and are designed to be operated with voice commands, displaying the same information that one would normally access on a smartphone or laptop computer. Industry estimates predict that these glasses could be available to the average U.S. consumer for about the price of a high-end smartphone by early 2014. So, soon you may be wearing these even as you read this book!"

The above quotation was included in the first edition of this book. However, chances are that you are not currently wearing a pair of Google Glass. This suggests a couple things about the rationale behind this book. First, technology changes fast. A tech that was discussed as futuristic when the first edition of this book was published has now been put to rest, in a span of less than three years (The Glass Project was cancelled by Google in January of 2015, although they have already announced a new Glass prototype—having filed a patent for the new device in December 2015). However, consistent with another reason behind the structure of this book, new augmented reality (AR) technologies are being developed, such as Microsoft's HoloLens. Thus, it seems that the nature of augmented reality is consistent with people's goals and provides something that people desire, even if the specific tools used to provide AR change quickly.

© Peppinuzzo/Shutterstock.com

Project Glass is a wearable Web browser in a pair of eyeglasses. The initial Glass project was ended in January 2015, but Google has already announced plans for a new device. Other companies, such as Microsoft and Sony, have also announced plans to release similar wearable devices.

Rogers (1986) also suggested other characteristics that new media share. The first is interactivity. There are many definitions that exist for interactivity, but the preferred one for us is "the degree to which users of a medium can influence the form or content of the mediated environment" (Steuer, 1992, p. 80). Thus, interactivity is a continuum, and all media have some level of interactivity, but newer media provide more interactivity than older ones. The second characteristic is known as demassification. This general idea is that media become less "mass," and allow for greater personalization and interpersonal content. Third, newer technologies allow for some levels of asynchronicity. This means that messages do not have to be received at the same time they are sent. Consider the prototypical mass medium, television; it is a synchronous medium, as messages must be received when they are sent. Interestingly, the classic interpersonal channel, face-to-face, is also a synchronous one. However, more and more options exist that break this constraint, (e.g., DVRs for television content and e-mails for interpersonal content), and the Internet allows for more of these types of asyncronicity.

Moving Toward MC

To this point, mass and interpersonal communication have been discussed as if they are separate from each other, and historically they have usually been considered as such (particularly in the scientific study of communication). However, there are also scholars who have suggested that this distinction is a false dichotomy (for example, see Reardon & Rogers, 1989). For example, when we communicate—whether through mass or interpersonal communication—we often have the same goals in mind. As noted in the very beginning of this book, communication is a goal-driven process. We may seek information; we may try to persuade others; we try to start, maintain, and/or end relationships; and we also seek entertainment, and each of these can be done through mass and interpersonal communication.

Although this distinction between mass and interpersonal may have always been somewhat false (see MC in Action: Was Dear Abby My Friend?), newer media have really blurred the lines between the two. For example, is Facebook a form of mass communication? Interpersonal? Neither? Both? It is these kinds of questions that led communication scholar Patrick O'Sullivan to suggest an idea known as "masspersonal" communication.

Masspersonal communication
Patrick O'Sullivan's idea that technology makes the division between mass and interpersonal communication blurry, and thus we should look for more useful distinctions in communication.

In general, the notion of masspersonal communication suggests that historically we have often used mass channels for interpersonal reasons and interpersonal channels for mass reasons. For example, based upon sheer audience size, the big screen in a major college football stadium during a game is a mass channel. However, if a person proposes to their significant other over that same screen, this would seem like the ultimate in interpersonal reasons. On the flip side, e-mail and telephones are often considered interpersonal channels. But when spam messages are sent over either one, they are generalized messages without regard for idiosyncratic information for each receiver and thus seem like a mass communication.

Based on this, O'Sullivan (2005) suggested that we delink, or separate, the channel of communication from the type of communication. Historically, mass has been linked with physical and electronic media and interpersonal has been linked with face-to-face (indeed, some even suggest that mediated interpersonal interaction is not true interpersonal communication because there is no

MC IN ACTION

WAS DEAR ABBY MY FRIEND?

There is always an answer; even if it's . . . you can't change anybody but yourself.

~Pauline "Dear Abby" Phillips

In early 2013, longtime newspaper columnist Pauline Phillips died at the age of 94. For traditional newspaper audiences, Phillips was known to the world as "Abigail Van Buren"—a renowned advice columnist who authored the world's most widely syndicated newspaper column, reaching over 1,400 newspapers and an estimated 110 million people each time it was published. From her first column—appearing in the *San Francisco Chronicle* in 1956—Phillips' columns were popular because of the pithy advice she gave readers. Readers were invited to write her letters describing their struggles in relative detail, and Phillips would select a few, publishing the complete letter text and a pseudo-name for the letter writer ("Troubled in Tacoma" or "Desperately Depressed") along with her advice.

From a communication perspective, we might consider what compelled so many anonymous strangers to write Abby about their lives. Most readers knew that Abby was not a real person—the pen name Abigail van Buren—and they were also aware that if Phillips did respond to their letters, she would publish the entire letter text in thousands of daily newspapers around the world. Common themes of these letters included stories about adultery, drug and substance abuse, and other social taboos that most people would consider highly private information, yet they shared openly with Phillips and, as a proxy, with the world . . . and she would respond with a similar level of detail and personability. So, is this an example of interpersonal communication—a letter to a friend and a response back—or is this an example of mass communication—a letter to a newspaper to be shared with the world?

Today, the voice of Abigail van Buren has been filled by Phillips' daughter, Jeanne Phillips, and is still one of the most widely distributed newspaper columns. And of course, she now has a Twitter handle: @DearAbby.

physical connection between individuals, although we disagree with this contention throughout the rest of this book). Again, newer technologies highlight that mediated communication is not always mass, and instead of differentiating types of communication simply based upon channel or audience size, it may be better to focus on more meaningful distinctions. Indeed, the masspersonal notion proposes two: message personalization and message access exclusivity.

Message personalization refers to the degree that a message is crafted to

Based on sheer size, a big-screen in a major college football stadium during a game is a mass channel.

a recipient in a manner that treats the recipient as an individual with distinctive interests, history, relationship network, and so on. Such an explanation is very similar to classic definitions of interpersonal communication, which argue that interpersonal communication takes place only when predictions about the interaction are made based on knowledge of the other and not on roles or on cultural

MC IN ACTION

MASSPERSONAL COMMUNICATION, CHARTED

In an unpublished essay from the International Communication Association (www.icahdq .org) convention in 2005, communication scholar Patrick O'Sullivan wrote about the increasingly blurred lines between mass and interpersonal communication. While never published in an academic journal, his essay has been read nearly 2500 times on the scholarship network service Academia.edu (https:// www.academia.edu/468715/Masspersonal_ communication_Rethinking_the_mass_inter-personal_divide) and has influenced many of the current studies examining how human communication works across a variety of different media.

As an exercise, let us consider a few different communication technologies such as e-mail, television, a social media application such as Facebook, and a handwritten letter. Can you think of where these different technologies would fit onto the preceding O'Sullivan's masspersonal chart? Do some technologies fit into different sections of the chart? Do any of these technologies fit into all four sections of the chart? Can you think of other technologies and where they also might fit?

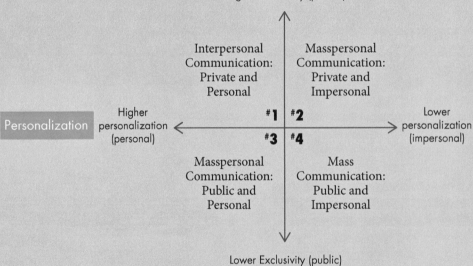

attributions (Miller & Steinberg, 1975). This is not unintentional, as interpersonal messages tend to be those with higher personalization and mass messages tend to be those with lower personalization.

Message access exclusivity involves the breadth of access to a particular message, or how public or private the message is. By traditional definitions, access to interpersonal messages would be exclusive to the intended recipient (private), whereas mass communication is by definition nonexclusive and accessible to a large number of recipients (public).

Overall, traditionally mass messages had low personalization and low exclusivity, and interpersonal messages had high personalization and high exclusivity. Yet, the masspersonal approach recognizes that there are many messages that cross the two (see MC in Action: Masspersonal Communication, Charted). In this way, O'Sullivan's concept allows us to explain traditional as well as new media technologies, and accounts for the entire communication process rather than merely focusing on the channel.

So What Is MC?

In our view, MC is simply communication that takes place using media. More emphasis is placed upon the C (communication) rather than the M (medium), although the particular channel (i.e., the computer or communication technology) provides interesting questions and answers that will be discussed throughout this book. Also, it is important to note that as a "communication first" perspective, the same goals and functions of communication in general—to inform, persuade, relate, and to entertain—apply to MC as well. This approach will also be discussed in greater detail in later chapters as well.

Key Terms

Communication (pg 2)
Audience-centered process (pg 2)
Source (pg 3)
Encoding (pg 3)
Message (pg 3)
Channel (pg 3)
Receiver (pg 3)
Decoding (pg 3)
Feedback (pg 3)
Noise (pg 3)
Mass communication (pg 7)
Bandwidth (pg 7)
Interpersonal communication (pg 7)
Mediated communication (pg 8)
Narrowcasting (pg 9)
Augmented sociality (pg 10)
Digitization (pg 10)
Binary code (pg 10)
Masspersonal communication (pg 12)

References

Bowman, N. D., Banks, J. D., & Westerman, D. K. (2016). Through the Looking Glass: The impact of Google Glass on perceptions of face-to-face interaction. *Communication Research Reports, 33*(4).

Bryant, J., & Thompson, S. (2002). *Fundamentals of media effects.* New York: McGraw-Hill.

Chaffee, S. H., & Metzger, M. J. (2001). The end of mass communication? *Mass Communication & Society, 4*, 365–379.

McCroskey, J. C., & Richmond, V. P. (1996). *Fundamentals of human communication: An interpersonal perspective.* Prospect Heights, IL: Waveland Press.

Miller, G. R. (1966). On defining communication: Another stab. *Journal of Communication, 16*, 88–98.

Miller, G. R., & Steinberg, M. (1975). *Between people: A new analysis of interpersonal communication.* Chicago: Science Research Associates.

O'Sullivan, P. B. (2005). *Masspersonal communication: An integrative model bridging the mass-interpersonal divide.* Paper presented at the International Communication Association annual meeting, New York, May 26–30.

Rearden, K. K., & Rogers, E. M. (1988). Interpersonal versus mass media communication: A false dichotomy. *Human Communication Research, 15*, 284–303.

Rogers, E. M. (1986). *Communication technology: The new media is society.* New York: Free Press.

Shannon, C. E., & Weaver, W. (1949). *The mathematical theory of communication.* Champaign, IL: University of Illinois Press.

Steuer, J. (1992). Defining virtual reality: Dimension determining telepresence. *Journal of Communication, 42*, 73–93.

Watzlawick, P., Beavin, J. H., & Jackson, D. D. (1967). *Pragmatics of human communication.* New York: Norton & Co.

CHAPTER 2

What Is the Internet?

In the 2001 movie *Jay and Silent Bob Strike Back*, the characters Jay (played by Jason Mewes) and Silent Bob (Kevin Smith) discover that a mutual friend—Holden (Ben Affleck)—has written a comic book about their lives called *Bluntman and Chronic*. Moreover, the comic book has been adapted into a film and is getting very negative reviews online. Confused by the situation and not understanding the notion of "online," Jay asks Holden to explain what the Internet is (to paraphrase around his more colorful language). Holden responds:

The Internet is a communication tool used the world over where people can come together to bitch about movies and share pornography with one another.

Chances are that you have used the Internet at some point in your life—likely at some point in the last hour. In fact, you may have been online before reading this. You might be online while reading it. But have you ever thought about what this tool—that you likely use every day—actually is?

> **Internet** As a common noun, a network of networks; as a proper noun, the global network of networks. It is a communication tool that is used for a variety of purposes.

First a word of warning: this is neither a computer science book, nor is it an engineering book. It is a communication book. It is our contention that the Internet is a communication tool. It allows us to perform many functions in our human lives. Thus we will focus on describing what the Internet is from a communication perspective, as we believe this is a central piece of understanding what MC is, as it is such an important technology for considering mediated communication. We will highlight the hardware as necessary in pursuit of that goal. But the things that make the Internet work will not be the focus of this chapter . . . or will it?

Before continuing on, go back to Holden's description of what the Internet is. How good of a definition is this? Does it explain the concept of the Internet (what it is) as well as the function (how it is used)? Think about this as you read the rest of the chapter, and we will return to this question later on.

Before reading this chapter, think about the following questions:

- What is the Internet?
- Who runs the Internet?
- What are social media?
- What do we mean when we describe the Internet as social space?
- How did it come to this?

What Is the Internet?

TCP/IP Transmission Control Protocol/Internet Protocol; this is a common method of formatting and sending data around the Internet. It is not a single protocol but rather represents a series of common protocols that standardize the way data are handled from all computers on a given internet.

As mentioned previously, you likely use the Internet every day. You may not remember a time before the Internet was a mainstream tool for communication (the authors of this book certainly recall a time when the Internet was not much more than a collection of rarely updated personal Web pages and technical documents), but have you ever thought about what it is fundamentally? This is an important question to think about for many reasons, but one of the biggest is that an understanding of what it is can help you think about how it is and can be used, and thus what mediated communication "really" is.

The question "What is the Internet?" is a big one, probably a lot bigger than it initially seems. An internet as a common noun—note the lowercase "i"—is simply a network of networks. We can think of telephone networks as internets, for example, or even small groups of individuals who share information about a specific topic (such as a network of communication scholars). In this definition, there are lots of internets that exist. Although the Associated Press has recently decided that it should no longer be capitalized (they argued in early 2016 that both "internet" and "web" are often used as generic terms), when we capitalize it and talk about the Internet, we are referring to a global interconnection of these networks that uses Transmission Control Protocol/Internet Protocol (TCP/IP) to share information between and within all of the networks. There are some important things to consider here, the biggest of which is the fact that the Internet exists to promote connection.

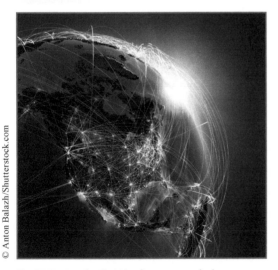

The Internet can be thought of as a series of information networks connected to each other, serving computers around the world with information.

The Internet can be thought of as a series of information networks (internets) connected to each other, serving computers around the world with information. Yet, do you think this is a satisfying answer to what the Internet is? Does this definition

© Anton Balazh/Shutterstock.com

really explain what the Internet is, how it is used, and the role it plays in our lives? Or is there more to it? If you found this definition unsatisfying, then we agree with you—it seems to explain the mechanics of the Internet as being something that connects, but it fails to really explain what those connections are, why they exist, and how they are used. We will take a somewhat roundabout way to answer this question more completely, but first we start by considering another question.

Who Runs the Internet?

In *The Spider and the Starfish*, authors Ori Brafman and Rod Beckstrom (2006) recount a story from a man named Dave Garrison who was the CEO of Netcom, an Internet service provider similar to AOL, in 1995. Garrison was trying to get start-up capital from a group of French investors to help grow his nascent Internet company, but the investors wanted to know who the president of the Internet was before they would consider the proposal. That is, the French investors wanted to know who was ultimately in charge of the Internet so that they could more carefully consider the investment opportunity, just as an investor in a restaurant business might want to know who is responsible for managing the supply chain of food and drink necessary to keep the business stocked from night to night. Flummoxed, Garrison tried to explain that there was no president of the Internet—that there was no one person or entity in charge of managing networked information. The investors seemed stunned by this and continued to ask questions about who made content decisions, logistic decisions, and other decisions to manage the Internet. In response, Garrison kept insisting that there was no president, and the investors in turn insisted that something must be getting lost in translation. Finally, realizing that they were not going to invest without having this question answered to their liking, Garrison simply told the investors that he was the president of the Internet. He then got his money.

Why were the French investors so stunned by the idea that there was no president of the Internet? Because they did not understand a simple yet fundamental core of how the Internet operates: the Internet is a decentralized organization (see MC in Action: The Law of Decentralization). It does not operate in the top-down, unidirectional manner that most traditional organizations operate, but rather it is largely controlled and managed by the very users themselves. Just as a starfish can live, grow, and survive when severely damaged in part because of its decentralized brain and other vital organs, the decentralized organization can live, grow, and survive because there is no one part of the system that is more or less important than any other—all are equally vital and located within the network, not at the center of it. Moreover, when some parts of the organization fail, other parts can split up the failing bits and support them until they come back online—just as a starfish can take pressure off of damaged parts until they are able to grow and take back responsibilities. As users, we might argue that a piece of the distributed "brain" of the Internet is within each of us as individuals, each time we log on and use it.

So, we know of course that Garrison was not and is not the president of the Internet, but who really does run the Internet? The answer might be apparent to you now: You do (see MC in Action: Person of the Year). The Internet is a system

Decentralized organization A company or organization in which there is no one main leader, president, or operating officer. Rather, the organization's leadership is broken up in several different parts of the organization itself.

You The most important thing for this book; used this way it refers to the idea that users are in charge of open systems like the Internet and thus have the freedom and responsibility for their success.

MC IN ACTION

THE LAW OF DECENTRALIZATION

According to *The Spider and the Starfish*, decentralized technologies have certain principles

- When attacked, a decentralized organization tends to become even more open and decentralized.
- It is easy to mistake starfish for spiders.
- An open system does not have central intelligence; the intelligence is spread throughout the system.
- Open systems can easily mutate.
- The decentralized system sneaks up on you.

- As industries become decentralized, overall profits decrease.
- Put people into an open system and they will automatically want to contribute.
- When attacked, centralized organizations tend to become even more centralized.

Can you think of organizations that you are a member of that might benefit from a decentralized organizational structure? Share your thoughts with us on Facebook at https://www.facebook.com/groups/234255823447372/ or on Twitter, using the #MediaAsTools hashtag.

MC IN ACTION

PERSON OF THE YEAR

In 2006, *Time* magazine named you their annual Person of the Year, an honor normally reserved for individuals who have had significant impact on world events. Past honorees have ranged from Mahatma Gandhi (1930) to Adolf Hitler (1938) and have included research scientists, former U.S. presidents, poets, investors, and even the computer (1982). While the magazine has not shied away from controversial picks in past years (Hitler, along with honoring the Iranian Ayatollah Khomeini in 1979 in the wake of the Iran–U.S. hostage crisis in Tehran and the Endangered Earth in 1988 to raise awareness for environmental issues), 2006 marked the first time that the individual reader—literally you—was honored as the Person of the Year for your individual contributions to the World Wide Web . . . a great résumé builder for you for sure!

largely controlled by the individual users, and it is those individual users and their collective actions that determine the direction of the Internet. This has become especially true in the era of social media, as the Internet has expanded as a social tool in which users can not only share bits of data and information with each other, but they can also form relationships and engage each other's thoughts, feelings, and even behaviors in a persistent and networked space.

MC IN ACTION

ILOVEYOU?

Considered by some to be one of the most successful computer viruses to date, ILOVEYOU was a computer worm (a virus that crawls from networked computer to computer without the need for an actual program) that played on computer users' romantic sentiments. Masquerading as a love letter sent via e-mail, once the user opened the message a hidden program infected their computer, corrupted many system files, and then automatically sent itself to the next fifty e-mail addresses stored in that user's contact file. Although it might sound strange that one would open up a love letter on a work e-mail, remember that many of these contacts would have been personal acquaintances, and so it would not have been too surprising for them to send personal messages to each other.

It was estimated that in the 10 days following its May 5, 2000 detection ILOVEYOU had infected as many as 10 percent of the world's networked computers at the time, causing nearly $9 billion in damages as companies invested time and money to repair infected computers. Fortunately, the virus itself was rather harmless and was easy to repair—many experts suggest that the virus' creator merely wanted to see how many computers he could get his program to "infect," perhaps to demonstrate to computer users the weakness of their security protocols. Yet, such stories show us the potential danger of a truly generative system and the power of the individual user in the network.

Have you ever had a computer, tablet, or smartphone infected by a computer virus? Share your thoughts with us on Facebook at https://www.facebook.com/groups/234255823447372/ or on Twitter, using the #MediaAsTools hashtag.

The Internet as a Social Space

Given Garrison's story, we can ask another question: if our earlier definition of the Internet—the more technically focused TCP/IP definition—is unsatisfying, what is the Internet really? Or put another way given the focus of this book: what is the function of the Internet as a communication tool? We would suggest that it is a space, not a physical one but a virtual one, for people to connect and create, and to do so socially. In other words, it is a tool that people use to accomplish their communication goals.

Importantly, much of what today's Internet looks like (and most likely, what tomorrow's Internet ends up looking like) was not necessarily planned. After all, if the Internet is a decentralized organization, who would do the planning? However, as Harvard law professor Jonathan Zittrain (2008) points out, much of how the Internet functions today is a result of a shared ethos—or code of ethics—held by many of the technology's founding fathers and early users. He points out some important features to note.

1. **Generativity** One hallmark of having the Internet set up in this way is something called the generativity principle. This is the idea that users are able to generate, or create, their own content (this is a good enough definition for our purposes). Thus, the system is a very open one, allowing users

to both consume and create content. Typically, this is seen as a good idea, because users often know what they want (and potentially, how to make it happen) better than a central "president" or organization does. However, this freedom certainly leads to the potential for users to hurt the Internet and its users by creating programs such as malware, spyware, and computer viruses (see MC in Action: ILOVEYOU?).

2. **No control of behavior** Designed in this open and distributed way, the system is not set up to control the user's behavior; it is designed to be free. In fact, many have suggested that the Internet (especially in the earliest days) was similar to the Wild West of 1800s. Just as many U.S. frontier towns were ruled by the settlers, cowboys, and lawmen who inhabited them, the only laws on the Internet are often the behavioral norms established by the users themselves. Perhaps it makes sense then that those inhabiting these new spaces—be it the U.S. frontier or the new Internet—would be in a unique position to know how to best govern themselves. However, there are consequences, likely positive and negative, of such a setup. On the one hand, all users are free to innovate and customize the network to satisfy their needs; on the other hand, not everyone's needs are for the greater good—such as the viruses and spyware mentioned previously.

3. **Simplicity** The Internet was designed to operate in a fairly "simple" manner in that it was created largely without many restrictions or regulations, and Zittrain points out two principles underlying this simplicity.

   a. **Procrastination principle** First, many of the earliest founders subscribed to the very simple notion that "if it ain't broke, don't fix it!" . . . and even further "don't try to fix it before it's broke." By this, they decided that instead of trying to foresee all potential problems with the Internet and implement policy and procedures to intercept them, they would leave the network(s) open and fix problems after they come up. The logic was that if a system is left open, the users may come up with better solutions to a problem than any one governing body, and you will not choke off their creativity when things are not broken. A good example of this in modern-day management practice would be the automotive company General Motors, which in the 1980s implemented a series of incentive programs to encourage lower-rank employees such as assembly-line workers to suggest improvements in the manufacturing process that would reduce costs. In many instances, workers recommended ways to better assemble or organize factory floor plans to minimize downtime—or time spent not actually manufacturing a vehicle.

   b. **Trust your neighbor principle** As a generative system, the Internet is only as functional as its users, which is perhaps one of the most remarkable aspects of the technology. On one hand, the Internet should not work at all. Think about how much trust this kind of open system requires in order to work effectively! Barring few legal restrictions, users are given near-infinite rein to create and generate content and programs for all others to use, often with no real personal consequences (other than having a "bad" Internet or a "good" Internet, which might or might not be a

concern for the average user) for the damage or enhancements done by that content and those programs (although we might argue that this is also true of all communication systems, including face-to-face). So, the Internet only works to the extent that its users are willing and able to make it work, and the founding fathers of the Internet believed that they could rely on this, and this was the best setup, because again, this is what keeps the system open. Remember, when "You" are in charge of the Internet, it means "You" are in charge of both its positives and negatives. This requires you to be a lot more vigilant and critical in what and how you use the Internet (see MC in Action: I Didn't See the Sign!).

MC IN ACTION

I DIDN'T SEE THE SIGN!

The many rules strip us of the most important thing: the ability to be considerate. We're losing our capacity for socially responsible behavior.

~Hans Monderman, in an interview with *Der Spiegel*.

How is it that removing limitations can encourage pro-social and beneficial behavior? In his book *The Future of the Internet*, Jonathan Zittrain wrote about an interesting traffic experiment in the Dutch town of Drachten in the latter half of 2005. In an attempt to increase traffic safety in the city center, this town of 45,000 moved to remove all road signs, markings, and even parking space lines from the area—in a sense, the town is now "verkeersbordvrij" (literally, a Dutch phrase translating to "free from road signs").

Many who hear this story try to imagine such a scenario in their own town or college campus and cringe at the thought. However, this experiment was a real-world test of civil engineer Hans Monderman's notion of "shared spaces"—a philosophy that argues for the removal of restrictions so that individuals might actively pay more attention to their surroundings rather than mindlessly responding to "arbitrary" restrictions and rules. In a sense, we all have a desire to get safely and quickly from Point A to Point B,

and in the absence of rules, we tend to self-organize for the greater good (which incidentally, serves our own goals as well). A good example of this would be watching a group of students trying to pour into an on-campus concert or sporting event—many times the hall or stadium designers will include small design cues such as shrubs or different-colored pavement bricks to guide students safely and efficiently through a queue. That is, it is not usually against the law to rush through a line (although it might be against social norms to do so), but the design of the entryway often facilitates our organization into lines.

The result? Traffic accidents were reduced to a single incident within one year of Monderman's experiment. While there are likely a number of different variables at play here (e.g., people might be overcautious in the beginning of such a new system), such data speak to the possibility of people self-organizing for the mutual benefit of the system.

Web 2.0

Web 2.0 A term that reflects changes to a more collaborative Internet, referred to colloquially as "create and collaborate."

Web 1.0 A term that refers to the earliest functions of the Internet as being a space for posting information, referred to colloquially as "read and retrieve."

Narbs Short for narrative bits; a term coined by Wake Forest University communication professor Ananda Mitra that refers to "an item of personal information posted online, particularly as it contributes, often unwittingly, to a personal narrative that individual is creating online."

To capture changes in how the Internet functions today, technology author Tim O'Reilly (2005) has suggested that we consider today's network as Web 2.0 in order to distinguish it from yesterday's Web 1.0. Referencing myriad social media platforms such as Wikipedia (in which individual users create and edit encyclopedia-style entries on subjects of their own choosing), Facebook (in which members create and share narbs—or narrative bits (Mitra, 2010)—with one another in a persistent, online social community), blogs (in which writers journal and report citizen commentary on any number of issues), and YouTube (in which users produce and share video with others), O'Reilly argued that the digital media landscape was one that featured the users as the center of both media production and consumption. In contrast to the "read and retrieve" nature of Web 1.0 in which users logged on to find static information more as a convenience, the "create and collaborate" nature of Web 2.0 features Internet users actively posting and sharing new content in an interconnected space. Consider for example that over 300 million pictures are uploaded by the over one billion daily Facebook users (over 1.5 billion people use Facebook at least monthly)—all massive numbers—and we see that social media are no longer about reading content produced by some, but rather produced by all (at least possibly by "all").

Yet the term Web 2.0 is a controversial one, with some suggesting it is simply a marketing ploy to "sell" us on the Internet's usefulness and others suggesting the distinction to be altogether meaningless. However, there do seem to be some important differences between the so-called Web 1.0 and Web 2.0, even if these differences may be more about usage than the technology itself; that is, the technology of the Internet has not really changed beyond its original scope, but the way we use it certainly has. New media writer and consultant Clay Shirky (2008) suggested that the many social tools now available allow for things to take place today (both online and offline, see MC in Action: I Stole a Sidekick!) that were not possible before due to the sheer scope of possibilities allowed by these social tools. This is a change in quantity that is so large that it looks like a qualitative change. Importantly for our discussion, Shirky further suggests that these tools do not really change human motivations and goals, just how we are capable of achieving these goals.

In defining Web 2.0, O'Reilly (2005) suggested seven core competencies that best characterize his philosophy. These competencies fit nicely with the discussion of how the Internet got to where it is today:

1. **Services, not software** This is sort of the idea of cloud computing—or computer programs that are housed in central servers rather than individual computer machines. (Facebook is a good example of this, as users do not have to install a Facebook program but rather are able to access Facebook by logging on through a Web browser.) Here the focus moves away from selling software to individual users and more toward the concept of shareware and providing users with a platform to accomplish what they want to do, in the manner in which they want to do it. An example of this is meetup.com. Meetup.com is a platform for people to create groups online with the express purpose of getting together to "meet up" with each other

MC IN ACTION

I STOLE A SIDEKICK!

I got ball this is my address 108 20 37 av corona come n do it I am give u the sidekick so I can hit you with it.

~Sashacristal8905

In his book *Here Comes Everybody*, Clay Shirky discusses how a small rant on a personal blog about a stolen cellular phone demonstrates perhaps one of the most important aspects of Web 2.0—the ability of network users to create and collaborate on their own information.

In early June 2006, New York City resident Evan Guttman had a friend Ivanna who misplaced her cellular phone (a $350 Motorola Sidekick, an early smartphone with an onboard camera; quite an expensive and luxurious phone for the time) in the back of a taxicab. After replacing her phone and in the process of configuring her replacement, Ivanna noticed pictures of a strange woman on her account, including the woman and her family, as well as her contact information. In short, another woman (in fact, a 16-year-old girl) had found Ivanna's Sidekick and rather than returning it to the taxicab company or reporting it to the police, she started using the phone as if it were her own.

Ivanna and Evan tried contacting the girl to ask her to return the phone, and after she ignored their requests, Evan took to social media to seek help. Writing a short blog about the phone and its new owner, he shared his story with anyone who might be interested in reading it. Quickly, his Web page was shared among other network users who had similar experiences with losing their phones, and they empathized with Ivanna's situation. Other network users began tracking the girl down, eventually finding the names of her family (including her brother, a military policeman) and her home address in Queens along with her MySpace and AOL accounts. Within days, literally thousands of people began offering Ivanna and Evan legal and procedural advice (police officers and lawyers, for example, offered pro bono advice on filing property reports with the local NYC borough police), while others took to harassing young Sasha both at her home and online, even resorting to driving by her home and calling her a thief in public.

In the face of an increasingly escalating situation, police eventually arrested the girl and charged her with possession of stolen property (although it was never clear if this was actually a theft, as Ivanna had indeed lost the phone in the back of a taxicab and the girl repeatedly suggested that she purchased the phone from a sidewalk sale). As Sasha's mother put it in a *New York Times* interview, "I never in my life thought a phone was going to cause me so many problems."

This story demonstrates perhaps one of the most important principles of Web 2.0—users create and collaborate on information in order to drive action, both virtually and in the real world. It also reaffirms the notion that information flows through an increasingly large and connected network, driving us more and more toward the notion of the "global village." The technology allows for this possibility, but you may ask yourself, did Sasha get what she deserved here?

You can read the original version of Evan's blog at http://www.evanwashere.com/stolensidekick/original/

MC IN ACTION

METCALFE'S LAW

One way to think about the utility of a network is to consider the number of unique connections within that network. As far back as the early 1980s, electrical engineer Robert Metcalfe proposed that the potential value of a communication network could be defined as the square of the number of connected users of the network, or n^2 (with n representing each unique connection, not each individual user). For example, a network with only one user would have no value since there is no connection between that user and any other, a network with two users would have a value of one (one unique connection), a network with five users would have a value of 25 (25 potential connections between the five users of that network), and a network of 500 users would have a value of 250,000 (a quarter-million potential connections between those 500 individual users. If we consider that as of 2016 there were an estimated 1.59 billion monthly active Facebook users, we might estimate the value of the entire Facebook network as having potentially 2.5281 quintillion (2,528,100,000,000,000,000) unique connections!

To see a graphic of Metcalf's Law, visit: http://en.wikipedia.org/wiki/File:Metcalfe-Network-Effect.svg

face-to-face. Groups can be set up and searched for around pretty much any organizing principle desired. Thus, rather than create the groups that they thought might be important, the creators of this Web site let the users decide what would be important characteristics for meeting up. Meetup.com is the platform, and it gives the users the service of meeting up with people with similar characteristics they themselves find important.

2. **Control of data that get better with use** In general, it might be argued that the more people use something, the more useful that something gets. Consider a pathway through a forest: the more people who choose to walk the same path, the more worn down and clearly marked that path becomes for future users. In terms of the Internet, let us consider Facebook. How useful would Facebook be if only one person was using the program or if the users only logged on once or twice a month to share information? (See MC in Action: Metcalfe's Law.) Google Maps is another example of this process. While the program is great as a traditional map, what makes Google Maps different from other maps you can purchase at a fuel station or pick up at an interstate rest stop (besides that it is digital) is that other users can tag locations of interest to them. It offers the possibility for users to find novel and useful ways to incorporate Google Maps into what they want to do, such as a user-created list of interestingly shaped rocks or good places to

Users can tag locations of interest on a Google map.

have a candlelight dinner or see certain species of florae or faunae. These are often not particular functions that the developers of the application thought of when originally designing the technologies, but they allowed for the possibility that users would generate their own uses.

3. **Trusting users as co-developers** Similar to the "trust your neighbor" principle discussed previously, one aspect of Web 2.0 is that Web developers have to work with and trust the users to help co-develop and co-create the technology. Consider a Web site like Wikipedia (www.wikipedia.org), an open-source and open-access Web-based encyclopedia written by users rather than by editors. For such a site to have credible information, the audience of users must contribute accurate information and correct the accuracy of posted information. Indeed, Wikipedia works only if we as the users are trustworthy, willing, and able participants in its creation.

4. **Harnessing collective intelligence** Another aspect of Web 2.0 is that co-creation and collaboration force us to accept that relying on the ideas of the many can outweigh those of the few, and it also allows for the possibility that useful information can come from a variety of sources. This is the basic idea behind the notion of "crowdsourcing." As Shirky (2008) pointed out, crowdsourcing makes sense in today's new mediascape as we are now able to get contributions from anyone who has them to offer regardless of their social stature and regardless of how small each unique contribution may be, because the costs of creating, distributing, managing, and sharing these ideas have been greatly reduced. Again, let us consider Wikipedia. First, because of the open nature of the platform, any reader who might know something about a particular subject—no matter how small—can make a contribution. And when an individual adds false information to a topic, we can (hopefully) rely on the collective intelligence of the group to correct the inaccuracy, and it becomes increasingly likely it will be found because so many people use the platform (similar to the second point, the data get better as more people use them).

5. **Using the long tail** In using the long tail, O'Reilly is referring to our ability to look to people on the fringes (often, people who have more specialized knowledge about a topic) in order to get more specific, accurate, or more complete ideas and information about any given topic. If we consider again Wikipedia, we might suggest that although a research scientist studying the human immunodeficiency virus (HIV) might know a great deal about the biology of the virus itself and how it affects the human biological system, an individual living with HIV might be able to tell us a small bit about his or her experiences with the virus. This notion goes along with harnessing collective intelligence, as in this example we can combine the scientist's and the individual's experiences to provide us with a more holistic view of HIV. Notably, using the long tail has become increasingly simple as we see more and more Internet users creating their own information, such as posting Facebook and Twitter updates on any number of topics (see MC in Action: Google "Flu").

6. **Non-device specific software** Referring back to the notion of cloud computing, O'Reilly argues that yet another key component of Web 2.0 is that the many different software programs are not dependent on one particular

MC IN ACTION

GOOGLE "FLU"

Throughout history, influenza—commonly referred to as the "flu"—has been a seasonal plague, with no known cure. It infects three to five million people annually, 500,000 of which do not survive. Influenza is a virus that often spreads rapidly during colder seasons when people tend to congregate indoors in large quantities. In response, many agencies—such as the Centers for Disease Control in the United States—often work to track the flu and other illnesses so that they can better prepare and protect the population from infection.

Add to this list of agencies Google. By tracking the prevalence of flu-related search terms, Google's nonprofit sector (www.google.org)

developed an interactive map that attempts to track the potential spread and scope of the flu by mapping individual Google users' search activity (http://www.google.org/flutrends/us/#US). Of course, such data would need to be interpreted with caution as it is just as likely that people use more flu-related search terms during so-called flu seasons, but it does speak to the power of the long tail to inform us about greater societal trends.

Have you ever used Google Flu? Give it a shot (especially during influenza season) and tell us about the experience, on Facebook at https://www.facebook.com/groups/234255823447372/ or on Twitter, using the #MediaAsTools hashtag.

device to be used. Considering Facebook, many users are able to log on to their accounts through any number of devices—such as a desktop or laptop computer, tablet computer, smartphone, or even an Oculus Rift.

7. **Lightweight interfaces** When we think about a lightweight interface, we can think about how much cognitive effort is required to use the technology as well as how many resources it requires in general (such as the physical size of the device, energy consumption, and storage space). Let us consider Apple's iPad for a moment. What can you do with it? Pretty much everything, as long as you have a network connection. How big is it? Most iPads are not much larger than an average 80-page spiral-bound notebook and weigh about the same, so you can take it anywhere. This increased mobility allows for some pretty amazing things to occur—both virtually and physically, online and in real time. For example, consider the real time "from the source" information that became available during the Arab Spring uprising in Tunisia, Egypt, Libya, and Yemen in late 2010 and early 2011. While these will be discussed in detail later in our text (Chapter 5), they each gave us an example of individuals harnessing lightweight technologies to take them into the battlefields and protest zones and share personal experiences in real time and across a myriad of different technologies.

Taken as a whole, all of these concepts led us to propose two notions that we would consider to be the main points of the Internet today, both the network in general and perhaps even the notion of social media more specifically.

1. **The more Internet users—or "netizens"—there are, the better the Internet can be for each user** To reiterate what has been said previously, the usefulness of the Internet to each user increases as more people spend more effort on it. Remember, as the people who run the Internet, "You" are the ones who are in charge of how useful it is.

2. **Socially creating channels and content** As has been reinforced by O'Reilly's Web 2.0 notion (which we do not see as simply a marketing ploy or empty statement), we are no longer simply passive consumers of media but are active producers of content as well. However, this creation and collaboration is more than just creating our own isolated content, but rather we are able to collaborate on things that we would have found remarkably difficult to work together on before, such as a holistic discussion of the biological and social ramifications of HIV via Wikipedia as described earlier. New media have given so many of us possibilities of participation in the creative and collaborative process; as Shirky and others point out, we tend to use it to do things we already wanted to do, but maybe were unable to do.

In fact, when we think specifically about the Internet as a functional technology, we are seeing some discussions about Web 3.0, referred to by many as "the semantic Web." If we consider that a Web 2.0 approach to the Internet suggests potentially billions of users are adding and editing small bits of information on a near-constant cycle in order to create and collaborate on collective information, we can also consider that the sheer volume of this information might be overwhelming to sort out and make sense of it. To this end, many programmers have begun designing technologies to better gather, organize, and even predict patterns in the big data generated by everyday users. Examples such as Google Flu show us how such programs can be used for good, but semantic Web programs have also given rise to concerns about data privacy—such as retail stores gathering information about shoppers' purchasing habits without the shoppers' knowledge and using those observed habits in their marketing efforts. Truly, the future of the Internet will be deeply rooted in understanding the functions of the technology moving forward.

In conclusion, it is important to remember that not only do you have a stake in the success or failure of the Internet, but for all intents and purposes **You are the Internet**. This is a great power you have, so use it wisely. As we all learned in *Amazing Fantasy #15*, Spider-Man's Uncle Ben taught a very young Peter Parker that "with great power, comes great responsibility."

Web 3.0 A term that refers to the manner in which networked technologies can be programmed to analyze large trends in the massive amounts of data provided by their users, referred to colloquially as "the semantic Web."

Big data A term that refers to the large quantities of information organizations can retrieve from Internet users regarding their usage patterns and preferences.

Key Terms

Internet (pg 17)
TCP/IP (pg 18)
Decentralized organization (pg 19)
You (pg 19)
Web 2.0 (pg 24)
Web 1.0 (pg 24)
Narbs (pg 24)
Web 3.0 (pg 29)
Big data (pg 29)

References

Brafman, O., & Beckstrom, R. A. (2006). *The spider and the starfish: The unstoppable power of leaderless organizations.* New York: Portfolio Trade.

Mitra, A. (2010). Creating a presence on social networks via narbs. *Global Media Journal, 9*(16), article no. 7.

O'Reilly, T. (2005). What is Web 2.0. Available at http://oreilly.com/web2/archive/what-is-web-20.html.

Shirky, C. (2008). Here comes everybody: *The power of organizing without organizations.* New York: Penguin.

Zittrain, J. (2008). *The future of the Internet—And how to stop it.* New Haven, CT: Yale University Press.

CHAPTER 3

Media as Tools

The Early Adopter's Dream Technology

It was hard to believe. A fully portable, shareable resource, which would radically alter the way we think, work, and live. The early adopters, indeed, would be so vastly empowered that there were great fears in the land concerning fairness, access, and equality. Subject to local protocol matches, groups of users could cheaply share information and coordinate activities across vast disconnections in space and time. Totally human-centered, deliberately matched to the strengths and weaknesses of our biological brains, able to evolve and alter to become easier to learn and deploy, the new piece of kit was, in fact, so simple that even a child could use it! Yet it would allow us to learn quicker, to grasp concepts otherwise beyond our reach. And— wonder of wonders—it would allow us to begin actively to think about our own thoughts and problem-solving strategies. As a result, it would invite us to systematically and repeatedly build better worlds to think in.

Many feared the new resource. They felt it was sure to encourage great laziness and to stop people thinking for themselves. If you could just ask someone for the answer, who would bother to learn anything? In the presence of such potent resources, wouldn't our "real" memories simply wither away? Where would it all lead? Might we not turn into a race of lazy, desensitized "post-humans"—hybrids who had traded flesh and spirit for artifice, abstraction. And power?

The above excerpt is taken from Andy Clark's (2003) book *Natural Born Cyborgs* (p. 80). What technology do you think Clark is referring to? Perhaps the Internet? The personal computer? Or maybe we go all the way back to the telegraph, or even the printing press? Actually, this story is about the development of language. Surprised? Our guess is that you may have expected the story to end with a discussion of a different communication technology, perhaps Facebook or Twitter. Instead, Clark makes the case that language—which is likely not something that we immediately think of as a technology—was a disruptive technology with great power, and that many feared it. In this way, it seems very much like many newer technologies that people have discussed being afraid of—such as oversharing using social media. However, it is our hope that throughout this chapter that you will come to see communication technologies (media) as tools we can use to accomplish our goals—they are neither inherently good nor bad for us. Of course, this doesn't necessarily mean all goals are good or that all types of usage are productive.

Consider the following questions:

- What are some of the central debates concerning the relationship between people and machines?
- What do we mean when we say that we use media as a tool?
- How is this different than how we used to look at media?
- Why are uses and gratifications especially important when we are examining MC?
- Are we inclined to think about MC using the assumptions we use in face-to-face exchanges?

If you are reading this book, you probably realize that technology changes very fast. As a college student, you probably remember a time before Facebook existed, and if you are a bit older (such as the authors of this text), you may even remember a time before the Internet was a mainstream technology, or perhaps, before it was a technology available to the public at all. Yet, it is pretty amazing (at least, to us) to take a step back and think about how fast some of these technological changes have occurred. As recently as 1995, mainstream magazines such as *Newsweek* were covering the Internet with great skepticism, suggesting it would never be "a mainstream thing" (see MC in Action: The Internet? Bah!).

Yet, here we sit little more than 20 years later, and the Internet has evolved into a technology that continues to impact so many people's lives on a daily basis—whether they realize it or not.

So, what happened? How was *Newsweek's* estimation so far off? Certainly, they were not the only skeptics of the new technology, yet their published commentary in 1995 has been almost categorically refuted in practice, even if similar criticisms often still remain. Futurist Ray Kurzweil (2005) offers a possible explanation in his Law of Accelerating Returns, suggesting that technological change

happens exponentially rather than linearly. As a result we often overestimate early benefits and underestimate long-term impacts. This occurs because technology builds upon itself. New inventions in one realm allow for newer inventions in other areas that would not have been possible previously (see MC in Action: Law of Accelerating Returns). So the ability to have new inventions in the future is greatly sped up by things that are invented now. Most people see technological change as a straight line; they see a current rate of change and assume that it will continue to be the same in 5, 10, 50 years, and so on. Instead, the exponential growth means that change will likely occur even faster during the next 5 years than it has in the previous 5 years.

MC IN ACTION

THE INTERNET? BAH!

Do our computer pundits lack all common sense? The truth is no online database will replace your daily newspaper, no CD-ROM can take the place of a competent teacher and no computer network will change the way government works.

In February 1995, an article published in the popular news magazine Newsweek suggested that the emerging Internet technology was more of a faddish interest of computer technicians than an actual social force. The author of the article lamented that technology could never replace "human contact" and that networked information was too clunky and cumbersome for the average person to be able to use without frustration. What do you think?

The Internet has evolved into a technology that continues to impact so many people's lives on a daily basis—whether they realize it or not.

© Ollyy/Shutterstock.com

The original article has been reproduced from its original print version (ironically enough) at: http://www.thedailybeast.com/newsweek/1995/02/26/the-internet-bah.html

Looking at the state of mediated technology today, tell us—do you think technology has been able to replace or impact (a) news media, (b) education, or (c) interpersonal relationships? Share your thoughts with us on Facebook at https://www.facebook.com/groups/234255823447372/ or on Twitter, using the #MediaAsTools hashtag.

MC IN ACTION

Law of Accelerating Returns

Author and futurist Ray Kurzweil has suggested that one way in which technological innovation is often misunderstood has to do with the linear manner in which we assume the world operates. In this, Kurzweil suggests that many individuals tend to overestimate the immediate and short-term influences of a technology (leading to disappointment and rejection of many innovations) and they also tend to underestimate the lasting and long-term influence (leading to rejection of older technologies that are in fact still quite relevant).

We might apply Kurzweil's law to understand the evolution of Facebook and de-evolution of MySpace. Today, Facebook and its one billion plus daily users has supplanted MySpace and its shrinking user base as the "go to" social media platform, which tends to lead many to discuss how Facebook "won" and MySpace "lost" the social media battle, to the point where many of you reading this might not even remember MySpace that well. However, re-examining the evolution of both programs reveals a logic completely in line with Kurzweil's thinking. Launched in 2003, MySpace is considered by many to be one of the first large-scale, open-access social media platforms in the world and enjoyed early success as a novel approach to the Internet—for the first time, Web users could own (for free) a personal and persistent presence on the Internet without having to learn any computer programming

language. From their 2003 launch, the platform swelled to over 100 million unique visitors in 2006 before declining in the face of a new platform: Facebook. Indeed, the potential "death knell" for MySpace came when the Facebook platform expanded from a college-only audience to consider anyone over the age of 13 (the same audience as MySpace). As Facebook eventually swelled to its over one billion daily active user accounts, the MySpace platform continued to shrink down to only a few million active users.

So, was MySpace a failure, and did Facebook "kill" it? Kurzweil might argue that if not for the invention and widespread adoption of MySpace as the first mainstream social media platform, there would never have been a Facebook. After all, prior to MySpace, the notion of having a personal profile on a persistent network space was more or less a foreign idea, reserved largely for a small segment of computer-savvy individuals building Angelfire pages (a web hosting service in the 1990s) or posting comments in bulletin boards. In other words, it took a MySpace to introduce consumers to the notion of social networks, and only then was another company (Facebook) able to improve on the original technology to make it more desirable to users. Think, what were the main differences between your MySpace and Facebook pages? And what might be the next social medium to challenge Facebook's user count?

Kuzweil's complete essay about the Law of Accelerating Returns can be accessed at: http://www.kurzweilai.net/the-law-of-accelerating-returns.

Exponential curves are those that appear as (nearly) straight horizontal lines for a long period (suggesting a stable period of innovation) and then quickly spike up in a nearly vertical line when they reach a critical point (suggesting a time of great innovation and rapid change). Communication technologies can be seen as

such a curve, based on this notion of accelerating returns. For most of human history, new inventions in communication occurred very rarely—for example, the time gap in innovation from writing to printing is estimated to have been as much as 4,000 years. With the arrival of mass media, however, these innovations came more and more frequently, such as the rather short 18-year gap between the first radio broadcast (an experimental transmission from the Metropolitan Opera in New York City on January 13, 1910) and the first regularly scheduled live television broadcast (images of windup toys and faces in motion, also originating in New York City on August 14, 1928). In general, media innovations came more and more frequently, and in recent years, technological change has begun to explode. In fact, some might argue that we are currently in the bend, or elbow, of the curve, where it has just started moving from a horizontal line to a vertical line. Consider that in today's media scene we can measure the distance between the introduction of MySpace (2003) and Facebook (2004) in a matter of months and describe and explain the growth of one technology to another in these terms. For a more dramatic example, consider that Google's social network Google Plus took only one month to reach 25 million unique users, while Twitter and Facebook needed nearly 36 months to accomplish the same user base benchmark.

> **Exponential curves** A term describing a pattern of technology adoption where the number of people using the technology suddenly spikes at a given historic moment.

What does this mean for the study of MC? First, it means that we are likely to see rapid growth in communication technologies in the near (and distant) future, perhaps even faster growth than we have seen in the last decade (if we truly are in the "bend" of the communication technology innovation curve). Second, because we perceive an exponential trend as a linear one, we are likely to overestimate what may happen with a technology in the short term but also underestimate the changes that come in the long term; of course, with accelerating returns the amount of time that is considered long term gets shorter and shorter as well. Third, and perhaps most importantly, this rapid change means that you as a user of communication technology will need to stay on top of these changes. You will likely need to have frequent and constant re-education about the latest advances to stay competitive in job markets and social situations alike; that is, you will need to adapt to a quickly shifting technology scene if you wish to meet your communication goals both today and tomorrow.

These incredibly fast changes in the technology itself can be difficult to stay on top of and that may only get harder as they speed up. Yet, it is also important to focus on what does not change as much—that is, the user and their goals. This is why this book takes the approach that it does. Do not forget that while technology changes at a faster and faster pace, people (in general) do not.

Natural-Born Cyborgs

There are many approaches and debates as to the relationship between people and technology. For example, technological determinism focuses on how technology changes people (e.g., Ellul, 1954). This approach tends to focus on the effects that technologies have on users and suggests that technology determines and shapes what people do with it and, eventually, society itself. An example of this approach might be an argument that the printing press led to the spread of literacy by making printed materials more available to individuals and thus introduced them to

> **Technological determinism** A perspective that suggests that technology drives society and culture.

Social shaping of technology A perspective that suggests that technology and society shape each other.

the written word. An alternate approach is that of social shaping of technology (SST). According to this approach, technology and society develop together, with each shaping the other (e.g., Williams & Edge, 1996). Referring to the printing press again, a SST approach might argue that the printing press grew from a greater societal need to have access to knowledge and printed words and that as people began to desire this common goal, printing technology was developed to meet public demand.

Perhaps consistent with this notion, according to Rogers (2003), technology tends to have two components: a hardware aspect and a software aspect. The hardware is the physical tool, whereas the software is the information of the tool. The hardware component is what we often think of when we think of technology, but the software piece is extremely important to remember and consider.

© phoelixDE/Shutterstock.com

The printing press led to the spread of literacy by making printed materials more available.

MC IN ACTION

WHAT TIME IS IT?

In *Natural-Born Cyborgs*, Clark talks about the invention of the wristwatch—and by extension, the notion of time itself—as a prime example of technology making us more rather than less human. Consider that in the modern era, we use time as a metric to organize, plan, and motivate our activities across an entire day, month, or even year (indeed, the very notions of days, months, and years are themselves inventions of the very concept of time). Prior to time as a "thing," early humans would organize their lives around their ability to hunt during the day and sleep at night, and they would make inferences about different climates based on obvious changes in air temperature over long periods. Yet, they did not schedule appointments around hunting, gathering, eating, and sleeping. These "day-to-day" activities were largely at the whim of impulse and opportunity—early humans hunted when they saw prey and slept when they were tired.

Fast forward to today, when we have set defined periods for breakfast (mornings, for sake of argument we will say 8:00 A.M.), lunch (noon), and dinner (6:00 P.M., although these meal times might not match up well with your daily habits). Having such a set schedule allows us to plan the rest of our work and sleep schedule so that we can arrange an efficient and productive daily routine, coordinating time for college courses as well as a vibrant social life. In fact, Clark would argue that this reliance on time is part of our cyborg nature: a biological species that has integrated an artificial (that is, not biological or natural to us) tool into our lives in order to help us live. How do you think your life on campus would change if there was no concept of time?

Technologies can also be re-invented, although some are hard/impossible to re-invent. Reinvention is the "degree to which an innovation is changed or modified by a user in the process of adoption and implementation" (Rogers, 2003, p. 17). A technology tends to diffuse more quickly when it can be re-invented. Perhaps this is one reason for the rapid diffusion of social media such as Facebook. Although the notion of affordances would suggest that a technology cannot be used for everything and might force/inspire some uses of the technology, Facebook is also a technology that has allowed for a great amount of re-invention as well. So, technologies tend to privilege some uses over others, but users can come up with new uses for many technologies. For example, a hammer is designed mostly to drive nails into wood and aid in the process of building things. However, a user could re-invent that hammer and use it as a weapon. The nature of the hammer does not allow for all re-inventions, as it would not allow a person to fly, for example. Communication technologies seem the same: Many allow for a great deal of re-invention (and even promote it); however, that re-invention possibility is likely bound to the affordances of the technology, both the hardware and software aspects.

> **Reinvention** The degree to which an innovation is changed or modified by a user in the process of adoption and implementation.

Still another approach comes from *Natural-Born Cyborgs*, in which Clark (2003) suggested that the distinction between technology and person is not nearly as clear as might be assumed; in fact, Clark suggests that it is our use of tools that makes us more rather than less human (see MC in Action: What Time Is It?). This is different from many other approaches, which note the dehumanizing effect of technology, with technology being something that separates us from our own humanity. However, recall from earlier in our text (Chapter 2) that we consider technology as a tool, and tools are merely devices used to accomplish goals—they have no objective value attached to them. Consider further that communication is a goal-driven pursuit, and you can begin to see how Clark's notions on technology might be extended to explain communication technology. In this way, communication technology is a tool that allows us to do the very things that make us human, such as share social information, form relationships, attempt to persuade others, and entertain ourselves and each other.

Thus, according to Clark, not only is technology not the antithesis of humanity, but *the use of technology and other tools are our natural state*. Our brains are wired to be cybernetic in that we are programmed to use tools as part of our daily lives; in essence, we are all "cyborgs." This does not necessarily mean that we are cyborgs in terms of the popular depiction of artificial metallic parts implanted into a human host, Terminator-style (although it could), but it does means that we extend ourselves through our tool usage, whether that tool is a hammer, a book, a wristwatch, or a Twitter account.

> **Cyborgs** Short for cybernetic organisms; refers to the fact that people utilize technology to "extend" themselves.

One way in which our brains are wired to be cyborgs is due to their inherent "plasticity"—their ability to physically change and adapt. The neural pathways, neurons, and nerve synapses in the brain can all be reworked, and probably with greater ease than was once thought. This plasticity allows us to deal with changes and utilize things that other species cannot (such as tools). One demonstration of this plasticity offered by Clark is to sit at your desk and place your left hand under the desktop. Have someone else tap on the top of the desk with one hand while tapping your left hand with their other hand. Do this long enough and your body will start to associate hitting the desk with the feeling. Now, have that other person hit the desk with a hammer, and see what happens.

> **Plasticity** The ability of the body, and the brain, to adapt and change.

This plasticity allows us to use our tools, and especially our communication tools, to extend our minds. Because our brains are changeable, we can use tools to overcome the limitations of our biological brains. And interestingly, it seems that we always have. For example, the ability to speak allows us to do many things we otherwise would not be able to do. The written word allowed us to write things down so we did not have to remember them, freeing up brain space to do other things. Consider taking notes in a class. Why do you do it? So you do not have to remember everything at all times, but can instead "extend" your memory out into this medium and free up brain space to do other things (at least until it is time to study and recall things for an exam or other assignment). We also use other media (be it television, video games, or the Internet) to do the same thing.

Given enough time and usage (and given an intuitive design), technologies can become seamless to the point where they are no longer registered by users as technologies and instead seem like a part of the "natural" human perceptual system. A common example of this might be verbal communication. The ability to communicate using language has not always been a part of the human experience, as early humans communicated only through the use of nonverbal signs and symbols, if at all. Over the course of our earliest evolution, humans began to experiment (in the loosest interpretation of that phrase) with different grunts and noises that came to represent different thoughts and feelings—recall our definition of communication as the act of stimulating meaning in the mind of another. As these early utterances developed and as human physiology developed along with them—for example, as the structures of the diaphragm, esophagus, larynx, lips, palate, tongue, and vocal pipe changed to be more conducive to producing a wider range of noises—humans continued to refine and reinforce patterns of speech and language to overcome the limitations of relying purely on nonverbal communication (such as the requirement of a clear line-of-sight in order to communicate). Over time, verbal communication became a "natural" mode of communication, and today we rarely consider language to be anything other than a default mode of human interaction. In this way, verbal communication would be what Clark would consider a transparent technology. Transparent technologies are ones we do not notice as we use them, as they seem almost intuitive and invisible in their use.

In contrast, opaque technologies are those that for whatever reason (be it poor interface design, a lack of requisite skills, or a lack of experience on behalf of the user), keep tripping the user up because they require constant and apparent attention. Using the language example from earlier, we might consider the learning of a second language as a communication technology that starts off as decidedly opaque. One of this book's authors lived in an older town in eastern Germany for an extended period of time as part of a study abroad program, and he struggled mightily with communicating in German throughout the trip. Although the languages share most of the same alphabet, the sentence structures, verb conjugations, and pronunciations are so different from the author's native English that the Germanic language seemed . . . well . . . foreign. Yet, with practice and patience (and about 3 years of time), the author was able to become proficient in this new language—this new tool for communicating his inner monologue to stimulate meaning in the mind of German-speaking others effectively.

Transparent technologies Technologies that have become so integrated, or seamless, into one's use that they are no longer noticed or recognized. An example of one for most people is the use of verbal language.

Opaque technologies Technologies that are still noticed during their use.

Indeed, this story points out another important feature of Clark's arguments: what starts out as opaque can become transparent, and what is opaque to some people is transparent to others. For example, is the Internet opaque or transparent? It is probably pretty transparent to most people reading this—one can think of the common answer to trying to solve a debate between friends as "why don't we Google it?" wherein we look up facts and information on Google just as simply as checking a wristwatch for the time of day (another of Clark's transparent technology examples). Yet, consider how your parents or grandparents might interact with the Internet, or consider how somebody living in a country without widespread computer access might feel about the transparency (or opacity) of the Internet? Another interesting example to consider here might be the use of emoji, Emoji are cartoon-like images, similar to emoticons (which are instead made using buttons on your keyboard) and represent a sort of shorthand language used in various forms of mediated communication (see MC in Action: Emoji: A New Language?). Like other languages, if you understand the generally accepted meanings represented by the symbols, then emoji are very transparent. If you don't, like the authors here, then emoji are incredibly opaque. The important consideration here is that, while interfaces can be designed to encourage more or less transparency, the variable is every bit as psychological as it is technical.

One of the best ways to think about extending our bodies and minds through technology is by considering those things our brains are best at and those things that our technology is best at. And in this way, also consider how we can use tools as scaffolding for the brain. In fact, we use a whole lot of things to "prop up" our brains. Some of those are simple internal tricks like mnemonics (you might remember the popular Roy G. Biv mnemonic to remember the colors of the rainbow in order from dark to light: red, orange, yellow, green, blue, indigo, violet), and others might be more external, like our media. We use written language and printed books to write down a story so as to not forget it, and so we will be able to

Scaffolding Tools that are used to bolster recall and manage relationships.

tell that story to others in the same way that we originally wrote it. In this way, we might also think of communication technologies such as Facebook as a form of scaffolding. For example, we can use Facebook to help us manage social connections with friends (strong ties) as well as other acquaintances and classmates (weak ties), and we can use our smartphones to store phone numbers so that we remember people's names rather than a seemingly random string of 10 digits when we want to contact them. Such technologies can bring us closer together by allowing us to focus on people rather than data, if we choose to use them that way.

© Alexey Boldin/Shutterstock, Inc.

We use Facebook to help us manage social connections with friends and other acquaintances.

MC IN ACTION

In many ways then, we can say that we are our tools—the scaffolding of our brains with our technology—working together to create who we are (as has been a theme in this book), for better and for worse. To state clearly, it is our approach that the tools themselves are not inherently "bad" or "good," but rather they allow us to do things that might be characterized as "bad" or "good." The tool may increase our ability to accomplish the goals that we want to accomplish, including many that might have previously been incredibly difficult, if not completely impossible. In the end, it comes down to the people using the tool. Thus, the best combination of our cybernetic selves—we being natural-born cyborgs to borrow Clark's metaphor—is for us to use our physical selves and brains for what they are best able to accomplish and use our tools for what they are best able to accomplish.

Using Our Tools

Uses and gratifications theory An approach to the study of communication media that focuses on what people do with media, rather than what media does to people.

As alluded to earlier in this chapter, different theories of media focus on the relation between media and people. Many of these theories discuss what media do to us and how we are affected by the media that we use. However, a theory called uses and gratifications theory (U&G: Rubin, 2009) focuses more on what we do with media. Borrowing from sociologists Katz, Blumler, and Gurevich (1974), the U&G model can be broken down as follows:

1. **The social and psychological origins of** As can be expected, there are many things in our environment that likely impact what we want to do at any given moment. Some of these include ourselves (physical and mental characteristics that make us each who we are) and our society (the people and traditions around us that inform our thoughts, actions, and behaviors).

2. **Needs, which generate** Who we are individually creates unique needs for each of us. Some of them are simply because we are human (for example, all of us have to eat and rest in order to ensure our continued survival), and some are more specific to each of us, such as an extroverted person wanting to have a large circle of friends in order to satisfy the need for the energy that comes from interacting with a lot of people (see MC in Action: Maslow's Hierarchy of Needs).

3. **Expectations of** Over time, and because of who we are, we develop expectations about how we can satisfy our needs. Many of these expectations come from watching others make media decisions for similar purposes and witnessing the results of those decisions (such as choosing to watch a somber movie and crying afterwards), and others come from our own past experiences with the same media products. Many of these expectations come from a trial and error process, where we end up seeing what products are able to gratify our needs. If it is has worked for us in past, we are likely to assume that it will work for us again in the future.

4. **The mass media or other sources, which lead to** As can be perhaps inferred by the general focus of this chapter and book, there are a great many things in our environment that can be used to accomplish our goals. Yet, we might argue that mediated communication (recall our discussion of that labeling in Chapter 1) is a particularly malleable part of our environments; that is, we have a good amount of control about the media tools we choose to use. An example of this might be watching an individual try to cope with a bad day at work. While this person could certainly choose to quit their job and no longer expose themselves to the source of their frustration, this would likely not be an easy choice to make. It might be easier (and more reasonable) for this person to instead choose to watch their favorite sitcom on television or play a video game for a few hours in order to distract them from the source of their frustration (see Chapter 13). Indeed, this goal-oriented use of media is the focal point of this book.

5. **Differential patterns of media exposure (or engagement in other activities), resulting in** Based on our needs and what we expect will be able to satisfy those needs, we purposefully select the tools that we think will work best or, at least, the best tools that are available to us. This pattern of exposure will vary depending on the needs and expectations associated with them.

6. **Needs gratifications and** One likely result of using a media channel to satisfy a need is that the need is gratified; that is, there is an effective match between gratification sought (expectations) and gratification obtained (results) by the user. In such a case, an individual is far more likely to choose the same channel in the future to satisfy the same need, and this feeds back into the expectations around what behaviors are likely to lead to gratifications. However, it can also be the case that gratifications sought do not match up with gratifications obtained, and in such situations, we will likely not repeat the choice in the future.

MC IN ACTION

MASLOW'S HIERARCHY OF NEEDS

One of the most popular discussions of human needs is that proposed in 1943 by developmental psychologist Abraham Maslow. In his "theory of human motivation" Maslow was among the first psychologists to suggest that human action is driven in large part by a need to feel self-actualized, that is, to feel as if we are maximizing our potential as individual humans. Such an approach was part of an emerging positive psychology movement that argued that humans are intrinsically motivated beings (they could be generally happy and satisfied without external gratification) but only after satisfying a number of basic psychological needs, including:

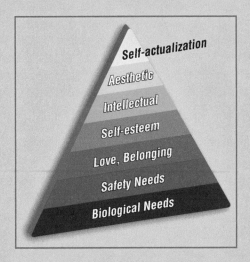

From College & Career Success, 5th Edition by Marsha Fralick. Copyright © 2011 by Kendall Hunt Publishing Company. Reprinted by permission.

1. Physiological needs, such as eating, sleeping, and procreation
2. Safety needs, such as having employment and shelter in order to ensure that their physiological needs are met on a consistent basis
3. Love and belonging needs, such as having healthy friendships and family connections
4. Esteem needs, such as a sense of confidence and accomplishment as well as the respect of others
5. Self-actualization needs, which represent the highest levels of human motivation such as creativity and spontaneity

7. **Other consequences, perhaps mostly unintended ones** Beyond a matching of expectations and effects, we might also consider the unintended results of usage that might also affect the individual user. For example, one might seek out a profanity-laden metal song in order to get over a fight with a boyfriend or girlfriend, but in doing so, one might also drive one's car faster and

become more hostile toward other people in the room. While the song did an excellent job of helping the person get over their romantic fight, it also has caused this person to become abnormally aggressive.

Face to Face: Standard?

As we close our discussion of media as a tool for communication, we should point out a final debate in the field of MC. As suggested by cognitive scientists Jim Hollan and Scott Stornetta (1992), it seems to be the case that many people hold face-to-face (FtF) communication up as a sort of "gold standard" of communication, especially for interpersonal interactions. Such an assumption might make sense, as we have been using face-to-face interaction as the norm for communication throughout most of our social evolution. As such, our communication systems are often designed in a manner to make them similar to FtF. A common point of contention raised by these people is that there are few, if any, communication technologies that can communicate the same sort of nonverbal elements of a conversation that an interpersonal conversation can, and thus, there is something "missing" or "lacking" from interpersonal computer-mediated communication. Technologies such as the telephone can only relay spoken language (perhaps voice, as well as tone and rate of speech), and text messaging can only relay textual information (basic words and perhaps a few emoji to express basic emotions). However, such a perspective limits how we think about mediated communication by confusing social cues with communication functions, and it does not acknowledge that there may be things that are accomplished even better online, even when we are discussing interpersonal communication.

As alluded to in the introduction of this textbook, notable computer-mediated communication scholars Joseph Walther and Art Ramirez Jr. (2009) have recently pointed out another important idea in the study of computer-mediated communication. In what we will dub their "functional" approach, they suggest that advancement in the field of commuter-mediated communication research is more likely to come by consideration of theoretically relevant, general characteristics of communication channels rather than simply comparing each new channel to FtF (or in comparing each new channel to the ones that it purports to replace). In this functional approach, Walther and Ramirez suggest that it is more important to focus attention on the why and how we use technologies for various functions, rather than looking only at the channels being used. We would argue that this approach is useful for considering all forms of mediated communication as well.

Functional approach The basic approach that this book takes to technology. It suggests that technology is best understood through the basic communication functions it helps people to accomplish.

To summarize this section of the book and to lead into the next chapters, there are three takeaway points to consider in the study of MC.

1. Media matters to people (it is real life). Often, we hear debates between students and working professionals alike that suggest (to paraphrase) that "Facebook is just a stupid program" and "that sort of thing only happens on Twitter," and in response, we are quick to remind these individuals that there is no inherent functional difference between our virtual and offline lives. The information, relationships, persuasion strategies, and entertainment media that we consume is made of the world and has real-world consequences, and we use them with real-world goals in mind.

2. Media are a tool, and they are neither a "good" nor a "bad." Here, we are reminded of recent debates surrounding the usage of social media in the workplace as a distraction or arguments that suggest violent video games to be a cause of antisocial and hostile behavior in children. In both cases, we suggest that media tools do not have an inherent pro- or antisocial application but rather are merely tools used to accomplish a goal. It is up to the user, and perhaps to society at large, to determine whether or not these uses are for the benefit or detriment to the personal, social, and public interests.

3. FtF is not the gold standard. Just because we have grown accustomed to using FtF communication as part of our daily interpersonal interactions, this does not necessarily mean that FtF is a superior form of communication as compared to MC. In fact, there are many circumstances where FtF interactions have been found to limit communication because they often introduce (sometimes, unintentionally) many extra elements to a conversation that can be thought of in terms of the Shannon–Weaver model (see Chapter 1) as noise in the communication process. We will address this elsewhere, but suffice it to say that we do not subscribe to the belief that FtF is by definition superior to MC for communication.

Key Terms

Exponential curves (pg 34)
Technological determinism (pg 35)
Social shaping of technology (pg 36)
Reinvention (pg 37)
Cyborgs (pg 37)
Plasticity (pg 37)
Transparent technologies (pg 38)
Opaque technologies (pg 38)
Scaffolding (pg 39)
Uses and gratifications theory (pg 40)
Functional approach (pg 43)

References

Clark, A. (2003). *Natural-born cyborgs*. New York: Oxford University Press.

Ellul, J. (1954). *The technological society*. New York: Alfred A. Knopf.

Hollan, J., & Stornetta, S. (1992). *Beyond being there*. Proceedings of the ACM CHI'92 Conference on Computer-Human Interaction, 119–125.

Katz, E., Blumler, J., & Gurevitch, M. (1974). Utilization of mass communication by the individual. In J. Blumler & E. Katz (Eds.), *The uses of mass communication: Current perspectives on gratifications research* (pp. 19–34). Beverly Hills, CA: Sage.

Kurzweil, R. (2005). *The singularity is near: When humans transcend biology*. New York: Penguin Books.

Maslow, A. H. (1943). A theory of human motivation. *Psychological Review, 50*, 370–396.

Rubin, A. M. (2009). Uses and gratifications perspective on media effects. In J. Bryant and M. B. Oliver (Eds.). *Media effects: Advances in theory and research*, 3rd ed., (pp. 165–184). New York: Routledge.

Rogers, E. M. (2003). *Diffusion of innovations* (5th ed.). New York: Free Press.

Walther, J. B., & Ramirez, A., Jr. (2009). New technologies and new directions in online relating. In S. W. Smith & S. R. Wilson (Eds.), *New directions in interpersonal communication research* (pp. 264–284). Newbury Park, CA: Sage.

Williams, R., & Edge, D. (1996). The social shaping of technology. *Research Policy, 25*, 865–899.

CHAPTER 4

Information Literacy in the Digital Age

Picture it. Southwest Connecticut, summer 1991. A young man is trying to decide his future. He needs to decide where to apply to college and does not even know where to begin. No one in his immediate family has attended college, and (except for a distant cousin) he plans on being the first person in his extended family to pursue higher education—some of you might have been in a similar position when deciding where to go to school as well. It will prove to be an enormously important decision in the way his life will unfold.

Having just obtained his driver's license, he decides to put on his Bugle Boy jeans, jump in his hatchback, and drive to the local shopping mall so that he can visit his nearest major chain bookstore. Curled up in a corner of the bookstore, he pines over stacks of college and university guides—giant manuals that attempt to reduce the campus experiences at hundreds of institutions down to a few pages. He looks for the books that contain information about everything from SAT score ranges for incoming freshmen to campus life, since he wants to make sure he is a good fit for a school before even applying (after all, completing paper-and-pencil applications takes a good deal of time and requires frequent trips to the post office). In the end, he walks out of Waldenbooks with three giant college guides, each one clocking in at over 1,000 pages and costing somewhere in the neighborhood of $20 apiece. He lugs them back to his car and returns home, where he will spend the next 3 months wading through page after page, eyes blurring as he takes in data concerning admissions criteria, academic programs, campus life, location, costs, and extramural activities.

Maybe the way this guy researched different colleges and decided where to apply seems a bit foreign. It is our assumption that when you searched for a college or university (perhaps the very college or university asking you to read this paragraph), you jumped online and visited the Web sites of various institutions in which you had an interest and followed a series of simple links to find the same information our guy found buried in his college guides. By using nonlinear navigation—that is, reading through information organized in terms of your specific topics and interests rather than through a predetermined flow or structure—you were able to find the information you needed quickly, instead of spending hours reading through the complete profile of every school in which you were interested. You probably did not even think of looking for a giant, print document containing this information, and indeed you might even be a bit surprised to know that they are still printed today (and they retail for as much as $25 each). Even if you wanted a large-format print document, you would likely be more inclined to download it onto some kind of electronic device, such as your laptop or e-reader.

The young man in the preceding story is one of the authors of this book (we will not tell you which one). Although he likes to think that 1991 was not all that long ago, he does recognize that the ways that someone can research colleges and institutions of higher learning has changed completely in the last 20-plus years. Although the information necessary to make a good decision might be similar—that is, SAT scores and college living information are still important to today's incoming freshman class—the ways in which people acquire that information are radically different. This illustrates a few of the fundamental tenets of information literacy and serves as a demonstration of information literacy in the digital age. In a very brief period, the ways that we acquire information have changed dramatically. This chapter will discuss the concept of information literacy. It will then go on to discuss the implications of information literacy in navigating our everyday lives, the centrality of information literacy in the workplace, and the potential problems posed by a lack of information literacy.

Information literacy
The ability of an individual to apply critical thinking skills to properly evaluate information.

Before we begin this chapter, think about these questions:

- What is information literacy, and why is it important?
- How do we become information literate?
- What skills are typically associated with information literacy?
- Why is information literacy so critical in the workplace?
- What disadvantages would you face if you were less information literate?

Information Literacy

Information literacy has been broadly defined as "the ability to recognize when information is needed and to locate, evaluate, effectively use, and communicate information in its various formats" (SUNY Council of Library Directors, 1997). Information literacy advocate and education scholar Mike Eisenberg (2008) adds that while many in academia and the workplace have become more computer literate over the past few decades, this does not necessarily translate into information literacy, as there is a difference between knowing how the hardware operates and knowing how to acquire the information necessary to make good decisions. As the amount of information online continues to expand at an exponential rate, it becomes more important to be information literate.

A number of conceptual models have been forwarded in terms of how we ought to think about information literacy and how institutions of higher learning should train people in information literacy. The most widely used of these is that forwarded by Eisenberg and Berkowitz (1990). The Eisenberg and Berkowitz model, which they dub the "Big 6," offers us a means of understanding information literacy as a process (see MC in Action: The Big Six). It begins with task definition. In order to understand how to acquire information, you first must know what it is that you are looking for and what the task you hope to accomplish looks like. You also need to be able to identify the information that is necessary in accomplishing this task. To return to our college search example, when you began looking at schools you probably determined that a number of key factors would be important in your decision—such as cost, distance, academic reputation, campus life, activities, and facilities. It may be the case that you figured this out from talking to friends, parents, or your guidance counselor, but in any case you needed to know what you were looking for before you started looking for it. You would not want to waste a lot of time looking at information that would not help you accomplish your goal, like reading all about economic policy in Moldova, if your goal was to decide what college to attend.

The second stage in the "Big 6" model involves the identification of sources. Here is a place where the norms and expectations regarding information literacy are in flux. At this stage, users identify all available sources of information and make determinations regarding what information will work the best. Of course, there are varying ways of defining what information is "best." For relatively unimportant decisions, we may be happy with the information we can get the fastest. For example, if we are trying to find a movie to watch tonight, a simple Google search for "movies and show times" might reveal the options in your area, and the first link might give you all you need to know—no need for further investigation. On the other hand, if you were buying a car, running a search for "used cars" and jumping on the first link would probably not be your best course of action. Interestingly, with incredibly important decisions, like matters of life or death, speed also plays a crucial role in the information we need. For example, if a bear is loose on your college campus, you may want to know this, as well as other information about it, as quickly as possible, and so you may not be able to take the time to search through many sources.

This is consistent with what we know about information processing from a persuasion standpoint too (see Chapter 11). With the exception of dire

Big 6 A six-stage model of information literacy designed by scholars to aid in the problem-solving process.

MC IN ACTION

THE BIG SIX

At www.big6.com, Eisenberg and Berkowitz define their approach to information literacy as "a six-stage model to help anyone solve problems or make decisions by using information." Their model is broken down as:

1. Task definition
   1.1 Define the problem
   1.2 Identify the information needed
2. Information seeking strategies
   2.1 Determine all possible sources
   2.2 Select the best sources
3. Location and access
   3.1 Locate sources
   3.2 Find information within sources
4. Use of Information
   4.1 Engage (e.g., read, hear, view)
   4.2 Extract relevant information
5. Synthesis
   5.1 Organize information from multiple sources
   5.2 Present information
6. Evaluation
   6.1 Judge the result (effectiveness)
   6.2 Judge the process (efficiency)

Reviewing the arguments on their Web page, what do you think of their arguments? Does this seem like a useful way of understanding information literacy? What do you think—if anything—is missing or unclear from their approach? Please share your thoughts on Facebook at https://www.facebook.com/groups/234255823447372/ or on Twitter, using the #MediaAsTools hashtag.

circumstances (like those mentioned above) we tend to devote more attention to the things that are of higher consequence to us. When we care about the matter in question we may turn to multiple sources and scrutinize the information. When it is less important (a more common occurrence) speed may be of greater importance than detail or arguments.

Source credibility
Perceptions of the source of a bit of information as being a believable one.

This also raises the issue of source credibility, which is a central component of this second stage. It is critical that information-literate individuals understand the difference between statements of fact and statements of opinion and the persuasive intent of advertising and marketing (again see chapters 10 and 11). The rise of the Internet has presented us with limitless sources of information, many of which are completely unreliable and/or may have ulterior motives for providing information. We are bombarded with advertising, spam, blog posts, rants, and attack pages every time we run a simple search. Learning how to sift through this information and identify credible and useful information then becomes critical. Always remember that it is YOU who are in control of the Internet, and so you need to pay more attention and be more vigilant about understanding the veracity of the information you utilize (consider again the verkeersbordvrij, Chapter 2).

Next come location and access. Information-literate users must be able to find the sources that make the most sense to use and to locate the information they need within those sources. Think back again to your college search. With a little research, you probably found your way to your university's home page. If you wished to find information on admissions standards, you probably knew (or could figure out) that clicking on the link to "Undergraduate Admissions" (or words to that effect) would lead you to this information. Likewise, "Financial Aid" would take you to information concerning finances, and "Sports and Recreation" may have taken you to information about on-campus activities. So you were able to find a credible source and then extract the necessary information from that source for your purposes.

You may also have been able to locate sources of "non-official" information about your university. Take, for example, the social media feeds associated with student organizations. The Twitter account associated with a student newspaper may have given you an idea of campus life and the prevailing conversations and debates on campus. Feeds from individual students with a significant number of followers could give you an inside look into a day in the life of a typical student. In a multimedia world, location may include both official and unofficial sources, as those with strong information literacy skills will understand that official sources will present the best image possible of the organization. At the same time, others outside might also have ulterior motives, such as intentionally presenting the university or organization in the worst possible image—or some version of the university that best fits their own personal goals.

This does, however, raise a sticky issue that we will tackle: discrepancies in access to information. It is impossible to extract the information you need from a source if you cannot access it. It may even be the case that you know where to find the information but cannot get to it. We will come back to this issue in a few pages.

Fourth, Berkowitz's model describes a skill set revolving around using the information. This is subdivided into two components—first, people must know how to physically engage in the material (read, listen, watch, search, etc.). Think about coming across a link to embedded video; you would probably click on the arrow in the middle of the page to begin video play, without giving it a second thought. However, somebody from an area with limited Internet access might stare at the screen wondering what it was that they were supposed to be reading (this technology would then be opaque, rather than transparent, for that user; see Chapter 3).

Second, information use includes extracting that which is relevant. At this stage, we are working into a finer level of specificity than simply finding information about our topic of interest—now we are looking for precisely the information necessary to make the decisions at hand. For instance, universities have a habit of burying the cost of tuition at the bottom of the financials page; information concerning financial aid can also be difficult to locate, as can the breakdown of tuition, room and board, and fees. In determining the costs of your university, you likely had to sift through some important, but less central, information in order to find it.

The Big 6 identifies synthesis as the next step in the information literacy process. At this stage, it is important to organize and present information from multiple sources in order to arrive at a decision. It may be the case that you were able to find and extract all of the information about your current university from the university Web site—and that is great. But simply finding out about your institution is not enough; you were comparing it to others in order to arrive at a decision. You likely repeated this process numerous times in order to gather the

information necessary to make comparisons. Furthermore, you likely did not rely only on information from the official university Web pages, but also consulted people you knew in college, especially at the colleges you were looking at, as well as friends, teachers, parents, clergy, and whomever else you thought might be able to weigh in on the decision. Verifying or reviewing information gleaned from a mediated source through an interpersonal relationship is very common, as we tend to believe that trusted others have our best interests at heart; decades of persuasion research suggests that interpersonal connections are more trusted than those that are purely mediated. Synthesis also involves the presentation of this information. This presentation can be of a formal or informal nature. In the workplace, you may be asked to research and present information about a certain product or organization, and this would be done in a very formal manner, complete with you wearing your nicest business attire. However, if you are trying to make personal decisions, you may need to make comparison lists in order to figure out what makes the most sense as a course of action, and this would likely be much more informal, perhaps written on the back of a napkin or envelope (like one of this book's authors often does). It could even constitute a mental checklist of pros and cons. In any case, you are taking the information you uncover and distilling it down into a concise, deliverable package, even if it is only meant for delivery to yourself.

Finally, the Big 6 model advocates an evaluation process during which individuals look back on what worked and what did not, both in terms of the process and the result. This stage also hones and sharpens our information literacy skills. By critically reflecting upon our own information seeking and acquisition, we can figure out how to do things better the next time (similar to the uses and gratifications process discussed in Chapter 3). As we repeat similar information-related tasks, they eventually become routinized. As bizarre as this probably seems to you now, there was a time when you did not know how to navigate a Web page, check your Facebook timeline, or post a tweet. Through trial, error, and self-assessment, they became things you do so routinely that you do not actively think about them (we might say they have become transparent; a term mentioned in an earlier chapter). Notably, changes to our information-seeking routines are often met with resistance, for exactly this reason. Everyone hates the new operating system, micro blog layout, site design, feed algorithm, and so on until they get used to finding what they need there. And then they do not.

Centrality of Information Literacy in the Workplace

Without a doubt, information literacy plays a central role in the workplace. In an increasingly media dependent, multinational economy, successfully navigating large-scale information and communication resources across time and cultural constraints is an essential skill.

In recent years, scholars have turned their attention to the ways in which information literacy can be conceptualized in the workplace. Bruce (1999) has identified what she calls the "seven faces" of information literacy in the workplace. The first of these—and perhaps most obvious—is the use of information technologies to stay informed and communicate with others in the workplace. For instance,

in a corporate setting people routinely use information systems to conduct business and manage workflow, records systems to manage human resources and payroll, and e-mail to communicate with both external and internal colleagues. The successful navigation of these technologies therefore involves not just learning the mechanical uses of the technology, but the placement of this technology within a vocational and cultural context. There are certain norms on the job that dictate how and when you use these technologies and the specific tasks for which they can be used.

Second, Bruce argues that knowing how to obtain information from appropriate sources constitutes another component of information literacy on the job, not unlike the information strategies stage identified in the Big 6 model. Bruce extends this model to go beyond information technologies and evaluate ideal information sources in a broader, organizational sense. For example, although you may be able to obtain necessary information about a project from online sources, it is likely the case that there is necessary information that must be derived from other sources as well. Someone in your organization likely has access to a budget, and your boss may have very specific ideas from a strategic planning standpoint. Understanding where (and sometimes who) to go for information, and that digital resources may not be the ideal source, is key.

Next, is understanding information literacy as a process leading to a solution or "deliverable." Bruce notes that given the variety of information resources available within an organization, there may be different, equally effective solutions derived from different sources. Depending on preferences, comfort with colleagues, familiarity with different data sources, and position within the organization, different individuals may have different but equally effective ways of accomplishing the same goals. Differences in these strategies sometimes create initial friction between colleagues, at least until results demonstrate their effectiveness.

The fourth "face" in this conceptualization is the control of information. Since individuals within organizations may get data from a variety of sources, the management of this information by individuals becomes critical. Keep in mind that in an organizational context, much of the information that is to be exchanged may be confidential, privileged, or at the very least managed by one individual. Not everyone has access to all of the information, as one would have with an Internet search for general information outside the workplace. Therefore, it is important that those who are in charge of gatekeeping (controlling information flow, see Chapter 5) information—electronically or otherwise—know how to release this information and get it out to people. In a way, the gatekeeping of information in a managerial context may actually be more important than the ability of others to locate it.

Fifth, it is likely the case that information literacy in the workplace includes the buildup of a personal knowledge repository that can be used to accomplish tasks or to help others accomplish theirs. From a media standpoint, it may be the case that one or more individuals within an organization become not only a knowledge source on the matter at hand, but also an expert in where to look for additional information. Think about your IT technician—the person in charge of technology at your school or workplace. Even if he or she cannot solve a problem off of the top of their head, they know exactly where to look, what searches and key terms to use, and myriad Web resources to explore, some of which you are likely not aware. Likewise, there may be information sources germane to your specific job functions that are largely unknown to the rest of the office. Knowing how to utilize these resources, and when and how to share them with others, then becomes a critical component of information literacy in the workplace.

Next, information literacy involves the merger of newly acquired information with existing expertise, not unlike the synthesis stage in the Big 6 model. In this experience, new information derived from electronic sources may be integrated into existing expertise, leading to new solutions. We might consider here that no one mode of learning is considered superior to another, but rather learning and information are additive—reading an old edition of Victor Hugo's *Les Miserables* with yellowed pages and handwritten notes in the margins can be combined with streaming video of a Broadway production of the musical to give the user a deeper and multimodal understanding of the experience.

Finally, Bruce offers an ethical experience associated with information literacy, that of knowing how to use the information wisely for the betterment of others. It may also extend to an understanding of intellectual property, knowing when to give due credit for obtained information, and the avoidance of plagiarism.

Clearly, the information literacy processes described in the Big 6 model have some applicability here, and if we think about the definitional issues surrounding information literacy, it is not difficult to see how critical this is for success in the workplace. In the context of media, the ability to identify, assess, and utilize electronic information is essential for success and advancement. There are a number of specific contexts in which the judicious use of information that is found online can be used to the advantage of organizations.

As stated earlier, information literacy in new media contexts is a learned skill. After our information-seeking habits become routinized, we do not think very hard about performing these tasks. As we will discuss later in this text, they become a tool, a means of manipulating our environment and maximizing positive outcomes for ourselves and those around us. But suppose for a second it was impossible for you to acquire these skills. Imagine that you found yourself in a position where you did not have access to or training in knowledge acquisition and information literacy. What if you turned on a computer for the first time and had no idea of what to do next? Would this not put you at a distinct disadvantage, academically and professionally?

Digital Divides and Knowledge Gaps

Digital divide An observation that there is a gap in technology access based on demographic and socioeconomic variables, creating digital "haves" and "have nots."

In 2006, Web usability expert Jakob Nielsen wrote about the digital divide, referring to "the fact that certain parts of the [world] population have substantially better opportunities to benefit from the new economy than other parts of the [world] population" (para. 1). In his essay, Nielsen expressed concern that so much of the world tended to focus on the digital divide—this division between the technology "haves" and "have nots"—purely in economic terms, that is, whether the average person could afford or not afford access to technology. To address this oversight, Nielsen proposed that we consider the digital divide at three distinct levels.

1. The economic divide, as explained earlier, deals simply with the ability for the average person to afford computing technology in order to access the Internet. Many experts such as Nielsen argue that with computer costs dropping to as low as $200 for a complete home computer system and with discounted Internet rates in some areas dropping below $20 monthly, we might consider the economic gap to be a smaller concern—in fact, a 2012 report by the Pew Internet & American Life Project (Zickuhr & Smith) reported that although one in five U.S. adults do not use the Internet, the primary reason for this lack of usage was not economic but rather a lack of interest. However, even though the price has dropped for computing power and Internet access and thus this divide may not be as big as it once was, it is still an important concern. Even if these economic divides are narrowing domestically, there is evidence that developing nations—as well as impoverished regions of developed nations—experience a tremendous disadvantage in terms of their access to electronic resources. For instance, a 2015 study suggests that only about 30% of the population of Africa is online, with some countries experiencing rates as low as 3% (see www.internet worldstats.com)

   Economic divide One dimension of the digital divide concerned with financial barriers to technology access, such as the ability to purchase a computer.

2. The usability divide, as Nielsen explains, is one's ability to functionally use a computer in order to access network technologies. Some researchers estimate that as much as 40 to 50 percent of the population might suffer from low technology literacy skills and that rarely are computers, computer programs, or Web pages designed with these users in mind. As discussed in Chapter 3, for people with low technology literacy, the tool will likely remain opaque and will thus not be as useful as it could be. Access to the technology is meaningless if one does not know how to use it effectively.

   Usability divide One dimension of the digital divide concerned with educational barriers to technology access, such as the ability to operate a computer.

3. The empowerment divide includes not only having physical access to technology and the basic skills to operate technology, but also considers the ability for an individual to use technology to satisfy their own goals and desires. Nielsen reports that for all of the social media users online, nearly 90 percent of them rarely contribute content to the networks and another 9 percent contribute sporadically (what Clay Shirky describes as a power-law function). If we consider our earlier discussions concerning the quality and value of a network, we can see the potential threat to the Internet that could happen if users are not empowered to participate.

   Empowerment divide One dimension of the digital divide concerned with understanding how to use technology to achieve specific goals.

As summarized in a report by the Nielsen Norman Group, "the economic divide is a non-issue, but the usability and empowerment divides alienate huge population groups who miss out on the Internet's potential" (Nielsen, 2006, para. 1). Given the centrality of information literacy in an increasingly global and increasingly technology-driven economy, the implications surrounding the privileging of

Some researchers estimate that as much as 40 to 50 percent of the population might suffer from low technology skills and that rarely are computers, computer programs, or Web pages designed with these users in mind.

MC IN ACTION

RESOLVING TO CLOSE THE DIGITAL DIVIDE

In November 1999, the National Communication Association (NCA)—the largest organization of communication academics in the United States—drafted and approved a Resolution on the Digital Divide. As one of only three recognized Resolutions in the organization's history, this was seen as an important step in the increasing importance of the issue at hand: more and more Americans were finding themselves divided by technology access—those who could afford digital content were enjoying the benefits of the emerging information economy far more than those without digital access. The original resolution called for greater awareness as to issues of technology access—the "economic divide" specified by Nielsen. However, and as Nielsen specified in his own writings, members of the NCA recognized that there was more to closing the digital divide than merely giving people computers and plugging them into the Internet. After deliberating, in November 2013 (in Washington, DC) the NCA approved the following amendments to the Resolution on the Digital Divide:

> "The National Communication Association (NCA) reaffirms its commitment to urge the development of free and low-cost ways of accessing the means for processing and distributing information in electronic forms. Moreover, NCA continues to urge the development of communication technologies that require minimal training but that still allow wide use of worldwide electronic resources. Additionally, as electronic resources continue to become increasingly demanding in terms of bandwidth, NCA asks that service providers ensure connection speeds necessary to competently

utilize said resources. Moreover, while many argue that economic barriers to technology have been greatly reduced, technology and information literacy barriers must be addressed with equal attention so that those with access to technology are able to use it effectively. Given these commitments, NCA resolves to take a leadership role in closing the Digital Divide through scholarship highlighting access, usability, and empowerment issues. NCA officers and staff will support legislation aimed at providing universal access to electronic means of communication. NCA will work with other organizations to ensure that communities in the U.S. and elsewhere have adequate electronic communication resources available to all. NCA members have a responsibility to increase awareness of the Digital Divide as a comprehensive social issue that considers socio-economic as well as literacy and empowerment dimensions. NCA urges its members to take an active role in increasing awareness of the Digital Divide through research, education, incorporating material on this problem into courses, through community consultation and education, and by advocating for appropriate policies at all levels of government, as well as supporting the production and distribution of open source software, as well as continued education on using said software."

Reviewing the new resolution, what elements of the digital divide do you see covered? Are there aspects of the resolution that do not address the digital divide?

information literacy are potentially severe. Indeed, the National Communication Association office has taken up a resolution on the digital divide and how scholars and practitioners should approach it moving forward (MC in Action: Resolving to Close the Digital Divide).

The Power of Numbers

Assuming one actually has the ability to access the technology and become information literate, one of the central challenges associated with information literacy revolves around separating "good" information from "bad" information. When we talk about the notion of user-created content, the central question we must ask is "do all of us always know more than one of us?" In the 1700s, French political scientist and mathematician Nicolas de Condorcet wrote of the power of group decision-making. His jury theorem proposed that the probability of a group of people making a correct decision is dependent on the individual probabilities of each group member making the right call. Expressed in terms of p_i where "p" is probability and "$_i$" represents an individual within a group, de Condorcet's theorem states that when p_i is greater than .50, the probability of a group making a correct decision increases with the addition of each new member—in other words, the group is statistically smarter than any given individual. However, if p_i is less than .50, the probability of a group making a correct decision decreases as it gets larger—that is, the group would be statistically dumber than any one of the individuals within it! In other words, we should not necessarily assume that groups will arrive at a better decision because there are more minds involved.

Jury theorem A mathematical proof that suggests that the probability of any group of individuals making a correct decision is based on the ability of the individuals within that group.

The Lesson of Wikipedia

Given the implications of de Condorcet's jury theorem, it might be natural to assume that the open-source nature of social media would lend itself to a collection of misinformation. Particularly with programs such as Wikipedia in which users are largely anonymous (at least, they are as anonymous as they choose to be), it might be difficult to trust that any information added to a group encyclopedia would be trustworthy. Yet, a 2005 article in the journal Nature found the average Wikipedia article to be about as accurate and reliable as the average *Encyclopedia Britannica* article—a study that Britannica publishers took great issue with (see MC in Action: Wikipedia = Trustworthy?). Although fact checking for accuracy is a challenging enough task, even more difficult is checking for completeness. For example, a 2011 study by Adam Brown discovered that while Wikipedia pages concerning politicians and candidates tend to be accurate, they also tend to omit significant amounts of information about the individual. We can check Wikipedia for accuracy, but we do not know what we do not know.

It is not difficult to see the challenges posed by crowdsourcing and user-generated content when it comes to information literacy. The final stage of the "Big 6," that concerning the evaluation of varying sources, is a complex and nuanced skill that may take a substantial amount of time to learn. Even if we assume that we have the access we need, the processes through which we discern the utility and quality of information are complex and largely unexamined through research.

MC IN ACTION

WIKIPEDIA = TRUSTWORTHY?

In 2008, Harvard law professor Jonathan Zittrain wrote about the lessons learned from Wikipedia, in particular what the program taught us about the power of using crowdsourcing for knowledge. He contended that the quality of Wikipedia pages could be understood in terms of how the users of the site saw their roles. Coining the term netizen, Zittrain argued that early users of the site saw themselves as part of a larger collective of individuals with a common goal—in this case, to provide accurate information from a variety of individual sources rather than one master source. Accomplishing this required each individual to recognize their place as a content co-creator and to recognize that the accuracy of content was more important than the individual writing the content, a focus on quality via content accuracy rather than quality via author credibility.

On first read, the concept of a netizen seems more metaphorical than practical.

However, Zittrain explained the function of netizenship by borrowing from a real-world example in the Dutch town of Drachten. In 2003, this mid-sized town of 43,000 residents tried a radical new experiment in hopes of reducing traffic accidents: they removed every traffic sign, light, and parking meter from the town (see Chapter 2). This line of "unsafe is safe" thinking suggests that

by removing legal restrictions on human behavior, we are forced to analyze our surroundings in order to accomplish our own goals. In the case of driving a vehicle, drivers are thought to pay more attention to their surroundings—the other passenger vehicles, turns and bends in the road, weather, and other traffic conditions—so that they can safely navigate from one point to the next. Indeed, traffic accidents in Drachten were found to be substantially reduced and other towns both in The Netherlands and in other countries have adopted similar models.

What can traffic deregulation teach us about Wikipedia? Zittrain expanded the general notion of awareness to the notion of being a netizen. If we consider the initial users of Wikipedia, it can be said that these initial editors had a common ethos, or core set of values, which they used to establish the inner workings of the program (see also Chapter 2). Including discussion posts with each article further helped these editors trust each other (the trust your neighbor principle), as each new edit was accompanied by an explanation of the reasoning behind it. When working with the editing interface, early users invoked the procrastination principle in allowing the users of the program to decide the most useful ways to format and structure articles rather than forcing articles to use a

---

Crowdsourcing Using larger groups of people—usually through social media technologies—in order to gather information on a given topic.

Netizen A notion that suggests all Internet users should consider themselves as residents of the Internet who are responsible for how the technology operates.

Ethos A core set of values used to extrapolate the details of a program.

Trust your neighbor principle In social media computing, this notion suggests that we must trust the other users of the network to behave in the same ways as we do. Such a notion is key to the concept of netizenship.

Procrastination principle In social media computing, the notion that one should allow users to decide ways to correct broken aspects of a technology rather than imposing rules or regulations for dealing with errors. Such an approach is thought to allow for more innovative solutions.

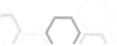

MC IN ACTION

WIKIPEDIA = TRUSTWORTHY? CONTINUED

predetermined template that might have choked off the creativity of the user base. Finally when dealing with article content, Postel's Law was invoked to suggest that accepting all edits—inaccurate as well as accurate—was preferred over strictly moderating new edits. Indeed, early research on this last point has shown the user base to be surprisingly adept at correcting bad information in articles, with

a study by IBM engineers finding that nearly half of errors on a sample of Wikipedia articles are fixed by other users within one minute of being posted.

How accurate do you think Wikipedia is? Share your thoughts with us on Facebook at https://www.facebook.com/ groups/234255823447372/ or on Twitter, using the #MediaAsTools hashtag.

Postel's law In communication technology, it suggests that a computing system should take a conservative approach in how it transmits data (being sure that it is standardized) but a liberal approach in how data are received (allowing any form of data so long as their meaning can be interpreted). This approach is often applied to management and organization, suggesting managers should be clear in their own instructions to others, but allow for a variety of different bits of information from those they manage.

The scientific community is only beginning to make sense of the ways in which we arrive at these judgments.

One important consideration that an open forum for information suggests is that users must be both willing and able to participate in order to maximize the quality of the final product (be a netizen, see MC in Action: Wikipedia = Trustworthy?). Hopefully, the realization that you can help create something better provokes your willingness to participate. The next section of this chapter will provide some short details into thinking about how to better assess (and thus add to) information.

Critical Thinking Basics

Richard Paul and Linda Elder have suggested that there are some universal intellectual standards to which we can hold arguments (2008). These standards of critical thinking might be even more crucial as today's media users have access to more information than at any other point in history—and not only more information, but more information more quickly. Indeed, some are even wondering if audience preferences for speedy information are beginning to trump their ability or desire to critically evaluate things such as breaking news—one example of this was a fake news story (or rather, Twitter headline) sent from a hacked Associated Press account which resulted in a momentary stock market crash on April 23, 2013 (see MC in Action: One Tweet, One Terrible Tuesday). As we attempt to assess information, these are good standards to think about. Ask yourself these things as you read and contribute to information online. This will help to make you a more critical contributor and put you on your way to being more able to do so.

The first universal standard is clarity. Clarity can be considered a gateway standard; that is, if a statement is unclear, we cannot determine whether it is accurate or relevant. In most cases, we simply stop evaluating the information

Clarity A dimension of critical thinking concerned with the vagueness of information; less vague information is usually considered more credible than more vague information.

MC IN ACTION

ONE TWEET, ONE TERRIBLE TUESDAY

*Breaking: Two Explosions in the White House
and Barack Obama is injured*

At 1:07 p.m. Eastern Standard Time on Tuesday, April 23, 2013 the Associated Press sent the above message out through their Twitter account. Although @AP almost immediately clarified that the Tweet was written by a hacker—somebody who broke into the account and posted the fake tweet— by then it had been retweeted (sent by other users) nearly 3,000 times, resulting in a good deal of public panic, and to the surprise of many, a nearly one percent drop in the Dow Jones Industrial Index. In other words, one false tweet caused the largest financial system in the world to momentarily crash. Following the initial tweet, stock markets recovered fairly quickly as news spread just as fast that the message was a fake.

How did this happen? How did so many people read, believe, and share this information and do it so quickly? And how were we all duped enough to ripple through the stock market? *Mental Floss's* Arika Okrent (http:// mentalfloss.com/article/50275/7-ways-we- could-tell-ap-tweet-was-fake) went back the next day and reanalyzed the message. She found seven ways in which the discerning news reader would have been able to spot the

fraud immediately. For example, AP news stories always write the word "Breaking" in all capital letters (i.e., BREAKING). Also, the AP would never refer to the president of the United States as Barack Obama without his formal title (i.e., President Barack Obama or President Obama). Looking closer, she also noticed that the tweet was not signed by the reporter who crafted it (AP tweets usually include the initials of the reporter), and also the tweet was not sent from the Social Flow media service to which the AP subscribes.

Although the markets quickly recovered— indeed they closed the day up 152.29 points (a 1.05 percent gain from the opening mark)— this "flash crash" has many analysts revisiting their computer algorithms and their own people to build more critical thinking barriers into the information processing equation.

Have you ever read something online that you knew was fake, but was spreading quickly? If so, how did you know that it was fake . . . and did you do anything to stop it? Share your thoughts with us on Facebook at https://www. facebook.com/groups/234255823447372/ or on Twitter, using the #MediaAsTools hashtag.

altogether (this is why your English instructors are so adamant about term papers having thesis statements). However, be careful not to just assume "well, I do not understand what that person is saying, so they must be smart." There are many people who try to pass themselves off as experts by purposely being unclear and by trying to use that ambiguity to their advantage.

Accuracy A dimension of critical thinking concerned with how correct information is.

The next standard that can be assessed is the accuracy of the information provided. Is what you are reading/writing/saying correct? You may attempt to figure that out by understanding who your sources are and considering what motivations they have for misrepresenting their information, checking multiple sources, and building an understanding of how information is created.

You might assume that accuracy is the highest standard to hold information up to, but Paul and Elder (2008) suggest six more standards that come after the accuracy has been assessed. The first of these is precision. How specific is the information or statement provided? Information may be accurate but it might be so vague that it is not very useful. For example, somebody might tell us that in a recent study one brand of diet pill outperformed all other brands in terms of total weight loss after a three-month trial. However, this information is a bit vague in that it does not tell us (among other things) information such as how much weight was actually lost, how many other diet pills were being evaluated, or how well all of the diet pills did against a placebo condition. If we told you that the "outper-forming" diet pill resulted in only two pounds lost after 3 months, this would not be nearly as appealing. Thus, we typically want information to be as precise as possible.

Next up, information can be specific, but not relevant, which is the fourth universal standard. In a political debate a piece of information may not actually be relevant, and if it is not, how does it help us at that time? For example, when politicians attack each other with name-calling—such as branding each other as "bleeding-heart Liberal" or "war-mongering Conservative" during a debate over the civil rights that should be granted to terrorists when they are in custody—these names might be accurate and specific, but are they really relevant to the issues of leadership? Sometimes they might be, but more often, they are not. In fact, many folks refer to the use of irrelevant information when debating an issue of impor-tance as throwing a red herring into the argument—as it is similar to how English foxhunters would train their dogs to better follow a fox's scent by tossing other objects such as pungent herring carcasses onto the hunting grounds.

The next standard to consider is depth. People often provide information that is superficial and not at a level consistent with the complexity of the argument. Put another way, people often give overly simple solutions to more complex problems. The classic "Just Say No" antidrug campaigns of the 1980s and early 1990s may be an example of this. Drug use and abuse is probably a much more complicated issue than simply just saying no, involving any number of socioeconomic issues and substance dependency concerns. If you are a drug addict, then your ability to "just say no" is likely greatly diminished. If you are a small child being pressured into drugs at a school or playground—the main target for the campaign—saying no might not be an option, or at least might not be a persuasive enough argument to convince a drug pusher to leave you alone. In general, the standard of depth suggests that you should provide infor-mation at a level of detail consistent with the issue you are discussing.

Along similar lines comes the next uni-versal standard: breadth of information. Does a position cover all of the necessary information? Information can be very deep, but not be broad enough because it does not cover all of the impor-tant angles. Again, politicians often have good arguments that provide a good amount of detail about a specific problem but do not consider other

Precision A dimension of critical thinking concerned with how specific information is.

Relevance A dimen-sion of critical think-ing concerned with information being related to the current topic of discussion.

Red herring A logical fallacy that employs extraneous or irrelevant informa-tion to an argument as an attempt to distract from the central issue of discussion.

Depth A dimension of critical thinking concerned with the level of detail given to a current topic of discussion.

Breadth A dimension of critical thinking concerned with the overall coverage of the complexities of a given topic of discussion.

In a political debate, a piece of information may not be relevant, and if it is not, how does it help us at that time?

associated bits of information. For example, we might hear a politician give an impassioned speech about why the closing of coal mines in West Virginia would help save workers' lives by getting them out of remarkably dangerous environments that they work in on a daily basis and give the audience accurate, precise, and detailed information regarding mine safety. Yet, such a speech overlooks the fact that closing mines might sharply raise unemployment in that state that has few other developed industries that can retrain and hire the displaced miners.

Combining different points of view leads to the next universal standard: logic. When we think and when information from various perspectives is brought together, we bring this variety together in some order. Logic exists when the combination of those thoughts is mutually supporting and makes sense in combination.

Logic can be a very difficult standard to achieve, but the final universal standard is often the hardest because it is often rooted in our own unconscious biases. That is the standard of fairness. Fairness implies treating all relevant viewpoints in a similar manner by holding all of them to similar standards of quality, without reference to one's own feelings or opinions. Basically, to be fair is to see all potential perspectives without bias until the information provided to you allows you to discount other perspectives critically rather than subjectively. This is very difficult because we tend to perceive things in a manner biased to our worldview—a notion referred to as egocentrism. However, with work, this fairness standard can be achieved.

Logic A dimension of critical thinking concerned with the internal consistency of the arguments being made during a given topic of discussion.

Fairness A dimension of critical thinking concerned with the objectivity given to different viewpoints regarding a given topic of discussion.

Egocentrism A logical fallacy in which individuals tend to process information in terms of their own viewpoints rather than reading the information on its own merits.

Conclusion

In sum, a lot of information exists online. In fact, more information exists than we can likely handle. However, as the duty for assessing and creating information falls more to YOU, it becomes that much more important to be willing and able to make sure the information you are consuming and contributing is of high quality. After all, while the sheer volume of information readily available to today's consumer is at an all-time high, the standards of evaluating that information—just as the goals of human communication itself—have not changed.

Key Terms

Information literacy (pg 48)
Big 6 (pg 49)
Source credibility (pg 50)
Digital divide (pg 54)
Economic divide (pg 55)
Usability divide (pg 55)
Empowerment divide (pg 55)
Jury theorem (pg 57)
Crowdsourcing (pg 58)
Netizen (pg 58)
Ethos (pg 58)
Trust your neighbor principle (pg 58)

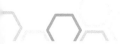

References

Bruce, C. S. (1999). Workplace experiences of information literacy. *International Journal of Information Management, 19*, 33–47.

Brown, A. (2011). Wikipedia as a data course for political scientists: Accuracy and completeness of coverage. *PS: Political Science and Politics, 44*(2), 339–343.

Eisenberg, M. (2008). Information literacy: Essential skills for the information age, *DESIDOC Journal of Library & Information Technology, 28*(2), 39–47.

Eisenberg, Michael B., & Berkowitz, Robert E. (1990). *Information problem-solving: The Big Six skills approach to library and information skills instruction*. Norwood, NJ: Ablex.

Nielsen, J. (2006, November 20). Digital Divide: The 3 stages. Retrieved December 1, 2013 from http://www.nngroup.com/articles/digital-divide-the-three-stages/.

Paul, R., & Elder, L. (2008). *The miniature guide to critical thinking: Concepts and tools*. Tomales, CA: Foundation for Critical Thinking.

SUNY Council of Library Directors. (1997). *Information literacy initiative: Final Report*. Retrieved May 16, 2013 from http://www.sunyconnect.suny.edu/ili/final.htm.

Zickuhr, K. & Smith, A. (2012). Digital differences. Pew Internet & American Life Project. Retrieved December 1, 2013 from http://pewinternet.org/Reports/2012/Digital-differences.aspx.

CHAPTER 5

News

In 1948—by some estimates about 50 years into the mass media revolution—communication theorist Harold Lasswell wrote on the function of media in modern society. For Lasswell, who was a normative theorist, the mass media were an agent of surveillance (providing information about the environment), correlation (providing different viewpoints and solutions to address problems in the environment), and transmission (providing a socialization to the environment). While later in our textbook we will address an area that Lasswell might have overlooked (Chapters 12 and 13 discuss the importance of entertainment), we can nonetheless see each of Lasswell's three stated media functions quite prominently in news media. From the earliest newspapers of the Han dynasty in China, to today's Reddit.com customized news ranking feeds, individuals continue to turn to news media to understand the complexities of their world. This chapter will explore all of these points in greater detail.

Normative theory/ normative theorist Theories that offer suggestions or explanations as how a particular phenomenon ought to be.

Before we begin, let us ask ourselves the following:

- What are the criteria for newsworthiness?
- How might new media technologies change the criteria we emphasize most?
- What is citizen journalism, and what does it say about the democratic process?
- What is the inverted pyramid approach to news writing? Is it the same in electronic news?
- What are some of the central theories associated with how we use and process news?

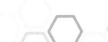

What Is News?

On its face, the concept of news seems simple enough—news is anything that is happening right now. When one thinks of news, one may think of late-breaking broadcasts, bold newspaper headlines, or frantic Twitter updates about important world events and unfolding stories. Yet, not all news is dramatic, worldly, or even necessarily important in an objective sense. News is usually written to appeal to the broad interests of the public, but understanding these interests can be a difficult process. In trying to define the essential qualities of a newsworthy event, several media scholars and journalism professionals have offered numerous lists of characteristics. For our discussion, we will focus on five: timeliness, prominence, proximity, consequence, and human interest.

Timeliness

Timing A component of news that refers to when a particular event happened.

As alluded to earlier in this section, one of the most apparent characteristics of newsworthiness is the timing of an event. Events happening right now are often the most interesting and novel to news audiences, and in general more recent events are considered more newsworthy. For example, news of a college student winning a prestigious scholarship last weekend is more newsworthy than news of the same student and the same scholarship award last year.

Prominence

Prominence A component of news that refers to how well-known the individuals in an event are.

Another characteristic of newsworthiness is the relative prominence of the event itself or individuals involved in the event. Prominence refers to the social import of something, or how famous it is. Often in news coverage we read about the daily lives of famous individuals because their prominence drives interest in the event they are partaking in (even if that event would not be news if the authors of this book did it). For example, it is not uncommon to read about a sports celebrity shopping at the mall or politicians eating at a public restaurant. Conversely, stories about regular people gaining notoriety through prominent events also gain newsworthiness—such as coverage of stadium food vendors preparing for a major sporting event or interviews with citizens attending a U.S. presidential debate. In each of these cases, the prominence of the people (in the former two cases) or the circumstances (in the latter two cases) drives interest in the stories.

Proximity

Proximity A component of news that refers to how close an event is to its audience.

The physical location of an event can also influence its newsworthiness. Proximity refers to the physical location of one thing in relation to another; in the case of news, we might consider where an event happened in relation to where we live. A story about freshman orientation at the University of Oregon might not have much of an interest to students at West Virginia University because Eugene, Oregon, and Morgantown, West Virginia are physically quite far away from each other (2,650 miles, according to Google Maps)—the story of Oregon's orientation is too distant from WVU for it to be important to the students in Morgantown. However, while

the two universities are separated geographically, it might be the case that the students at both universities have quite a bit in common: both are major land grant colleges with large student bodies, both have prominent athletic and academic programs, and both admit thousands of freshman students each year. In fact, these similarities might result in students from both schools having a semantic proximity to each other—that is, they might have similar thoughts and feelings about college that would make a story on freshman orientation have a universal appeal to both populations.

Consequence

Events that hold great consequences for people tend to be considered more newsworthy. Stories about war and suffering tend to dominate headlines because such events have a dire impact on how large segments of the population go about their daily lives regardless of where they are happening. Likewise, political events and crime stories tend to take precedence in much news coverage, as these stories inform us about changes to our legislative system or particularly dangerous events happening in communities around us. In general, the more people who are affected by a story, the greater the sense of newsworthiness associated with a given event.

Consequence(s) A component of news that refers to the impact of a particular event on individuals or society.

Human Interest

One of the more abstract characteristics of newsworthiness is the notion of human interest, or the extent to which a story talks about the human condition. Human interest stories tend to place intense focus on one person or group of people, usually with an emotional appeal or angle. Common human interest stories include reports about country or city life, exceptionally gifted or smart children, or the "common folk on the street" sort of interviews. Many refer to these as "soft news" stories because they tend to place less emphasis on the other characteristics of newsworthiness, but this is not always the case. For example, a story about U.S. President Barack Obama quitting his smoking habit might speak about the dual stresses that come from addiction withdrawal and living a public life, but the singular and emotional focus on Mr. Obama would likely qualify this story as a human interest one even though he is a prominent individual (the story might even have a semantic proximity to smokers or individuals who have recently given up smoking).

Human interest A component of news that refers to how a story might speak to the greater human experience.

It is important to realize that not all five of these characteristics need to be present for a story to be newsworthy, and under different conditions, some characteristics will dominate a news story over others (see MC in Action: What Is News?).

Earliest Sources of News

Although many people tend to think of newspapers and mass media as a relatively modern invention (indeed, most textbooks on the history of mass media connect the development of the modern mass communication age with the Industrial Revolution), it is important to note that elements of what we might consider "the news" have been around since as far back as ancient China.

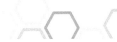

MC IN ACTION

As social creatures, people have always had a thirst for knowledge about the world around them. Spoken chronicles and fables are as old as speech itself, but the first written gazettes find their roots during the Han dynasty of China—one of the first government-produced news bulletins ("tipao" or "邸報") in the second century AD (Brook, 1998). Most of these were hand printed on ornate silk and were designed for official eyes only, usually containing economic, military, and political information (although as with any physical artifact, they often found their way into common hands). According to Infelise (2002), other similar one-page bulletins ("avvisi") were printed in the city-state of Venice and sold to the general public for one *gazzetta* (a small coin).

However, the invention and widespread distribution of the Johannes Gutenberg's moveable-type printing press made it economically viable for private organizations to enter the newspaper business. The printing press substantially drove down the cost of creating a newspaper by reducing the time and talent required to handwrite each individual gazette. Moreover, as the availability of native language printed materials had sharply increased in the two centuries following Gutenberg's invention (in Western Europe alone, nearly 200 million books were estimated printed in the 16th century and nearly 550 million in the 17th century), common folks and nobility alike had a newfound appreciation for the written word.

While not the first newspaper (this honor is typically given to *Relation aller Furnemmen und gedenckwurdigen Historien/Account of all distinguished and commemorable news*, a German-language newspaper started in Strasbourg in 1605), Sweden's *Post-och Inrikes Tidningar (PoIT,* translated roughly to *Post and Domestic Times*) has been published continually in Stockholm since at least 1645. The earliest correspondents for PoIT were postmasters who were asked to submit reports of what they and their employees had seen or heard. The publication thrived as ordinary Swedish citizens were able to read about happenings from around their country, and it still exists today (see MC in Action: The Oldest Newspaper?). It took only four decades later for American Colonialist Richard Pierce of Boston to begin publishing *Publick Occurrences Both Forreign and Domestick* on September 25, 1690. Pierce wrote critically of the British Crown and, although it was very popular with other Colonials, the newspaper was shuttered after one

MC IN ACTION

The Oldest Newspaper?

The Swedish Post-och Inrikes Tidningar (PoIT) is the oldest known continually published newspaper in the world, having started publication in 1645. However, as of January 1, 2007, the paper has shifted to an online-only publication format, which was regarded by former Editor-in-Chief Hans Holm as "a cultural disaster" (Associated Press, 2007). The paper can be accessed at: https://poit.bolagsverket.se/poit/PublikPoitIn.do

In the United States, the only copy of Publick Occurrences Both Forreign and Domestick was published in 1690 before being shut down by order of the British Crown. The full text of that edition has been transcribed and is available for reading at: http://en.wikisource.org/wiki/Publick_Occurrences_Both_Forreign_and_Domestick

What is the history of the printed newspaper in your hometown? Is the printed newspaper still a primary source of news for your family, or do you get news from another source? Let's talk about these questions with other students and scholars, on Facebook at https://www.facebook.com/groups/234255823447372/ or Twitter using the #MediaAsTools hashtag.

edition for, among other things, "sundry doubtful and uncertain Reports." Many historians point to this newspaper as being historically important for two reasons: (1) showing the power of the printed word to the early Colonials and (2) eventually leading to the Stamp Act of 1765, which required Crown approval via an embossed stamp to publish many works (Shaw, 1959).

Jacksonian Democracy and the Birth of Objectivity

For many modern news media consumers, the notion of objectivity in news reporting is considered a benchmark of journalistic practice and is something that we have come to expect from journalists and the news that they produce. Although debates ensue over the perceived bias in news programming (notably, research shows that the largest predictor of perceived bias is an individual's own political view), we can generally agree that the concept of fair and balanced news coverage is both respected and expected from Western news audiences. In fact, many journalism professionals suggest that just as human beings are rarely objective, it might not be plausible to expect a journalist to take a neutral position on a given story or event. However, as in their careers, reporters might be expected by news audiences to treat stories and events—and perhaps most importantly, the people in those stories and events—with a sense of fairness.

However, this was not always the case. As seen in the preceding examples, the earliest *tipao* were published by the Han dynasty and featured content favorable to the Emperor, and the rebellious *Publick Occurrences* was closed by the English Crown for being unfavorable to the King. Countless other newspapers and

Objectivity Related to the news, presenting a story or event in an impartial and unbiased manner. Objective news stories usually focus more on the facts and figures of a story or event, rather than the opinions of the person(s) delivering the news.

Fairness Related to the news, discussing the elements of a story or events in such a way as that it is free from discrimination.

MC IN ACTION

A POLITICAL VOICE FOR ALL?

The Fifteenth Amendment to the Constitution—the amendment removing voting restrictions based on "race, color, or previous condition of servitude" was not ratified until 1870, and the Nineteenth Amendment—giving women the right to vote—was not ratified until 1920. How do you think these developments might have influenced the manner of presenting content in newspapers? Did these new political audiences have unique goals related to seeking information from the media? Forming relationships with the media? Engaging in persuasion with media messages? Seeking entertainment?

Subjectivity Related to the news, presenting a story or event in a partial and biased manner. Subjective news stories usually focus more on the opinions a person(s) has(have) of a story or event, rather than facts and figures.

Jacksonian Democracy A political belief that recognized the democratic authority of everyday citizens; a contrast with aristocratic politics of the early 19th century that focused primarily on issues dealing with the privileged class.

Penny press Early newspapers that were printed during the late 19th and early 20th centuries that contained popular news and opinion articles and often cost only one penny. The penny press is considered the earliest form of the modern newspaper.

pamphlets published in the British Colonies during the Revolutionary War were unabashedly for or against British rule of the Colonies—Thomas Paine's famous *Common Sense* comes to mind—and there was no pause or pretense of non-bias. Publishers were viewed (and often viewed themselves) as influential persons, and they used their printing presses to lobby for their causes. After all, as newspapers were largely aimed at the economic and political elite (that is, those with political influence through their finances and their voting rights), mass media was less about information and more about persuasion. In short, these early publications tended to eschew objectivity and, instead, were written with a great deal of subjectivity.

It was not until a change in political philosophy that changes in journalism practice began to occur. The early 1800s saw a gradual shift from elite politics that placed focus on winning the opinions of societal elite to a new era of Jacksonian Democracy in which the political influence of the common man was recognized. As suffrage rights expanded to incorporate larger parts of society—eventually including all White male citizens (so there were still large parts of society not included at this time, see MC in Action: A Political Voice for All?)—there was an increased focus on the politics of the "common man." This common audience was far larger and diverse than the niche audiences (the political and economic elite) for which the earliest political pamphlets were targeted. For example, the common man was less concerned with commodity pricing and political dogma and more interested in what author George R. R. Martin might label "rain, healthy children, and a summer that never ends"; that is, the common man was chiefly interested in the weather (be it for planning the day or for nurturing crops), family, and a comfortable life.

This new political interest suggested a new type of news medium—the penny press—that, true to its name, sold more popular news and events for the cost of a penny. Publishers in turn sought out advertisers eager to reach a growing middle class consumer base to offset publication costs, and in this a fundamental shift in the production of news had begun. For the first time, messages were created for mass consumption, and mass consumption meant that they needed to appeal to the widest possible audience—hence, stories were written in an inverted pyramid style (see MC in Action: The Inverted Pyramid), and stories that focused on facts over fantasy, information over imagination, and news over narrative became increasingly normal.

MC IN ACTION

THE INVERTED PYRAMID

A hallmark of modern-day journalism is a method of story writing called the inverted pyramid. In this style, reporters are tasked with placing the most important elements of a story in the lead, or first paragraph, before expanding on the story in subsequent paragraphs. The lead usually contains the who, what, when, and where of an event, while the rest of the story tends to focus on and develop the why and how elements.

Why put all of the important information up front? Some media historians have suggested that early news stories tended to be sent over unreliable telegraph lines, so journalists were instructed to make sure that the most important elements of a story were included in the first paragraph in case the telegraph did not fully transmit. Others merely suggested that early newspapers were short on space, and as such, writing in inverted pyramid style allowed newspaper editors and producers to cut a story rather easily by simply deleting paragraphs following the lead.

Regardless of its origins, it is clear that this style of writing has been influential in shaping how the news is produced even today. Yet, as we see a change in news coverage from the printed newspaper to the online edition, many wonder if the inverted pyramid will become more or less popular as a method of news writing. What have your experiences been when you read online news? Do you see stories written in inverted pyramid style? Are there new styles you have begun to notice? And how do these styles influence how audiences read the news, in your opinion?

With a classmate, read the front page of your campus newspaper. How many stories are written in an inverted pyramid style? For stories that are not, can you identify a particular reason why the writer and/or editor might have chosen a different style of writing? Perhaps you're seeing a new style of writing for the Internet—share your findings and your thoughts with us, via Facebook at https://www.facebook.com/groups/234255823447372/ or Twitter using the #MediaAsTools hashtag.

News and the Electronic Age

Following the growth of printed newspapers, developments in communication technology helped grow the news industry. While a complete history of news and the electronic age is somewhat beyond the scope of this book (indeed, there are hundreds of volumes written on this specific subject), there are some important key points relevant to the study of MC.

Some of the earliest electronic mass communication messages can be attributed to electrical engineer Frank Conrad, a Pittsburgh native who in 1919 established the first licensed radio station KDKA from his garage in western Pennsylvania. For programming, Conrad and his family would play music, or he would play records from his personal collection (a likely copyright violation, given the "for private use only" commonly found on most music purchases from stores or downloaded online). He would also read football and other sports scores from

Inverted pyramid style A style of newswriting that presents the most important elements of a story in the first paragraph and adds more specific details in subsequent paragraphs.

MC IN ACTION

THE SEXIEST BLUES AND BLACKS

As early television was broadcast in black and white, often the makeup used by actors was not the familiar shades of red rouge and silver eyeliner we might expect. The earliest makeup artists found that the best way to accentuate facial features was to use shades of increasingly dark blue and black makeup, as darker colors retained their color depth on black-and-white film. As well, many common special effects such as blood in vampire movies were actually poured from bottles of chocolate sauce (which likely made acting out bloodsucking scenes quite tasty).

the daily newspapers of the time. Conrad even pioneered—albeit not intentionally—the first commercial sponsorship, by arranging to play records from a local music shop in exchange for promising to mention the shop by name on the radio. KDKA and its primary financial backer (and Conrad's employer) Westinghouse continued to be major force in the early days of electronic mass media, from their first live news bulletin (the results of the 1920 U.S. presidential election), the first live sporting event (an April 1921 prize fight between Johnny Dundee and Johnny Ray broadcast live from Pittsburgh's Motor Square Garden), and several other firsts. Importantly in all of these "firsts," radio audiences were able to experience events without actually having to be present for them; that is, radio transcended the limitations of space and (in some cases) time.

In a similar vein, the first television broadcasts in the 1930s and 1940s built on the notion of an electronic broadcast media system by introducing images and video to the system—audiences could both hear and see events without witnessing them firsthand. Experimental broadcasts in the 1920s led the way to the Federal Communications Commission (FCC, the same entity responsibly for licensing Conrad's KDKA-AM radio station) granting commercial broadcast licenses to WNBC and WCBS (both in New York City) and WPTZ (Philadelphia) in the early 1940s. Color television saw its way into commercial broadcast in 1953, adding a layer of familiar reality to the original black-and-white broadcasts (see MC in Action: The Sexiest Blues and Blacks).

Broadcast versus Narrowcast versus Tailoring

Electromagnetic spectrum In telecommunications, the available range of frequencies—such as radio television waves—that can be used to transmit information.

An important note about broadcast systems, however, is that they are regulated by the FCC because they are sent through public airwaves—legally, the U.S. government owns the electromagnetic spectrum, on which radio and television signals, as well as modern-day cellular phone signals, are reliant to transmit data (see MC in Action: The Fellas at the Freakin' FCC!). Thus, we often discuss the introduction of cable television as a break from the broadcast system; after all, cable signals are transmitted through physical cables connecting each receiver to a central

MC IN ACTION

THE FELLAS AT THE FREAKIN' FCC!

A 2005 episode of the popular FOX animated series *Family Guy* centered around Griffin family patriarch Peter broadcasting his own television channel, PTV, from his garage (in a very similar fashion to Conrad and the humble beginnings of KDKA-AM Pittsburgh). Producing questionable content such as "Dogs Humping" and "The Peter Griffin Sideboob Hour," Peter was trying to create content for folks with interests similar to his own. However, when he chose to broadcast these programs over public airwaves, the FCC intervened (assisted by a call-in complaint by Griffin matriarch Lois) and threatened to shut down PTV unless Peter substantially altered his programming.

This episode perhaps highlights a few key elements (and misconceptions) about how the FCC operates. First, we must recognize that Peter's programming, while potentially offensive to some, would have been acceptable for distribution in a narrowcast form such as a cable network. Second, we must recognize that the FCC does not actively monitor content; rather, it typically responds only after a complaint is registered with their office. In fact, the "complaint and respond" operation is an element of the FCC often lost on the average media audience—so long as a particular community does not find material offensive, then even broadcasters are free to distribute potentially questionable content provided it meets community standards of decency. Thus, while Peter and his gang lamented the FCC's censorship of their programming, one solution would have been to create a cable network instead.

[Link to video for the Family Guy song, from Hulu: http://www.youtube.com/watch?v=2NDPT0Ph5rA]

distribution system (the authors are reminded of ordering cable service and watching the line workers dig several trenches in front of their mountain home in order to physically connect their television receiver to a larger trunk cable, which ran under the highway to yet a larger cable).

Why is this important? Because cable signals do not use public airways nor are they accessible to the public at large (one must pay a subscription fee to receive cable signals), they are often considered to be narrowcast (sent to smaller and intentional audiences; broadcasts are sent indiscriminately for anyone with a radio or television receiver to use) and thus not subject to FCC regulation. Thus, as a narrowcast system, cable provided content producers with the ability to produce more nuanced (and perhaps controversial) content free from federal regulation, and it also allowed producers to know their audiences in much greater detail, producing content for smaller audiences that might not have been as popular for a larger one. In fact, from an early 1957 cable broadcast of a musical version of *Cinderella* to the widespread introduction of original cable programming in 1972, cable programs have almost always catered to smaller audiences, what media scholar Herbert Gans (1975) might call "taste cultures" of individuals with rather narrow information, relationship, persuasion, or entertainment goals.

Narrowcasting and Editorializing

In some ways, narrowcasting has also led to a growth of Web sites and smaller publications that are much more reminiscent of the older media landscape of the Colonial times—publications that are more directed at being influential and often targeted at specific audiences rather than distributing objective news reports for broad audiences. In part, this growth of more subjective news outlets closely mirrors the growth of digital media such as the Internet and the World Wide Web (see Chapter 2) in that as the relative cost and skill required to create an online presence have dropped significantly, more groups and individuals who wish to influence society are publishing their own editorial content. In the United States, two such Web sites that exemplify the growth of more openly biased editorial news Web sites are the *Drudge Report* (http://www.drudgereport.com) and *Huffington Post* (http://www.huffingtonpost.com), the former often identified as a more conservative publication and the latter as more liberal. *Drudge Report* began in 1995 as a weekly subscription-based e-mail newsletter, largely covering and distributing gossip that founder Matt Drudge was able to access using connections both in Hollywood and Washington, D. C. Readership of the *Drudge Report*, and perhaps the publication's credibility, increased substantially when in January 1998 Drudge became the first media outlet to report on former U.S. President Bill Clinton's sex scandal with White House intern Monika Lewinsky (archived at http://www.drudgereportarchives.com/data/2002/01/17/20020117_175502_ml.htm). *Huffington Post* launched in May 2005 as a online news outlet that many saw as the "liberal" version of the *Drudge Report*, and quickly grew into a 10-language, international media giant eventually purchased in 2011 by AOL for over $315 million. In 2012, *Huffington Post* became the first exclusively digital news organization to win the coveted Pulitzer Prize for their coverage of wounded U.S. soldiers called "Beyond the Battlefield" (available at: http://www.huffingtonpost.com/news/beyond-the-battlefield/). As of February 2016, both the *Drudge Report* (130) and *Huffington Post* (128) are among the top 200 Web sites visited on the entire World Wide Web, according to Alexa Web Analytics. The *Drudge Report* and *Huffington Post* are but two examples of a growing online market of advocacy newspapers that have eschewed traditional values of broadcast media such as objectivity in order to advance or oppose social issues. Notably, neither publication has been free of criticism. Some are concerned that such publications might not be as transparent with their more non-objective editorial missions, which might be seen as deceptive by media audiences not accustomed to reading subjective rather than objective news content (see also Chapter 4). Others have questioned the willingness of such publications to quickly publish and then retract controversial and questionably accurate content, such as incidents in which the *Drudge Report* has printed about high profile politicians' domestic disputes using claimed anonymous sources—in 1997, they reported on gossip regarding a Clinton White House aide's alleged domestic assault; in 1999, they claimed to have video evidence of Clinton's "love child" birthed with a prostitute. Both stories were quickly retracted. Some of these publications have been criticized for taking advantage of unpaid contributors to flesh out their products, with the *Huffington Post* facing both a content strike and a class-action lawsuit for engaging in the practice despite having been acquired that same year for over $300 million. Despite these concerns, such narrowcast publications continue to provide an emerging and compelling option for media audiences seeking additional angles to the stories and events of the day.

Conservative In the context of politics and news, a conservative publication would be more likely to feature editorials and stories that support traditional social attitudes and values; the "status quo."

Liberal In the context of politics and news, a liberal publication would be more likely to feature editorials and stories that support emerging social attitudes and values.

Gossip Information related to ongoing events or stories, or the people involved in those stories, that has been neither confirmed nor rejected as accurate.

Advocacy newspapers Publications, either online or offline, that intentionally and openly adopt a subjective or editorial approach to journalism. Advocacy newspapers tend to actively align their editorial coverage in support or opposition of social issues.

MC IN ACTION

THE INTERNET LIVES!

The WorldWideWeb (W3) is a wide-area hypermedia information retrieval initiative aiming to give universal access to a large universe of documents.

~Tim Berners-Lee, written at the top of the first Web site

On April 6, 1991, any computer user with the appropriate hardware and software would have read the above message upon logging on to http://info.cern.ch. This was the world's first Web site, written by the technology's creator, Tim Berners-Lee. Berners-Lee had invented the technology for the modern-day Internet as you and I know it as early as 1989 (see also Chapter 2 for more on the basics of the Internet). The early years of the Internet saw initially slow growth: 10 Web sites by the end of 1992, 130 by 1993, and just over by 2700 by 1994—perhaps one of the most famous being the January 1994 release of Yahoo!.

Courtesy of Internet live stats (http://www.internetlivestats.com), the growth of the Internet can be tracked by counting the number of individual domain names, such as "wvu.edu," "kendallhunt.com," or "moveon.org." Plotting the total number of Web sites for each year since 1991 shows that initially slow growth quickly spiked in 1993, likely a function of Berners-Lee releasing the World Wide Web technology into the public domain. This rapid diffusion of Berners-Lee's technology saw continued growth, with 17 million Web pages by the end of 2000, 206 million by 2010, and right at one billion pages in 2014—which Berners-Lee

recognized via his Twitter feed (@timberners_lee) "tp://www.internetlivestats.com/watch/websites/ recently passed a billion websites by their count . . ." (a message that received 161 likes and 341 retweets: https://twitter.com/timberners_lee/status/511988109211627520).

Is the Internet still growing? 2015 saw a nearly 11 percent decline in the total number of Web sites, and some estimate that as many as 75 percent of these sites are inactive. *WIRED*'s Chris Anderson and Michael Wolfe forecasted the decline of Web sites in 2010, explaining that the increased popularity of mobile communication and app-based interfaces along with social media applications has users more engaged with each other than with more traditional (i.e., mass media-style) Web pages. As of early 2016, two of the most popular Web sites in the United States were Facebook (#2) and YouTube (#3), both the two most popular smartphone apps as of 2015 (in order, #1 and #2). Much of this interaction via social media is less about mass audience content (Web-based news stories, for example) and more about user-generated content.

Does this mean that news media should abandon their Web pages? Unlikely. Internet live stats explains

Diffusion (of innovation) A process by which inventions are adopted for use throughout society. These diffusion processes often follow a very predictable pattern of slow initial growth, followed by rapid adoption, and followed by another slower growth period.

User-generated content Online content, both private and public, that is created by (usually) amateur media users, often without commercial influence. Sharing personal photos to Facebook or writing blog posts could both be considered forms of user-generated content.

MC IN ACTION

The Internet Lives! CONTINUED

that similar Web site reductions were observed in 2010 and 2013, often due to monthly fluctuations in how Web domains are calculated. They predict a return to the one billion mark by the end of 2016, with this being a stable prediction as of 2017 (a point at which the number will not dip below one billion). Other reasons to keep those e-publications online? The #1 Web site is Google (http://www.google.com) and the vast majority of all Web traffic comes in the form of a Google search. Notably, news aggregators such as Yahoo! (#5), Reddit (#9),

and Bing (#20) are immensely popular, as are more traditional news outlets such as ESPN (#21), CNN (#23), and the *New York Times* (#24), which remain primary destinations for news. Be it spoken, printed, digitized, or some technological medium not yet imagined, audiences will likely always have a curiosity and need to be informed about the stories and events around them. As one of our authors (a former newspaper reporter, both print and online) often tells his students, "newspapers specialize in news, not paper."

MC IN ACTION

The Epic Googleplex

At its best, EPIC is a summary of the world—deeper, broader and more nuanced than anything ever available before . . . but at its worst, and for too many, EPIC is merely a collection of trivia, much of it untrue.

~EPIC 2014

In 2004, new media commentators Robin Sloan and Matt Thompson presented a video presentation to the Poynter Institute (a U.S.-based nonprofit news education organization) on the future of news audiences. Inventing the hypothetical EPIC (Evolving Personalized Information Construct), they described a media system completely tailored for each individual Web user wherein the computer program EPIC searches and scans the entirety of online news in a given point in time, taking and rewriting existing news stories so that they can be tailored to meet the discrete personality, interests, and tastes of individual audience members. As the preceding quote demonstrates, such a news distribution system would likely be remarkably attractive for each user, but

could have a devastating impact on society as a whole as we might lose collective sight of the important issues of the day.

Yet, as we have argued in this book (and as Sloan and Thompson seem to suggest), media tools are not inherently "good" or "bad," but rather the individuals who use them can do so in a "good" or "bad" manner. What do you think? As you use more tailored media sources to learn, relate, persuade, and entertain yourselves and your friends, do you feel more or less informed about the world? Why or why not?

Talk to us about your experiences, either on Facebook at https://www.facebook.com/ groups/234255823447372/ or Twitter using the #MediaAsTools hashtag.

The original EPIC videos are available for viewing at http://epic.makingithappen.co.uk/

This broadcasting/narrowcasting dichotomy perhaps sets the stage for today's media landscape. First, this dichotomy is not restricted to electronic media—major daily newspapers are often considered analogous to broadcast information (intended for large and indiscriminate audiences), whereas magazines and books might be considered more narrowcast (intended for smaller and more intentional audiences). Second, the introduction of Internet-based media programs gave rise to a third type of tailored media content (see also Chapter 2). If we follow the logic that cable television broke somewhat from the traditional definition of "mass" communication by transmitting messages to a more intimate audience while also increasing the number of channels available to the audience (see Chapter 12), then we can see the shift to Internet media as continuing to break from this "mass" concept. Internet audiences can be large (such as the audience for CNN.com or USAToday.com, largely the same as their cable or newspaper audiences, respectively), but they can also be quite small (such as the audience for our research blog #ixlab notes . . .—http://comm.wvu.edu/fs/research/notes—which is not much more than a small handful of communication technology scholars). Given the estimated 1.01 billion registered Web pages as of September 2014 (which actually declined in 2015, but rebounded; see MC in Action: The Internet Lives!), we see a media system that is increasingly customized, or customizable, to fit the unique goals of each user (for better or worse, see MC in Action: The Epic Googleplex).

Social Media—Are We All Media?

It's about the many wrestling power from the few . . . and how that will not only change the world, but also change the way the world changes.

~Lev Grossman, *TIME Magazine* (2005)

As discussed in Chapter 2, in 2006 *Time Magazine* named you—literally, every Internet user—as their Person of the Year. While it can be debated if the Web 2.0 revolution happened before, during, or after 2006 (also see Chapter 2), it cannot be debated that the widespread adoption of social media technologies have dramatically shifted how people use and are influenced by media. It has also created a rise in what has been commonly called "citizen journalism."

Social media Communication technologies that allow users to create public profiles in order to connect and share content with other users, usually in a public fashion.

Citizen Journalism

In early 2012, popular technology magazine *WIRED Magazine* ran an editorial on major U.S. events that were reported on not by traditional journalists or news agencies but rather by Twitter users. Ordinary people armed with smartphones and a need to talk about their surroundings told us of U.S. Airways 1549 landing safely in the Hudson River (@highfours), an armed gunman on the loose at Discovery Channel's Maryland headquarters (@jdivenere), damage from a rare earthquake in Richmond, Virginia (@JordnJnkieJuice), and even a forewarning about a New York City SWAT patrol organizing blocks from Zuccotti Park—headquarters of the infamous Occupy Wall Street protests (Roots drummer @questlove). In fact,

even the death of Osama bin Laden was witnessed and reported live on Twitter long before any news crew or world media could know of the event. These citizen journalists served as the eyes, ears, and mouth for some of the most prominent and newsworthy stories of the early 21st century (see MC in Action: "Uh oh, now I'm the guy who liveblogged the Osama raid without knowing it").

What does this mean for traditional journalism? Some media critics have argued that stagnant and sliding subscriptions to major U.S. newspapers coupled with the speed of citizen journalists might spell an end to news media as we know it. That is, there are concerns that larger media organizations cannot compete with the collective knowledge and access of an entire social media network that is constantly texting, tweeting, and sharing pictures of the world around them. At the same time, many are wary to trust the word of untrained citizen journalists as they might often violate what new media researcher Vincent Maher (2005) has called the "three deadly E's": ethics (not having an understanding of the ethical principles of journalism), economics (not having the economic resources to produce quality and in-depth coverage of events), and epistemology (subscribing to an activist rather than an objective motivation to produce the news). Indeed Shirky (2008) talked cautiously about the "mass amateurization of information" that the Web 2.0 universe has ushered in wherein each Internet user has an equal stake in the creation of new information, as well as collaborating on this information to ensure its accuracy and utility for us all. In fact, the same Web 2.0 principles so critical to encouraging and enabling citizen journalism also led to the creation of many of the advocacy newspapers mentioned earlier in this chapter—indeed, many would consider individuals such as Matt Drudge to be among the first successful digital citizen journalists.

By the same token, it may be the case that this shift toward citizen journalism has changed the ways in which audiences think about their content, and even their expectations of that content. A number of scholars have proposed a model of "hybrid journalism," in which audiences relying on news delivered through mobile technologies such as Twitter do not necessarily expect objective reporting, but instead are seeking commentary, impression formation, and affective content associated with the events at hand. For instance, in their examination of Twitter news content associated with the 2011 Egyptian revolution, Papacharissi and de Fatima Oliveira (2012) propose that on-the-ground reports of the revolution were as important in terms of consensus building and galvanization as they were in providing factual information. It may be the case that part of the appeal of this kind of reporting is the affective sense of being in the middle of the action, and that this further serves to blur the lines between entertainment and news.

Theories of Information Effects

So, how might we be influenced by the information we receive from our media systems? And how might newer communication technologies change the way we previously considered information effects? The following sections will discuss some of the major theories of information effects as well as the role of communication technology in altering (or not) some of their fundamental precepts.

MC IN ACTION

The Flyswat Heard Around the Twitter

In the early morning hours of May 2, 2011, Sohaib Athar, an IT consultant living in Pakistan, was awoken by the sound of military helicopters hovering near his apartment window. Startled and a bit annoyed by the event, Athar did what many of the 140 million other Twitter users tend to do late at night and took to the social media platform to complain. One-hundred and forty characters at a time, @ReallyVirtual hopped online and wrote about the strangeness of a helicopter hovering over the normally quiet town of Abbottabad and at one point wrote that the helicopter had better leave or he would smack it with a huge flyswatter. Distracted by the commotion, Athar watched the events in front of him and tweeted his thoughts and reactions. From helicopter noise came an explosion, a crash, and reports from other Twitter users that the helicopters were not even Pakistani. Reports of a family that perished in the crash and then the spotting of a second helicopter continued to grab Athar's attention, and Twitter users began to retweet his comments, transforming the humble-and-humorous IT consultant into an ad hoc correspondent for a growing global audience. Athar confirmed reports of a helicopter crash and other details of the event by reporting what he was seeing and hearing before the big news came across: it was revealed by international news services that Osama bin Laden was killed in a U.S. Navy SEAL raid on a compound in Abbottabad, Pakistan. The Mashable archive of his tweets is at: http://mashable.com/2011/05/01/live-tweet-bin-laden-raid/

Agenda Setting Theory

The press may not be successful much of the time in telling people what to think, but it is stunningly successful in telling its readers what to think about.

~Bernard Cohen, *The Press and Foreign Policy* (1963)

The preceding quote is often considered one of the most clear and concise explanations of the influence of news media's coverage on individuals and society—coverage of news stories tends to influence the type of stories we pay attention to far more than it influences how we actually feel about the stories themselves. Studied prominently in coverage of politics and elections, the landmark study on agenda setting theory was conducted by Maxwell McCombs and Donald Shaw in Chapel Hill, North Carolina (both were associate professors at the University of North Carolina, Chapel Hill at the time of the study). McCombs and Shaw (1972) were interested in how newspaper and television coverage of the 1968 U.S. presidential election was shaping the political opinions of people in the region, the so-called "agenda" of the election. Their study found a significant correlation between those issues of importance to the average Chapel Hill resident in October

1968 (shortly before the election) and coverage of the very same events in June 1968 (five months prior to the election); more importantly, the correlation between voters' opinions in June and newspaper coverage in October was not significant. This data demonstrated that prior and prominent newspaper coverage of a given issue increased the salience of these issues in the minds of news media audiences. Follow-up stories over the next 40 years have generally been consistent with the agenda setting hypothesis.

What increases salience? One major component is the *placement* of a story in a particular news medium. For newspapers, stories placed on the front page (the headline stories) tend to command more attention from the audience than stories placed inside the newspaper. Another component of salience is the *amount of time and space* that news media devote to a particular issue. During the 2012 Summer Olympics in London, many online news sources such as www.usatoday.com and www.msnbc.com created special sections specifically for coverage of the Olympic Games, athletes, and related stories. A third component of salience is the *duration of coverage* of a given event. A prominent example would be the National Football League's Super Bowl championship game, which tends to receive international coverage for weeks leading up to the actual game (typically played in early February of each year). Indeed, the intense media focus on the Super Bowl is likely one reason why live broadcasts of the game regularly set audience records—the February 5, 2012 game between the New York Giants and the New England Patriots was viewed by an estimated 166.8 million people in the United States, almost one-half of the entire population.

Might the notion of agenda setting be changing in an increasingly Web 2.0 world? Traditionally within any news organization, the placement of news stories was determined by a few gatekeepers who chose news coverage items based on any number of different variables—including the newsworthiness characteristics from earlier in this chapter as well as different local and regional interests, as well as advertising and corporate influences. Decisions to give priority coverage to some events over others were driven by these variables as well as physical constraints, such as the limited number of professional reporters available to cover the events as well as physical limitations on the space available in any given newspaper or news segment.

Fast forward to today's social media landscape, and we see examples of citizen journalists and other regular people creating and sharing their observations about the world around them. As content is increasingly published by the masses and shared with the masses, one might question the role of mass media organizations as agenda setters—after all, some of the biggest events of the 21st century have been covered by the masses first and the news media elite second (again, the story of @ReallyVirtual and the death of Osama bin Laden). At the same time, emerging research has suggested that the majority of Twitter messages—as many as 50 percent of all shared Web links, for example—are generated by fewer than 20,000 Twitter users (consider that in light of Twitter's nearly 250 million users as of December 2013), with traditional media sources creating the majority of content (Wu, Hofman, Mason & Watts, 2011). Such a distribution of content is indicative of what famed Italian economist Vilfredo Pareto called the 80–20 rule (since renamed the Pareto principle) by which 80 percent of economic capital, specifically land in his studies, tends to be controlled by a smaller 20 percent of the general population. Considering that the capital of our Information Age is content,

Salience Whether or not a particular thought or belief is on one's mind.

Gatekeeper An individual such as a newspaper editor or television producer who is responsible for the selection of different stories over others.

80–20 rule/Pareto principle A principle borrowed from economics that suggests that a majority 80 percent of capital tends to be controlled by a minority 20 percent of elite stakeholders. Pareto principle distributions have been widely applied to understand how land and wealth are distributed in several countries, as well as how Internet traffic can be understood.

one might suggest that traditional sources of information still control a good bit of influence in today's networked society. At the same time, as more citizen journalists begin to create persistent presences in the media landscape—such as creating and sustaining advocacy publications like those discussed earlier in this chapter—one might begin to see a shift in the major gatekeepers of the 21st century, just as Revolutionaries such as Benjamin Franklin and Thomas Paine did in the 1700s!

Exemplification Theory

In 1968, scholar George Gerbner established his "mean world effect" to explain why heavy users of mass media believed that the world around them was a particularly dangerous place despite crime statistics suggesting violent crime to be on a nationwide decline (Gerbner, Gross, Morgan, Signorielli, & Shanahan, 2002). His cultivation theory suggested that media users' perceptions of the real world were heavily skewed in favor of the view of the world on television—specifically, as more crime television and news broadcasts began to dominate, the media audiences naturally assumed that there was more crime around them. Particularly as stories including base-rate information about crimes were largely nonexistent in the news, stories about crime lead to beliefs and fears about the same.

> **Base-rate** Information concerning the typical incidence with which an event takes place in the social world.

A look into the mechanics of the mass media through exemplification theory explains this process in more detail. Consider the characteristics of a story as being newsworthy. Stories of news value often attract the attention of media producers specifically because of their uniqueness—a violent home invasion in a quiet suburban community or a child from a lower-income family getting accepted to a prestigious university to pursue his or her education. For different reasons, both of these stories capture our attention because they are unexpected events; they are exemplars of extraordinary events (Zillmann & Brosius, 2000).

> **Exemplars** Single observations that people make, and subsequently use to draw assumptions about people, places, and things they observe later.

Moreover, it might be argued that the repeated usage of exemplars in mass media stories can result in a rather skewed view of reality. For example, if newspapers only cover stories of crime in a given area, it might suggest to media audiences that the given area is particularly dangerous—regardless of whether or not the area really is any more or less dangerous than its surroundings. In other words, as newspapers continue to focus on unique exemplars we begin as an audience to believe that the exemplified stories represent daily occurrences. Back to our crime example, we believe there is a mean world around us because we are constantly reading about it and we are rarely provided with evidence suggesting the rarity of these events.

And yet again, we might consider how the Web 2.0 media system is changing our access to different exemplars. Considering again the Arab Spring revolutions of 2010 (see Chapter 2), many social media audiences based in the United States were able to get information about the student protests and military responses not by following official statements from Arab officials or United Nations peacekeepers and overseers, but rather they were able to get firsthand accounts of many of the activities from the images, videos, and commentary provided by those people on the front lines of the revolution. Granted, the question could be posed that these youth might not have been representative of their entire nation-state's political interests (for example, those youth who had access to technology, the Internet, and who spoke English tended to be the ones most followed by and shared with international

audiences), but it can be argued that social media has given us access to a wider perspective on news events than ever before (if not by the sheer number of sampling contacts alone) which has the potential for us to look past exemplars to get a more holistic perspective on any given news event. As of 2016, nearly one in seven people on Earth have created a Facebook profile, suggesting that while Facebook users have more potential to contact a seemingly innumerable number of social connections without ever leaving their homes, nearly 85 percent of the world is not actively using this technology, allowing us to ask who is getting what news?

Framing Theory

When producing a news story for publication—be it in a newspaper, on a Web page, or in a broadcast format—writers and editors must choose how to "package" the story in order to satisfy any number of demands. What aspects of the story are most important to the audience? What elements of the story are more newsworthy than others? Which set of quotations or facts do we start with? How can we structure the story to make it most appealing to our readers? How can we highlight the "most important element" in a given news story?

Sociologist Erving Goffman attempted to explain this careful structuring of stories in his framing theory (Goffman, 1974). He contended that (a) stories are framed to highlight specific events and (b) these frames are influential in how audiences decode and make meaning of the story. According to politics and media scholar Robert Entman, a frame is the "[selection of] some aspects of a perceived reality [that] make them more salient in a communicating text, in such a way as to promote a particular problem definition, causal interpretation, moral evaluation, and/or treatment recommendation" (Entman, 1993, p. 52). Simplified, we can understand framing as the purposeful attempt to package a story to highlight some story elements over others.

When we study framing, a central concern is the role that story framing plays in making some story elements more salient than others and how this increased salience influences our ability to accurately process story information. For example, a story on a military conflict might label an antigovernment group as "freedom fighters" or "terrorists"—the former suggesting the group to be on the side of right and the latter suggesting the group to be on the side of wrong. In 2008, sports communication scholar Andy Billings wrote similarly about NBC's presentation of the Olympic Games for U.S. audiences, which often goes to great lengths to frame coverage in terms of dramatic narratives often rooted in geopolitical or even moral issues of the day in order to increase viewership of the Games. Such framing is often not so much rooted in terms of a political agenda as it is an economic one (see MC in Action: The Economics of Morality)—an attempt to make the Games as attractive as possible to the widest possible audience so as to recoup the reported $4.38 billion paid to the International Olympic Committee to exclusively broadcast the games in the United States from 2014 to 2020.

Once again, we can consider the potential impact of Web 2.0 technologies on the framing process. If it is argued that news producers carefully frame stories so that they can be presented to audiences with a certain meaning attached to them, how might this process be different when today's media audience does not always get news from large media organizations? For example, @ReallyVirtual's original

Tweets about the bin Laden raid were rather frameless from a political standpoint as he was merely reporting what he was witnessing (and he was not even really sure what we was witnessing), while the Tweets from the many Arab Spring activists were decidedly pro revolution. Tweets during the National Football League's short player lockout allowed sports fans to hear directly from their favorite athletes about their "side" of the labor dispute, allowing fans to circumvent coverage in major news services that might have suggested players to be greedy or selfish in their contract and labor demands. In general, we can see how the networked media landscape of today lends itself to an increased marketplace of ideas, perhaps making the influences of framing effects (as well as the agenda-setting function of the media and the notion of exemplification) diminished.

Marketplace of ideas A philosophy that suggests that ideas should be treated like free enterprise economic goods in that individuals should be able to read any number of ideas and decide for themselves those ideas that are useful and those that are not.

MC IN ACTION

THE ECONOMICS OF MORALITY

While much of the research surrounding the form and function of media framing tends to be situated around an assumption that different content producers have different personal and political interests, prominent media scholar Ron Tamborini proposes a slightly different approach: the economics of morality.

In his model of moral intuition in media entertainment, or MIME, Tamborini (2011) suggested that while the content in much of our entertainment and informational media is often rooted in moral issues—battles of moral right and moral wrong—the reasons behind these content productions are economic. Tamborini argues that content producers are aware that "drama sells," but they are also aware that different audiences have very distinct moral orientations, what he refers to as morality subcultures. For a broadcaster, producing content that violates the moral orientations of the intended audiences will likely result in very unpopular, unsuccessful, and potentially troubling broadcasts (for example, the program was reported to the FCC for violating community standards of decency—themselves often rooted in moral rather than legal considerations). Thus, producers are likely to create content that upholds and supports rather than violates and challenges predominant moral orientations. In fact, research applying MIME has suggested, for example, newspaper headlines in more liberal or conservative parts of the United States generally present news in a more liberal or conservative manner, respectively, and that many popular sitcoms and soap opera programs tend to present a more conservative view on such cultural taboos as alcoholism, adultery, and spousal abuse. In addition, there is emerging research to suggest that differences in media content and preference across cultures can often be attributed to differences in the moral standards between, for example, U.S. Latino and non-Latino populations (soap opera content) and U.S. and German television audiences (the former preferring more sitcoms and the latter preferring more news programming).

Yet, as media becomes increasingly narrowcasted or tailored, how important do you think it is for producers to understand the morality subcultures of their audiences? Do you think there few or many morality subcultures? Can you identify newer programs that seem to tap into larger or smaller morality subcultures?

Key Terms

References

Anderson, C. & Wolfe, M. (2010). The web is dead. Long live the Internet. WIRED.com. Retrieved April 16, 2016 from http://www.wired.com/2010/08/ff_webrip/.

Billings, A. C. (2008). *Olympic media: Inside the biggest show on television.* London: Routledge.

Brook, T. (1998). *The confusions of pleasure: Commerce and culture in Ming China.* Berkeley: University of California Press.

Cohen, B. (1963). *The press and foreign policy.* New York: Harcourt.

Entman, R. (1993). Framing: Toward clarification of a fractured paradigm. *Journal of Communication, 43,* 231–242.

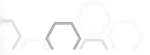

Gans, H. (1975). *Popular culture and high culture: An analysis and evaluation of taste*. New York: Basic.

Gerbner, G., Gross, L., Morgan, M., Signorielli, N., & Shanahan, J. (2002). Growing up with television: Cultivation process. In D. Zillmann & J. Bryant (Eds.), *Media effects: Advances in theory and research*. Mahwah, NJ: LEA.

Goffman, E. (1974). *Frame analysis*. New York: Free Press.

Infelise, M. (2002). Roman Avvisi: Information and politics in the seventeenth century. In G. Signorotto and M.A. Visceglia [Eds.] *Court and politics in Papal Rome*, 1492–1700. Cambridge: Cambridge University Press.

Maher, V. (2005). *Citizen journalism is dead*. Grahamstown, South Africa: New Media Lab, School of Journalism & Media Studies, Rhodes University.

McCombs, M. E., & Shaw, D. L. (1972). The agenda-setting function of mass media. *Public Opinion Quarterly, 36*(2), 176–187.

O'Dell, J. (2010, May 1). One Twitter user reports live from Osama bin Laden raid. Mashable.com. Retrieved September 12, 2013, from: http://mashable.com/2011/05/01/live-tweet-bin-laden-raid/

Associated Press (2007, February 6). *World's oldest newspaper goes purely digital*. NewsMax.com Wires. Retrieved January 30, 2014, from: http://archive.is/IuCxq

Papacharissi, Z., & de Fatima Oliveira, M. (2012). Affective news and networked publics: The rhythms of news storytelling on #Egypt. *Journal of Broadcasting and Electronic Media, 62*(2), 366–382.

Shaw, S. J. (1959). Colonial newspaper advertising: A step toward freedom of the press. *The Business History Review, 33*(3), 409–420.

Shirky, C. (2008). *Here comes everybody: The power of organizing without organizations*. New York: Penguin.

Tamborini, R. (2011). Moral intuition and media entertainment. *Journal of Media Psychology, 23*(1), 39–45.

Wu. S., Hofman, J. M., Mason, W. A., & Watts, D. J. (2011). Who says what to whom on Twitter. *Proceedings of the 20th International Conference on World Wide Web*, 705–714.

Zillmann, D., & Brosius, H-B. (2000). *Exemplification in communication: The influence of case reports on the perception of issues*. Mahwah, NJ: LEA.

CHAPTER 6

Media as Educators

One challenge to education is getting learners to engage educational material. As students, we often get distracted during course lectures and discussions, as we have other thoughts and emotions on our minds—distractions from the course material that ultimately hinder our ability to process lessons and knowledge. However, as an autotelic process, media is often seen as a particularly useful channel for education. Most of us consume a fair amount of media in our daily routines, and we can assume that by an early age we have become adept at internalizing knowledge gleaned from media. Studies on children's media use suggest they spend nearly seven and one-half hours in front of a computer or television screen daily, and another full hour using cellular phones for texting or talking; these numbers do not drop off substantially through early adulthood. While some might lament this increased reliance on mediated communication over "good old-fashioned" face-to-face communication, it is again important to consider that the goals of these mediated activities (as we have continually highlighted throughout the book) do not have to differ from one communication channel to the next. In fact, one might argue that this increased communication activity via technology is indicative that people today are actively seeking and attending to new information every day (perhaps because we have more information available to us than ever before). This chapter will discuss the numerous ways that media is and can be used as an educational tool.

Autotelic process A process or activity that is intrinsically motivated, having no external reward associated with its completion.

Questions to consider when reading this chapter:

- Why have some traditionally avoided thinking about media as a learning mechanism?
- What are cognitive and affective learning? How are they different concepts?
- Why is it important to consider social learning processes when we talk about new media?
- Why might video games be different than other media in terms of the learning processes associated with them?
- How can social media hurt and/or help the learning process?

Mr. Rogers and Big Bird: Learning through Television

By the 1960s, most estimates suggested that as many as 97 percent of households in the United States owned at least one television set. In a mere 30 years, television had replaced the radio as the "great storyteller of [the] age" (to borrow from an often-quoted passage from media scholar George Gerbner) and had quickly become a cultural force for information, relationships, persuasion, and entertainment.

This growth in popularity was especially apparent among children, who by the mid-1960s were estimated to spend upwards of 27 hours or more per week watching television. In response to this, many local television stations began to produce children-specific programming (or at least, programming aimed at children and adult audiences), but these programs were criticized for focusing on basal content, often highlighting slapstick violence (the authors can think of programs such as *The Three Stooges* as prime examples of this) or in general presenting simple storybook-style narratives with little educational value. Indeed in 1961, FCC chairman Newton Minow famously proclaimed that television content at the time was a "vast wasteland" of low-brow, commercially driven content designed to appeal to the base interests of its audience, and in particular not suitable for children (see MC in Action: Minow's Vast Wasteland). As television rose to prominence as a primary source of information and entertainment, many began to wonder about potential negative effects of television content on children. In the 1950s and 1960s, there were few television offerings designed specifically for children—yet children made up a substantial part of the viewing audience. Even comedies such as *The Three Stooges* were panned by some as focusing on violence and bullying behaviors that might have encouraged children to do the same to each other. Moreover, intense coverage of the Vietnam War—considered by many media historians to be the most uncensored and violent war coverage to date—and other political scandals and stories tended to dominate headlines in news media.

During this time, parents, producers, and scholars began to concern themselves with the potential negative influence of television on children's

development—both from a cognitive and from an affective perspective. It was clear that television was a popular form of media, so simply removing the television from children was not an answer. Conversely, simply removing children from television (or television from children) seemed shortsighted—after all, if television was having a negative effect on children's development, could it also have a positive one?

MC IN ACTION

MINOW'S VAST WASTELAND

I admire your courage—but that doesn't mean that I would make life any easier for you. Your license lets you use the public's airwaves as trustees for 180 million Americans. The public is your beneficiary. If you want to stay on as trustees, you must deliver a decent return to the public—not only to your stockholders. So, as a representative of the public, your health and your product are among my chief concerns.

~Federal Communications Chairman Newton Minow, addressing the National Association of Broadcasters annual convention in May 1961.

In 1961, FCC chairman Newton Minow delivered perhaps one of the most memorable speeches by any FCC official when commenting on his vision for broadcast television—his first speech as the newly appointed FCC boss. Labeled by some as the "culture czar," Minow called upon content producers of the time to offer more choices, more diversity in programming, and more alternatives to popular programming. He spoke in front of the most powerful and important broadcast leaders of the day and challenged them to watch their own programming for an entire day, ensuring them that the programs would be full of what newspaper columnist Doris Fleeson paraphrased as "violence and mediocrity and—worst of all from their point of view—they would end up being bored." While neither Minow nor his FCC directly worked to censor broadcast television, many media historians credit his FCC (for better

or worse) with driving network executives to carefully reconsider the programs offered on their stations or risk losing their broadcasting license when it was up for renewal (a process that worked in three-year cycles).

How big was Minow's impact on television? Some feel that his New Frontier approach to the FCC forced broadcasters to consider more carefully the public interest and to produce more socially responsible content, or at least be more judicious in their current offerings. Others feel that Minow only scared broadcasters into consolidating their operations, cancelling or refusing to develop new content that might be considered risqué, and as a result greatly reducing the choices, diversity, and alternatives for programming (precisely the opposite of what he set out to do). Yet, one impact is certain: the S. S. *Minnow* from *Gilligan's Island* fame? That too was named after Minow.

Minow's original speech can be accessed at: http://www.americanrhetoric.com/speeches/newtonminow.htm.

Cognitive Learning

What if you could create content that was both entertaining and instructive? What if it went down more like ice cream than spinach?

~television journalist Michael Davis

As television was growing in popularity, educational professionals and parents alike noticed a parallel—although not necessarily related—troubling trend in the cognitive development of schoolchildren. The achievement gap between children from low and high socioeconomic status (SES) was widening—suggesting that children from higher income families were also doing better in school than children from less privileged families. Concern was growing that this achievement gap would then widen SES differences, and education scholars began to explore alternative methods for teaching scholastic material to children. Surveys of children from lower SES families reported that across many demographic variables, one common connection was that these children watched more television than those children from higher SES families—one common reason reported was that in the lower SES families, parents usually worked longer hours and were away from their children in the early afternoon, as there was a time gap between school ending and parents coming home from work.

Recognizing both the increased popularity of television among children, particularly with lower SES children, and examining the educational achievement gap, accomplished television producer Joan Ganz Cooney organized financiers and researchers to form the Children's Television Workshop (CTW) in 1968 (see Fisch & Truglio, 2001 and Davis, 2008 for a complete history of *Sesame Street*'s development). Securing nearly $8 million in grants (about $55 million in 2016 dollars), CTW was able to produce high-quality children's programming that was similar in production standards to the most popular television shows of the time with an educational platform rooted in academics (including an educational curriculum designed by Harvard professors). From this, *Sesame Street* was born: a program focused specifically on children's cognitive development. By 1979, nearly nine million young children (under the age of six) were regular daily viewers of the show, with especially high viewership among children from low SES families. As of the 21st century, the show has enjoyed success internationally and expanded its educational views to reflect changes in cultural and social issues along with cognitive learning, including the 2010 introduction of an African American puppet who sings about how much she loves her hair (http://www.youtube.com/watch?v=enpFde5rgmw, a response to cultural stereotypes about ethnically Black

While *Sesame Street* focused on the development of educational achievement, concerns about children's social development were also emerging.

hairstyles) and a 2002 puppet named Kami on South Africa's *Takalani Street* who is diagnosed with HIV.

Sesame Street has been on television for a long time, but has it been successful? Did the program close the educational achievement gap? On one hand, children who watched *Sesame Street* did significantly better in school than children who did not watch the program, and the length of viewing was a significant positive predictor of achievement (i.e., the more *Sesame Street* a child watched, the better they did in school). However, research also revealed that the achievement gap between lower- and higher-SES children actually *increased*—a phenomenon known as the "Matthew" effect. Children overall were able to learn a great deal from entertainment television as compared to other types of programming, but children from family backgrounds that were more involved in their learning performed much better—showing the dual influence of media and one's social environment on child development. Of course, also worthy of note is that *Sesame Street* and other shows of its era were groundbreaking in other ways, offering lessons that went beyond academic proficiency, such as social awareness and emotional intelligence skills central to early childhood development.

Matthew effect In education, a process by which children who have early advantages—from greater reading and writing skills, to greater access to resources at home—tend to improve academically at faster rates than children without these advantages.

MC IN ACTION

DEATH OF A PET

On March 23, 1970, the beloved goldfish of Mr. Fred Rogers passed away. At least, this was the premise of *Mister Rogers' Neighborhood*, Episode 1101. In this episode, viewers watch as Mister Rogers discovered his pet goldfish lying motionless at the bottom of its fishbowl. After trying to revive the fish by pouring salt in the bowl (as Mister Rogers explained to the viewing audience, if the fish had merely been sick, adding salt to the water bowl might have killed pathogens in the water while not harming the fish itself), Mr. Rogers comes to the realization that his pet goldfish is dead. Sadly, Mr. Rogers removes the fish from the water, wraps it in a paper towel and—while discussing his feelings with the television audience—buries the fish in his backyard.

Why would Mister Rogers choose to show such a sad (and, for some, almost ghoulish) story on public television? To him, it was important for children to learn the value of discussing their feelings openly with each other and with their families. As well, Mister Rogers reminded the audience that it is okay to feel sad sometimes and even to cry—just as he did when his pet dog died when he was a child. Such lessons are core to learning how to feel and effectively cope with one's emotions. In Chapter 12, we will talk more about emotional reactions to television and other entertainment programming, but we would also like to hear from you.

Can you remember any television programs (or any other medium, such as movies, music, and video games) that contained similar messages? Consider sharing examples of this content with our Facebook group at https://www.facebook.com/groups/234255823447372/, or with our Twitter users, following the #MediaAsTools hashtag.

A video recording of the original broadcast can be found, courtesy of the Fred Rogers Center, at http://www.fredrogerscenter.org/resources/toolkit/activities/childrens-television-age-appropriate-content/

Affective Learning

While *Sesame Street* focused on the development of educational achievement, concerns about children's social development were also emerging. For example, while Minow's "vast wasteland" speech talked about declining test scores, he was just as concerned with television content showing "blood and thunder, mayhem, violence, sadism, murder," as well as advertisements "screaming, cajoling, and offending"—to many, this was a general concern as to the well-being of those watching so much television. If psychologist George Gerbner's claims about television as "the great storyteller of the age" were true (see Chapter 5), then one could only worry about the deleterious emotional impact of television content on children.

One particularly concerned individual was Mr. Fred Rogers, a Presbyterian minister in Pittsburgh, Pennsylvania, who expressed his concerns that children were not being exposed to positive role models in the media. In many ways mirroring Minow, Rogers was quoted as saying "I went into television because I hated it so, and I thought there's some way of using this fabulous instrument to nurture those who would watch and listen." Both men, among countless others, were equally concerned but hopeful about the impact of this new technology on all audiences, but particularly children.

Rogers hoped for a children's program that focused on the social world of children—one of imagination, inquisitiveness, and inspiration. From his first entry into the world of television in 1951 as a composer for NBC, Rogers developed much of his now-famous "Mister Rogers" persona in Toronto before February 1968 saw the first U.S. broadcasting of *Mister Rogers' Neighborhood*. Breaking from *Sesame Street, Mister Rogers' Neighborhood* exposed children to many facets of society, ranging from tours of factories and construction sites (to show children how the world works) to discussion about divorce, war, and—in a critically acclaimed 1970 episode—a frank discussion about coping with death (see MC in Action: Death of a Pet). Even noted media critic and scholar George Gerbner wrote that Fred Rogers' focus on real-world issues in a concrete and nurturing way held great promise for positively impacting children's socioemotional growth (Yates, 1999). His show was immensely popular, with 895 individual episodes taped from 1968 to 2000, and a viewing audience of nearly nine million households during the show's peak in the 1980s (Long, 2015). In general, research has demonstrated that children who regularly watched Mister Rogers reported fewer behavioral problems in school and were more open and in control of their emotional states—and these effects were particularly strong in children from lower SES families (likely due to increased exposure to the programming). Although Fred Rogers died in February 2003, his legacy of fostering compassion and creativity and encouraging affective learning among his audience continue on through the Fred Rogers Company (http://www.fredrogers.org) and a number of YouTube videos featuring original footage, remixes, and tributes to everyone's neighbor. As highlighted by Long (2015), perhaps the most famous and fitting tribute to Mister Rogers was produced by PBS Digital Studios' John D. Boswell in the form of a YouTube remix video "Garden of Your Mind" with nearly 12 million views as of April 2016 (https://www.youtube.com/watch?v=OFzXaFbxDcM)

Social Learning Theory

Learning would be exceedingly laborious, not to mention hazardous, if people had to rely solely on the effects of their own actions to inform them what to do. Fortunately, most human behavior is learned observationally through modeling: from observing others one forms an idea of how new behaviors are performed, and on later occasions this coded information serves as a guide for action.

~Albert Bandura

When we discuss learning from media, we are assuming that people can learn by watching something rather than actually doing it. Consider the preceding examples of *Sesame Street* and *Mister Rogers' Neighborhood*—in both cases, children are thought to be learning cognitive or affective lessons (respectively) by watching the actions of others on-screen rather than performing and practicing the actions for themselves. This type of learning through vicarious experiences rather than direct experiences forms the basis of sociologist Albert Bandura's social learning theory.

At its core, social learning theory (SLT: Bandura, 1977) suggests that individuals learn by modeling the witnessed behaviors of others. In order to do this, an individual must pay attention to the behavior and devote their attentional resources to understanding the behavior script being watched. Second, an individual must be able to retain the behavioral script so that they can remember it when it is no longer in front of them. Third, an individual must learn how to and be able to physically reproduce this script on their own; at this stage, Bandura would likely argue that the witnessed behavior has been learned. Of course, individuals do not blindly reproduce every behavior they learn, but rather there must be a motivation (the fourth stage of SLT) in order for a script to be enacted or performed. One determinant of an individual's motivation is witnessing the consequences of the behavior on the behavioral model. For example, if a character in a popular television show consistently uses violence to solve his interpersonal problems (i.e., fighting with friends and loved ones) and is rewarded for this behavior (i.e., his friends and loved ones come to like and respect him more), individuals who watch the show might tend to believe that violence is an acceptable and useful method for solving interpersonal conflict. However, consider the same character and actions resulting in negative consequences (i.e., his friends and loved ones leave him); this would likely not encourage individuals to behave in the same manner. Bandura argued that individuals are more strongly motivated to reproduce learned behaviors that they see rewarded than reproduce behaviors they see as punished—and he also suggested that a lack of punishment for a given behavior was interpreted by most individuals as an implicit reward (see MC in Action: Bandura and Bobo). Another related determinant driving one's motivation to enact a learned behavior or not is the attractiveness of the model. Rewarded models are generally seen as more

Vicarious experience The notion that humans can experience the world through observing others rather than through direct experience.

Modeling The process of learning a behavior by observing others.

Script A cognitive shortcut that we rely on to understand how a sequence of events takes place in a given circumstance.

attractive than punished ones, but individuals might also perceive a model as more or less attractive based on their own interpretations. For example, research has shown that television audiences find characters of their own gender and race more interpersonally similar. From an SLT perspective, these findings would suggest that audiences are more likely to "copy" the behaviors of demographically similar characters (and less likely to copy the behaviors of demographically different characters).

SLT was later amended to the more encompassing social cognitive theory (SCT) in order to place more focus on the cognitive learning processes underlying the observed behavioral learning. In fact, some research has even applied SCT to the acquisition of different attitudes and beliefs (which might be more affective/emotional than cognitive in nature), further highlighting the flexibility and importance of Bandura's theories of observational learning. We should also point out that SLT/SCT were never conceptualized as theories of media psychology or mediated communication. That is, Bandura was not originally interested in understanding media's impact and role in observational learning, at least in his earliest "Bobo doll" research (see MC: Bandura and Bobo). However, it became obvious to media researchers that any theory so centrally focused on observation would be

MC IN ACTION

BANDURA AND BOBO

In 1961 and 1963, Bandura conducted a series of experiments to test his social learning theory. Using a Bobo doll—an inflatable doll approximately five feet in height with a painted clown face—Bandura was able to show that children who watched an adult model (model in the theoretical sense) behave aggressively toward the doll (hitting it with their fists, a toy hammer, and shouting angrily while hitting it) were more likely to mimic the behavior. His argument was that children are taught that adult behaviors are proper and accepted and thus they would reason that if an adult was allowed to engage in a behavior, then that behavior must be a proper one. In this way, he demonstrated that children learned through observation—particularly as the children who watch the adult play quietly in the room instead of attacking the Bobo doll also avoided attacking Bobo.

He followed up this initial study in 1963 by introducing two key elements to the experiment. First, he introduced a punishment or reward condition wherein the model (one of his laboratory assistants) was either offered candy or reprimanded for attacking Bobo. Second, he had children witness the punished or rewarded behavior on film rather than in person—thus changing the channel of communication to a mediated one. Indeed, Bandura found that only the children who witnessed the model (a) attack Bobo and (b) receive a reward for their attack were motivated to also attack Bobo.

Bandura and his social learning theory continue to be influential in the study of observational learning as well as mediated communication. And, finally, there is Bobo—whose unfortunate physical sacrifices to the study of human communication and behavior have resulted in one of the most robust theories of observational learning and media influence in the past 70 years.

applicable to the study of media—after all, mediated content is inherently observational (although we might challenge this later when we talk about video games in Chapter 13). This point is made most clear in Bandura's foundational research, in which he used videotaped interactions of adults being rewarded or punished for their behavior as a way to allow children to "observe" potential models of behavior. Perhaps it is unsurprising then that Bandura's writings on SLT/SCT are commonplace in the study of media, with Bandura himself even specifying aspects of the theory for media researchers in several writings (cf. Bandura, 2002).

In later years, social learning theory was re-labeled by Bandura as social cognitive theory in order to place more emphasis on the separation between cognitive and behavioral learning. Importantly, the theory does not necessarily predict that all learned behaviors are enacted—such as the case with watching a violent television show and behaving in a violent manner. Bandura was careful to highlight that, while behaviors can be learned through observation (likely at the reproduction stage of his model), there must be a motivation to enact the behaviors. In other words, learned scripts do not necessarily translate to enacted ones. Chapter 9 will discuss social cognitive theory in more detail.

How might this process be different when we discuss computer-mediated communication? One of the more obvious differences—discussed in part as follows—is the role of interactivity. All of Bandura's research is based on the notion that we can learn through witnessing rather than enacting different thoughts, actions, and feelings. Yet, when we think about a child using the Internet to look up information for a book report, or playing a video game that asks them to enact a particularly violent act, or even watching a television program while following an online conversation about the narrative on Twitter, are we still talking about observational learning? Or rather, do today's mediated communication technologies always require the user to do rather than simply witness actions? This is a question currently facing researchers today as we continue to examine Bandura's and other learning theories in the new media landscape. Of course, that doesn't mean that you don't have an answer for us now! *Share your thoughts on some of these questions using our official social media spaces—Facebook at https:// www.facebook.com/groups/234255823447372/ or Twitter using the #MediaAsTools hashtag.*

Video Games and Learning

If television was the dominant form of entertainment media for children in the mid-20th century, video games have emerged as a dominant form of entertainment media for the 21st century. As recently as 2010, nearly 70 percent of all U.S. households reported playing video games on a regular basis, with these gamers playing an average of eight hours weekly. In fact, the popularity of video games as a leisure activity among children has been considered such a large phenomenon that some scholars, such as Pew Foundation research fellow Steven Jones (2003), argued that a childhood without video games could actually have a negative impact on that child's ability to socialize with his or her peers.

According to technology and education researcher James Gee, video games are inherently educational in that they require the player to become familiar with a world not their own (see MC in Action: *The Legend* (Literally) *of Zelda*). Of

MC IN ACTION

THE LEGEND (LITERALLY) OF ZELDA

It's dangerous to go alone! Take this.

~Old man in a cave, *The Legend of Zelda*

The preceding quote is perhaps one of the most famous in video game history as it marked the start of the Nintendo Entertainment System's *The Legend of Zelda*, one of the most successful games (and franchises) in video game history. Released in February 1986, *Zelda* introduced video game players to perhaps one of the first open-world, nonlinear video games—that is, a video game that progressed not by moving left to right defeating monsters on-screen, but by navigating a persistent game world and finding one's one way through the puzzles, mazes, and directions of a world not too different from any child's neighborhood (save the swarms of dragons, bugs, and monsters).

While not at all designed as an educational game per se, *Zelda* is perhaps a prime example of Gee's claims that video games are by their nature educational. In the game, players are placed in the middle of an unfamiliar game world called Hyrule and given no direction as to where to go or—as they encounter monsters in the world—how to defend themselves. Players know only that they are supposed to locate and collect eight different pieces of a magical Triforce (again, whose locations are unknown) to defeat a

monster called Ganon (and this information is known only if players actually took the time to read the game manual or watch the game's opening credits). Beyond learning how to physically play the game, such as moving and attacking monsters, successful completion of *Zelda* requires players to coordinate memory and logic systems to continually navigate a large game map, making mental notes of the location of different dungeons, item shops, and safe houses (to heal themselves when damaged). As well, many of the game's challenges cannot be defeated merely through attacking and running and instead require the player to solve complex logic puzzles or recognize different audio or visual patterns on-screen.

The original *Legend of Zelda*, and countless games since it, represent perhaps the best combination of a video game that presents both a play challenge in mastering the game controls as well as narrative challenge in deciphering the game's riddles and landscape in order to restore peace to Hyrule. The game's lore continues to this day, with the remastered *The Legend of Zelda: Twilight Princess* HD release in March 2016 marking 30 years of Hyrulian gaming.

course, the question is what exactly is being learned. Just as the rise of entertainment television in the 1950s and 1960s caused parents to concern themselves with the content being taught to their children, many have lambasted video games for featuring decidedly antisocial content—fighting games and first-person shooters are often highlighted as examples of video games that place intense focus on violence and murder. Indeed, the 1995 release of *Mortal Kombat* in public arcades spurred the video game industry to begin rating video games according to their content (similar to television ratings). However, in another

parallel to concerns about television's influence on children, the question was raised: Can't the effects be positive as well as negative?

The notion of video games as an educational tool is not a new one. As far back as 1971, a movement was underway to use the interactive nature of video games to teach scholastic lessons (see MC in Action: *The Oregon Trail*). One reason that video games have been expected to be powerful educational tools is because of their inherent interactivity. Unlike television and other traditional media, video game play requires active and near-constant engagement in the experience—in many ways, video games force passive audiences to be active users, and active engagement is thought to be key to reinforcing educational lessons. In addition, video games appear to tap into the multimodal learning practices championed by many educational psychologists and teaching professionals—games present material textually, audibly, visually, and experientially all at once. Another area in which video games might prove to be particularly useful as educational tools is by serving as accurate simulations of real-world events and systems. Traditional lesson plans on complex issues such as a biology lesson on the circulatory system are quite adept at helping learners establish a basic understanding of system components, but video game simulations allow learners to see the systems "in action." A recent movement in developing serious games perhaps showcases these concepts quite well, with games such as the critically acclaimed *Darfur Is Dying* (discussed in detail in Chapter 9) placing players in the role of a starving Sudanese refugee struggling with the harsh reality of finding potable water to survive while avoiding threats far outside the reality of your average American child. In many of these games, a core learning objective is to encourage the player to develop a sense of authentic empathy for others by putting them in the position of others (such as the Sudanese refugee from *Darfur is Dying*). However, more recent theorizing (Banks, 2015) has suggested that having game players take the perspective of their on-screen character might not be the most effective way to foster empathy, because the psychological differences between the player's experiences and the avatar's digital world are often very distant from one another—it might be difficult for a college student in Fargo, North Dakota or Storrs, Connecticut to really understand and immerse themselves in the cultural and geo-political climate of the Sudan, to the point that empathy could suffer. Drawing from research in family psychology, Banks argues that a better strategy for fostering empathy might be to develop serious games in which the player acts as a caretaker or friends to the main character (an "Avatar-as-Other" orientation) rather than taking control of the character and pretending to be in their shoes (an "Avatar-as-Me" orientation).

In fact, even games not designed to be educational have been found to have real educational and developmental benefits. Emerging research on laparoscopic surgeons (surgeons who perform surgery with the aid of smaller and robotic tools) has shown that those surgeons with video game play experience had significantly better eye-hand coordination and a general understanding of human-computer interfaces. Indeed, several studies from the University of Wisconsin's Learning and Transfer Lab (http://psych.wisc.edu/CSGreen/publications.html)

As recently as 2010, nearly 70 percent of all U.S. households reported playing video games on a regular basis.

Interactivity Having control of both the form and content of a media message.

Multimodal learning Incorporating several different learning styles (i.e., visual learners, textual learners, etc.) into a single lesson plan or activity.

Simulation A virtual environment that is meant to replicate an actual environment or situation.

Serious games A specific category of video games that usually aims to teach a particular educational or social lesson.

Avatar In video games, the on-screen character that represents the player's space in the video game. Mario and Sonic would be considered avatars, as well as any character that the player created themselves.

Empathy The ability to understand and share the feelings of others.

MC IN ACTION

THE OREGON TRAIL
You have died of dysentery.

Such was a common fate for American frontier families in the early- to mid-1800s and a common fate befalling many elementary-aged students who first attempted to navigate the Oregon Trail in the video game of the same name. Funded by the Minnesota Educational Computing Consortium in 1971, educators Don Rawitsch, Bill Heinemann, and Paul Dillenberger wrote the first source code for a video game designed to teach schoolchildren about the harsh realities faced by the pioneer families who blazed and navigated the Oregon Trail.

While there is no concrete data as to the educational impact of *The Oregon Trail* on those students who played it—when asked, many of our students recall the game teaching them about the hardship of life on the Great Plains, but often discuss in greater detail the "action-packed" hunting segments and seem to have difficulty actually recalling what the Oregon Trail was or where it started (Independence, Missouri) or ended (the Willamette Valley in Oregon)—there is no doubt that the game was a prime example of an education-based video game that remains popular to this day (the most recent release of the game was in 2011 for Windows 7, and some mobile phone applications are free for download for Android OS and Apple iPhone users).

have archived the many developmental benefits of video games as tools for helping improve cognitive abilities, memory, eye/hand coordination, and a number of other different skills. Research on sex differences in cognitive skill sets—established patterns suggesting that men tend to be better at mental rotation ability (the ability to imagine objects from different angles) and women tend to be better at pattern recognition and verbal ability, for example—has found that playing video games emphasizing these skills can attenuate, or reduce, the gap between sexes. Thus, video games have been established as robust tools for training a variety of different mental abilities.

Massively multiplayer games such as *World of Warcraft* have been found to foster organizational and leadership skills among engaged gamers. The skills that are required to be competent and excel at these types of games such as coordinating other players in planned attacks, delegating game tasks to other players, and communicating using technology across many different genders, ethnicities, and age groups are exactly the kinds of skills that many employers are looking for, and these skills seem to translate into that job world. Might we see the day when you will be able to list that you are a level 90 Pandarian warrior with Zen master fishing and blacksmithing skills as past work experience on your résumé? Probably not (although if this were true, at least one of the authors of this text would be highly employable!). But, we might suggest that such a notion may not be as far-fetched as it seems at first glance.

Distributed Learning

One of the oldest, and most frequent, uses of mediated communication for education involves distributed, or distance, learning (Kelly & Westerman, in press). This type of education is designed to utilize technology to enable education across geographical distance limitations. In other words, it brings the classroom out of the actual physical classroom and suggests education can occur among people who are distributed across various locations (and times, as well). These date back at least to correspondence courses, where people would utilize snail mail as part of their educational process—mailing sample artistic sketches to Art Instruction, Incorporated (mailed to Minneapolis) or completing courses in everything from "Better Business Writing" to "Motor Traffic Management" through the International Correspondence Schools (mailed to Scranton, Pennsylvania; both of these ads, and scores more, were found in the pages of comic books from one of your author's extensive collections). More recent technologies—often called learning management systems—have obviously increased the possibilities for distributed learning, providing students with a secure and persistent space to engage class lessons from any environment with an Internet connection. Notably, these systems work well for teachers also. Much to the chagrin of their students, rather than cancel class sessions due to travel, the authors of this book have been known to lead course discussions from such remote locations as Belgium, Germany, Japan, and Taiwan.

Although distributed learning is rather popular for its flexibility of time and location (Kelly & Fall, 2011) among other reasons, challenges exist for success in an online class setting. Like most tools, these require the learner to be both willing and able to utilize the technology for educational goals. Basically, distributed learning will not work if one does not possess the technical know-how to use the technology that is being used for the class, and if one does not have the self-discipline to work through and learn using the independence often provided in online education (See MC in Action: Rules of Virtual Groups). Once more, in many ways, YOU are in charge of your online learning.

One other very important concept for successful distributed learning is social presence. This concept will be discussed in more detail in Chapter 7, but it generally is a feeling of being with others. This experience tends to increase a variety of educational outcomes, such as satisfaction with a course and instructor, perceived cognitive learning, affective learning, and retention (Richardson & Swan, 2003; Russo & Benson, 2005; Swan & Shih, 2005), and can be achieved through the use of technology. Recently, colleges and universities have been working with an organization named Quality Matters that offers training to help ensure that online courses are designed so that they can take advantage of the affordances of online learning (such as distance education for students who cannot otherwise attend class) while working to overcome constraints (such as the lack of social presence that some students report in online courses). Although the program details are proprietary, a general focus of the evaluation process centers around three components that seem relevant to social presence: student-to-teacher connections, student-to-student connections, and student-to-content connections. Of course, these principles are likely just as core to the in-person classroom as they are to the online one, perhaps further highlighting the importance of communication in our daily lives.

Learning management systems Computer programs that are often integrated with academic courses that allow for basic communication and instruction features to be delivered via the Internet. Systems often include online reading and lecture materials, as well as discussion boards and message systems to encourage student and teacher communication.

KHAN ACADEMY

Notably, not all distance or distributed learning involves the formation of learning communities or digital "replications" of the classroom, as some of the above examples suggest. Perhaps one of the more well-known distributed learning programs operates more as an online repository for knowledge than a classroom—in fact, even their founder openly suggests that his platform is not intended to "somehow constitute a complete education" (as told to Westervelt, 2016). That man is Massachusetts Institute of Technology graduate Salman Khan, and his platform is the immensely popular Khan Academy (http://www.khanacademy.org). Khan originally experimented with online learning in 2004, using the drawing function of an early messaging program (Yahoo!'s Doodle Pad) to help tutor his younger cousin in mathematics (Khan's degrees are in engineering and computer science). She and her friends enjoyed the simplistic chalkboard-style animations that Khan created, which inspired him to begin producing similar segments on YouTube. Following investments in the form of

educational development grants from both the Bill & Melinda Gates Foundation and Google (among others), Khan Academy was born in 2006 as a nonprofit and open-access educational resource. Although the early content was mostly focused on mathematics, the content has since broadened to focus on a variety of topics, including physical and social sciences (e.g, biology and economics) as well as fine arts and humanities (e.g., art history and music). The Web site's content has been translated into over two dozen languages, and their official YouTube channel (http://www. youtube.com/user/khanacademy) has nearly 2.5 million subscribers, with videos in over five dozen languages. As Khan explains in his introductory video, "Nobody's born smart. We all start at zero." As of April 2016, Khan Academy is one of the 500 most visited Web sites in the United States, and one of the 1200 most-visited sites in the world. For a platform completely focused on education that has to compete with Grumpy Cat videos and Kim Kardashian gossip, that is a lot of traffic!

Social Media and Learning

As mentioned in Chapter 5, social media technologies have influenced the way that many of us read and share news and current events. One of the more unique aspects of this influence is the increased co-production of media content by today's media user. Consider a platform such as Facebook, which as of 2012 was estimated to have nearly one billion individual users. Content posted to Facebook is not created by a central organization (although certainly many organizations—in particular media organizations such as CNN—maintain a strong Facebook presence) but rather is created by the users of the program (see Web 2.0, Chapter 2). As well, Facebook does not distribute content but rather provides a networked platform for users to share content with one another based on how they are connected. In

MC IN ACTION

RULES OF VIRTUAL GROUPS

Group work is often one of the biggest challenges and complaints that students have. And although it can be a challenge in traditional FtF classes, it becomes especially challenging given the fact that students in an online class may not be physically located in the same city, state, or even country (which also creates possible time issues). However, working in groups is a fact of life for most people post schooling—as the famous saying (sort of) goes, "no person is an island, complete unto themselves." Thus, if you find yourself struggling to work in a group, especially a virtual one, Walther and Bunz (2006) provide six "rules" for more effective management of working in a virtual group or team (pp. 833–835):

1. Get started right away.
2. Communicate frequently.
3. Multitask getting organized and doing substantive work simultaneously.
4. Overtly acknowledge that you have read one another's messages.
5. Be explicit about what you are thinking and doing.
6. Set deadlines and stick to them.

These are likely good suggestions for non-virtual groups as well, but become especially important online, where things often take longer and nonverbal cues are often lacking (see also the discussion of Social Information Processing Theory, in Chapter 8). As teachers ourselves, we often hear from students that group work is one of the most challenging and frustrating elements of college, with many students upset that others are often not available at mutual times for face-to-face meetings. To this end, perhaps the asynchronous elements of mediated communication technologies can offer students a solution?

Consider sharing your advice and experiences using mediated communication as part of group projects. Do you use social media such as Facebook and Twitter? Learning management systems such as Blackboard or Moodle? Maybe your groups use online work programs such as Google Docs to share and edit documents together?

Let's talk! Share your ideas to the official course Facebook group at https://www.facebook.com/groups/234255823447372/ or via Twitter, using the #MediaAsTools hashtag.

Asynchronous (communication) Communication that does not happen in "real time"—that is, communication that often takes place with some time delay. E-mail is a good example of an asynchronous communication channel.

both ways, Facebook behaves less like a mass media organization and more like a medium in the truest sense—a channel (or platform) for others to send messages to others. The majority of social media programs—Twitter and Google Plus, for example—operate using the same general principle as does Wikipedia: users create and collaborate on content.

Facebook in the Classroom

Among students, Facebook is the "killer app" for social networking—many studies report that as many as 95 percent of college students and similarly high numbers of high school students have an active Facebook page. Early research examining Facebook's influence on class performance tended to focus on the displacement hypothesis, arguing that time spent using the social network was negatively associated with academic achievement and largely found support for this hypothesis (Junco, 2011). Indeed, these findings mirrored earlier research on television's influence on academic achievement in schoolchildren—increased television viewing was associated with decreased academic performance.

However, many of these studies did not consider the way in which media was being used by students. For example, studies on television usage found that students who watched more news and documentary-style programs significantly outperformed their peers, suggesting that a focus on the type of usage rather than merely time spent using it is an important variable. Likewise with Facebook, studies looking at types of usage have found the program to positively influence student learning in several ways. Research has found that students engaging in class-related Facebook groups have increased motivation to learn material and felt closer to both their classmates and teachers—both aspects of affective learning considered important to academic success. In terms of cognitive learning, Facebook is thought to increase academic outcomes because it provides students with a persistent space to engage in class materials (a "ready space" for learning as described by Selwyn, 2009) that provides students an additional space to learn and study in their own space and time. This latter point is of particular importance when we consider students as digital natives—a term coined by educational psychologist Marc Prensky (2001)—who seem adept at using technology to satisfy any number of goals. Assuming that today's learners are living in a digital world, emerging evidence suggests that purposively connecting with students in these "native" and persistent spaces may provide an additional avenue for learning.

Indeed, early research results from Bowman and Ackaoglu (2014) have found that students who voluntarily sign up for a closed class-related Facebook page (about 50 percent of a class of 323 volunteered to join the group) scored six points higher on their course exams in an introductory mediated communication class (sort of like the one you are likely taking) than students who chose not to join the group. While these results are still preliminary, common themes discussed by those students who joined the Facebook group were that they felt a greater sense of accessibility and connectivity to the class material, their fellow classmates, and their professors. More recent data from the same research team even found evidence that students who use Facebook as part of their college courses thought that

Displacement hypothesis The notion that time spent engaging in one activity necessarily results in less time spent engaging in other activities.

Affective learning The feelings associated with the learning process.

Cognitive learning The act of storing and understanding new information.

Digital natives Individuals born into a technological age who are experts at using and adapting to technology for a variety of end goals, including a preference for communicating through technological devices.

the content was more relevant to both their daily lives and their future careers! However, other research has found that using Facebook for nonacademic purposes in the classroom can severely distract from academic performance. Again, we see an example of technology as a tool—social media does not inherently increase or decrease academic performance, but it can be used as a tool to do either (or both).

Of course, Facebook is not the only social media technology that can impact the classroom. Noted instructional technology scholar Reynol Junco (also cited above) has conducted a number of studies on costs and benefits of using social media in the classroom, showing a number of benefits. He and his colleagues (Junco, Heiberger, & Loken, 2010), found that the use of Twitter for extending and supplementing class discussion led to higher levels of both student and faculty engagement when compared to a control group (a similar class, not using Twitter), as well as higher course grades. However, there are still active debates about the role of social media technology in the classroom, as there are two important caveats of both Bowman's and Junco's work: (1) the social media discussions are curriculum-focused, and (2) the technology usage often occurs outside of rather than during class.

MC IN ACTION

BE SOCIALLY HERE, NOT (DIGITALLY) THERE!

"Your former lover tagged a photo you are in" vs. "The Crimean War was the first conflict significantly affected by use of the telegraph." Spot the difference?

~New York University professor Clay Shirky

Speaking from our collective experience as professors, rarely is it the case that a news outlet such as *The Washington Post* gets excited about a simple course format change. However, entering the Fall 2014 semester, noted media studies professor Clay Shirky made a seemingly paradoxical decision (at least, for a professor known for his mostly positive and progressive writings on technology and communication): he asked his students to stop using laptops, tablets, and phones while in class.

He outlined his position in an early-semester editorial for *Medium* (a popular online technology publication), which was quickly picked up by news outlets around the world, including the Post. In his writing, Shirky observed that his students seemed increasingly disconnected from class (less social presence, perhaps?) and increasingly involved elsewhere. The students' bodies were physically in class, but their minds seemed at best distracted from course lessons and at worst unable to process even basic course content. For Shirky, both were problematic.

Regarding distraction, Shirky explains that at a fundamental level the majority of social media content is likely more socially relevant (and therefore more enticing) for students in a classroom setting, because this content is an organic part of their daily lives—as Facebook founder Mark Zuckerberg once famously quipped, "A squirrel dying in front of your house may be more relevant to your interests right now than people dying in Africa." Shirky saw this as inextricably

MC IN ACTION

BE SOCIALLY HERE, NOT (DIGITALLY) THERE!

CONTINUED

linked to the larger concern of information processing, arguing that the attentional pull of this extraneous information (at least, to class content) was causing students to engage in multitasking, either intentionally or unintentionally trying to both follow along in class and pay attention to their social network feeds. As Shirky summarized in his editorial, psychological research has generally shown that multitasking is very inefficient, often resulting in overall poor performance at all tasks involved. One of the reasons for the lack of effectiveness is that when people attempt to multitask, they often instead engage in code-switching—continually diverting their attention between several different pieces of information without taking time to fully process any of them on a deeper level. Although such surface-level processing might be effective for understanding friends' Facebook status updates and admiring their Instagram photos, it is likely not nearly enough attention necessary to fully understand more complex class lessons. Shirky equates this to the infamous "elephant and rider" problem, in which the brain (the elephant) is trying to process all of the information that it thinks it can (no pun intended), while the student (the rider) is left to wrangle the powerful beast/brain into attention. For this reason, Shirky—along with many other teachers—have begun to restrict (or even outright bar) the use of communication technologies in their classrooms. Supporters argue that such policies help students break their almost compulsive reliance on social media and communication technologies, while opponents argue that these "technology abstinence" policies do little to teach students how to successfully manage and use mediated communication tools to their advantage. As a student, we wonder what you think about this debate.

Do you have classes that either encourage or prohibit the use of social media and other technology in the classroom? Share your stories and experiences on our official Facebook group at https://www.facebook.com/groups/234255823447372/ or via Twitter using the #MediaAsTools hashtag. Of course, make sure that if you're doing this during class, that you're allowed to do so!

Shirky's complete *Medium* editorial can be read at https://medium.com/@cshirky why-i-just-asked-my-students-to-put-their-laptops-away-7f5f7c50f368#.4hvu5bfen

Multitasking A process by which a person tries to complete several different tasks at one time, usually resulting in poor overall performance from splitting one's attention to suboptimal levels for each individual task.

Code-switching A process by which a person switches their attention quickly from one task to another.

Some companies, such as Ann Arbor-based Seelio (http://seelio.com), have even attempted to create social media platforms specifically focused on student homework and projects. The program is very similar to LinkedIn in that students

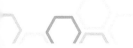

are able to create searchable profiles that document their class projects, creating a digital portfolio of their college coursework that can be shared with classmates, teachers, and potential employers. Within Seelio, classmates and teachers can collaborate and comment on each other's assignments, perhaps fostering a sense of social presence discussed earlier in the chapter.

Massive Open Online Courses

The notion of extending the classroom beyond the "brick and mortar" school building is not a new one. Mail correspondence courses such as the LaSalle Extension University offered distance education courses and complete college degrees from 1908 to 1982, and schools such as the University of Phoenix operate online courses for several hundred thousand students every year. Even some high schools have started this practice, with online charter schools such as Ohio Virtual Academy offering a virtual alternative to traditional primary and secondary education systems. In each of these cases, educators have recognized that technologies can allow potential students access to knowledge without being constrained to a physical classroom that might not be accessible to everyone for a number of reasons. In 2008, the University of Manitoba launched what might be considered the first massive open online course (MOOC) to an audience of over 2,300 non-tuition paying students. Following in 2011, Stanford University launched three online courses to an open audience of over 100,000 students—eventually leading to the development of a MOOC-specific software called Coursera. In 2012, the University of Miami's online high school started MOOC courses to help prepare students for college entrance exams such as the SAT. Perhaps one of the most prestigious science and engineering schools in the world, the Massachusetts Institute of Technology, has made the vast majority of their course content freely available online since 2001, via the MIT Open Courseware platform (http://ocw.mit.edu/index.htm).

So, what are MOOCs, and why would universities want to use them? First, MOOCs are not generally designed with the intention of offering certified accreditations or degrees, nor are they meant to replace the traditional education system. Rather, they are designed to provide convenient and persistent access to information on demand—often as a supplement to an existing education system (such as Miami's SAT prep courses) or as an extended learning project (such as Stanford's courses). MOOCs tend to take two forms. The cMOOC, or collectivist MOOC, is an approach that embraces the Web 2.0 notions of creation and collaboration between students and instructors by approaching the MOOC as a shared space for learning. cMOOCs tend to place less focus on the instructor as the locus of expertise and rather reframe the instructor as a facilitator of a larger conversation between students, a sort of "guide on the side" to help students with their own engagement. The xMOOC, or traditionalist MOOC, is an approach that more closely resembles a traditional on-campus learning environment, with students logging in from locations to attend lecture sessions (either live or prerecorded) before interacting with instructors with follow-up questions. In this vein—and largely in line with the core principles of this textbook—the MOOC is meant to be another tool for education, to function as a space for engagement (with each other, with teachers, and with course content) by those students who desire more.

Extended learning Educational endeavors (such as classes or workshops) that attempt to provide training to individuals across physical and temporal boundaries, similar to the concept of distributed learning.

Key Terms

Autotelic process (pg 87)
Matthew effect (pg 91)
Vicarious experience (pg 93)
Modeling (pg 93)
Script (pg 93)
Interactivity (pg 97)
Multimodal learning (pg 97)
Simulation (pg 97)
Serious games (pg 97)
Avatar (pg 97)
Empathy (pg 97)
Learning management system (pg 99)
Asynchronous (communication) (pg 101)
Displacement hypothesis (pg 102)
Affective learning (pg 102)
Cognitive learning (pg 102)
Digital natives (pg 102)
Multitasking (pg 104)
Code-switching (pg 104)
Extended learning (pg 105)

References

Bandura, A. (1977). *Social learning theory.* Englewood Cliffs, NJ: Prentice Hall.

Bandura, A. (2002). Social cognitive theory of mass communication. In J. Bryant & M. B. Oliver (Eds.), *Media effects: Advances in theory and research* (pp. 94–124). New York: Routledge.

Banks, J. (2015). Object, me, symbiote, other: A social typology of player-avatar relationships. *First Monday, 20*(2), doi: 10.5210/fm.v20i2.

Bowman, N.D., & Akcaoglu, M. (2014). 'I see smart people!': Using Facebook to supplement the university mass lecture. *Internet & Higher Education, 23.* doi: 10.1016/j.iheduc.2014.05.003

Davis, M. (2008). *Street gang: The complete history of Sesame Street.* New York: Viking Press.

Fisch, S. M., & Truglio, Rosemarie T. (Eds.). (2001). *"G" is for growing: Thirty years of research on children and Sesame Street.* Mahwah, NJ: LEA.

Jones, S. (2003). *Let the games begin: Gaming technology and entertainment among college students.* Washington, DC: Pew Foundation.

Junco, R. (2011). Too much face and not enough books: The relationship between multiple indices of Facebook use and academic performance. *Computers in Human Behavior, 28*(1), 187–198.

Junco, R., Heiberger, G., & Loken, E. (2010). The effect of Twitter on college student engagement and grades. *Journal of Computer Assisted Learning, 27*(2), 119-132. doi: 10.1111/j.1365-2729.2010.00387.x

Kelly, S., & Fall, L. T. (2011). An investigation of computer-mediated instructional immediacy in online education: A comparison of graduate and undergraduate students' motivation to learn. *Journal of Advertising Education, 15*, 44-51.

Kelly, S. E., & Westerman, D. (in press). New technologies and distributed learning systems. In P. L. Witt (Ed.), *Handbooks of communication science, Vol. 16 Communication and learning.*

Long, M. G. (2015). *Peaceful neighbor: Discovering the countercultural Mister Rogers.* Louisville, KY: John Knox Press.

Prensky, M. (2001). Digital natives, digital immigrants. *On The Horizon, 9*(5). Retrieved from: http://www.marcprensky.com/writing/prensky%20-%20 digital%20natives,%20digital%20immigrants%20-%20part1.pdf.

Richardson, J. C., & Swan, K. (2003). Examining social presence in online courses in relation to students' perceived learning and satisfaction. *Journal of Asynchronous Learning Networks, 7*, 68–88.

Russo, T., & Benson, S. (2005). Learning with invisible others: Perceptions of online presence and their relationship to cognitive and affective learning. *Educational Technology & Society, 8*, 54–62.

Selwyn, N. (2009). Faceworking: Exploring students' education-related use of Facebook. Learning, *Media and Technology, 34*(2), 157–174.

Swan, K., & Shih, L. F. (2005). On the nature and development of social presence in online course discussions. *Journal of Asynchronous Learning Networks, 9*, 115–136.

Walther, J. B., & Bunz, U. (2005). The rules of virtual groups: Trust, liking, and performance in computer-mediated communication. *Journal of Communication, 55*, 828–846.

Westervelt, E. (2016, January 5). A bit of a Montessori 2.0: Khan Academy opens a lab school. NPR.org. Retrieved April 17 2016 from http:// www.npr.org/sections/ed/2016/01/05/461506508/sal-khan-on-learning-coding-and-why-virtual-ed-is-not-enough

Yates, B. L. (1999, March). *Modeling strategies for prosocial television: A review.* Paper presented at the Association for Education in Journalism and Mass Communication Southeast Colloquium. Lexington, KY.

CHAPTER 7

Relationships in a Digital Age

Sal 9000 knew she was the one for him. Nene was beautiful, she didn't fight with him, and she attended to him as he wished. In fact, Sal referred to Nene as his dream woman. So he knew that he had to marry her. And when the ceremony took place, it was broadcast live to thousands of people online in Japan.

Anything seem strange yet? If not, keep reading.

The most interesting part of this story is not that two people got married. It is not even that the ceremony was broadcast live online (which is a growing phenomenon, as is broadcasting funerals, for reasons we will discuss later in the book). No, what you will likely find to be the strangest part of this story is that one of the "participants" in this wedding is not a person at all. Can you guess which one?

Sal 9000 is a real person, a 27-year-old from Japan. But his beautiful bride? She is a video game character from the Nintendo DS *Love Plus*.

Now does anything seem strange to you? If you are like most of the students we have discussed this with, you will likely think it is incredibly strange and maybe even a little (or a lot) creepy.

But is this creepy? Sal says he does not feel the need for a human girlfriend, even suggesting that Nene is better than a human girlfriend, stating "she doesn't get angry if I'm late in replying to her. Well, she gets angry, but she forgives me quickly." CNN's Kyung Lah has a short interview with Sal 9000—complete with photos and videos of his wedding—available at http://www.cnn.com/2009/WORLD/asiapcf/12/16/japan.virtual.wedding/index.html?iref=allsearch

Creepy or not, we believe this story highlights and illuminates a lot about relationships in the digital age and relationships in general, for that matter. This chapter (and the next) will discuss this phenomenon and will give some reasoning behind how and why we might use MC for relationships, both close and acquaintance, and even with ourselves. After reading it, come back and ask yourself again: is the story of Sal 9000 creepy? If you are saying yes now, you will likely still be saying yes later. But hopefully, you will also maybe gain a little understanding into what might be going on in Sal's relationship with Nene and maybe will think a little bit differently about your own relationships as well.

When reading this chapter, consider the following:

- Think back to our earlier discussion of Maslow's hierarchy of needs (Chapter 3). Is there a connection between Maslow and our desire to use new media to connect to others?
- Are online relationships "bad" or "good"?
- How have our assumptions regarding online dating changed in recent years?
- Why is presence important when thinking about the ways we connect online?
- What does the "media equation" tell us about our interactions with mediated individuals?

We Are a Social Species

So, why might Sal 9000 choose to "marry" a video game character? First, it is important to consider a general truth about people. We are social animals. On the whole, we desire interaction with other people. In fact, this is something that is necessary for our survival—so goes the old saying "no man is an island, complete unto himself." Psychologists Edward Deci and Richard Ryan suggest that the need for relatedness—that is, our desire to engage in meaningful relationships with others—is one of the primary factors that motivate people to do things. Thus, it should come as no surprise that people use a communication tool such as the Internet in order to connect with other people. Whether it is an alphabet of symbols for spoken language, books and telegraphs so that we can send written communications, a television show so that an organization can broadcast messages to large audiences, or a message posted on a social media profile, technology allows people to communicate in new ways and have a profound impact on the ways humans communicate with each other. But regardless of the technology itself, a main purpose is to communicate with each other—to engage in decidedly interpersonal communication (see MC in Action: The Nicest Place on the Internet).

MC IN ACTION

THE NICEST PLACE ON THE INTERNET

Having one of those days? Yeah, been there too. And sometimes, a little pick-me-up is hard to come by. So come on by to turn the sad into happy and the happy into a celebration. Cause this is a nice place to visit on days like today.

~The Nicest Place on the Internet Web Site

No doubt, many students are familiar with the darker side of the Internet, with incidents such as catfishing and cyberbullying often populating headlines and leading to a general concern about safety in an increasingly online age. Although such a discussion might seem a bit outside the focus of a book chapter on entertainment, so much of our online activity blurs the lines between information-gathering, relationships, persuasion, and entertainment that one person's goof-off fake Twitter account might be another person's secret crush (identity scholar Jaime Banks might talk about differences in how these individuals relate to their on-screen personae, as discussed in Chapter 6). After all, for many people browsing the Internet is a common leisure activity—a modern-day version of channel-surfing.

For those fortunate enough to web-surf over to the nicest place on the Internet (http://thenicestplaceon-theinter.net), trolls and trash-talk are replaced by something decidedly more positive: a simple digital hug, from a seemingly infinite number of strangers in a video loop. While very little is known about the motivation for creating the Web site, December 2011 saw the launch of one of the more creative and compassionate living art projects online.

One way that we might understand this page could be through the lens of communication scholar Thomas Socha, a recognized leader in the study of positive communication. While his research tends to focus on what can be done interpersonally between people to foster a greater sense of closeness and support (Socha & Pitts, 2012), one might wonder if these sort of seemingly frivolous videos might really help media users feel a bit better after a particularly long and taxing day. Indeed, there is some research to support this concept—as far back as the 1950s, Horton and Wohl (1956) found that media audiences often formed imagined relationships with on-screen personae such as famed news anchor Walter Cronkite (often considered "The Most Trusted Man in America") as well as countless other radio and television celebrities of the day; we call these para-social relationships.

If you get a moment, visit the Web site, and share the experience on our official Facebook group at https://www.facebook.com/groups/234255823447372/, or with our Twitter users, following the #MediaAsTools hashtag. Maybe even consider adding a hug yourself, so that somebody else can get a good pick-me-up the next time they visit!

Para-social relationship A relationship that media viewers and users often form with on-screen characters that mirrors an authentic friendship or in-person relationship, but exists (by definition) only in the mind of the viewer or user.

ARPAnet The Advanced Research Projects Agency Network, this system of networked computers was started in 1969 with funding and oversight from the U.S. military. The network was designed to allow researchers to share data quickly and confidentially across large spaces.

E-mail A form of electronic communication in which users can send each other private messages to digital mailboxes, similar to sending a letter through a traditional mail service.

Perhaps surprisingly to some who assume all technology to be a form of mass communication, research has shown that interpersonal communication is a common use of the Internet. People use various Internet-based applications to connect and interact with other people, and this social interaction cuts across types of relationships: romantic partners, family members, friends, and acquaintances among them. Indeed, this is a bit different from the initial functions of the Internet, suggesting that the Internet is a tool capable of powerful re-inventions. When the Internet was first created as ARPAnet in 1969, it was designed as an interconnected computer mainframe network that would connect researchers who would have a "place" to share research and information more quickly and easily than by doing it face-to-face. Put another way, it was designed to overcome the space and time li mitations of face-to-face communication.

Then a funny thing happened. Two years later, in 1971, ARPAnet added an early electronic "mail" system so that individual researchers could contact each other with specific questions, similar to leaving memos in office mailboxes. As has been pointed out by communication scholar John Sherry and one of this book's authors in 2008, this e-mail system became the killer application that led to the early (and continued) expansion of what we today know of as the Internet. It turns out those early ARPAnet researchers, like most other humans, wanted to talk to people with whom they shared similarities. Messages about research would include increasingly interpersonal information as the scientists got to know each other over common work interests and shifted their conversations from being task-oriented to being more social-oriented over time.

We have come a long way since that early ARPAnet, and we have opened the Internet (and the many internets that comprise it) to a much greater number of users than ever before. For example, as of 2016, Facebook boasts over one and a half billion monthly active users, representing over one in every five people living on Earth. This number is up from 2013, which saw 1 account for every 7 people on Earth, suggesting that Facebook is not a dead technology. Although there is some debate as to how many of these accounts belong to "real" people, we can see that having such a large user base is staggering considering the platform was launched in 2004. Even technologies such as video games, which are not primarily designed for social interaction (or at least, were not designed for social interaction initially), contain a great deal of social communication. In general, people like to interact with other people, and they seem to do so even when the channel is not necessarily designed for this. This goes back to the creation of the Internet from the very first time it was turned on: scientists sharing data also wanted to share their thoughts and opinions on their projects, which evolved into the formation of social bonds across the barriers of one lab or one project. It is apparent when looking at communication technology that, although the tools might change, the people do not: people want to talk to people, and we do it even when the application or platform has been created primarily for some other purpose.

Online Interaction: Boon or Bane?

Although there seems to be some agreement that the Internet is indeed used to interact with other people, not all agree on the effects that this large amount of online communication has on users. There are scholars who have discussed how a reliance on online interaction will have detrimental effects on society. In his modern classic *Bowling Alone*, Harvard political scientist Robert Putnam argues for the ways in which media serves to reduce social interactions. The title of the book comes from his own observations in bowling alleys, in which he noticed that although more people seemed to bowling overall (at least as of 2,000), membership in bowling leagues was way down. In other words, people were coming to the bowling alley but often were alone: they were coming alone, bowling alone, and then leaving alone. Why is this important? Putnam argued that in the preceding decades people had begun to rely more on solitary leisure activities—primarily media such as watching television at home—to occupy their free time instead of engaging other people in social activities such as bowling. Thus, when folks did decide to go to a bowling alley now and then, they found that their lack of social interactions with others resulted in having to bowl alone; in simplest terms, they had no other friends to bowl with.

> Social interactions
> Conversations between people central to the human communication process.

More recently, another criticism has been offered by scholar Sherry Turkle, who suggests that we come to expect more from technology and less from people. As we come to rely more and more on technology for our connections, we lose the ability to be alone to reflect and also the ability to truly converse with others, thus losing valuable intra and interpersonal abilities. For more about Dr. Turkle's thoughts, please see her TED talk at http://www.ted.com/talks/sherry_turkle_alone_together.

Although Putnam and Turkle ask important questions and get us thinking as researchers, many criticisms have been laid against these positions. The most common one can be summed up by Barry Wellman, (e.g., Wellman, Haase, Witte, & Hampton, 2001) a sociologist at the University of Toronto, who has pointed out that communication technologies such as the Internet can in fact be tools that not only allow and encourage communication between people (we can think specifically of social media programs here), but they can also aid in the creation of new communities that are not restricted to the boundaries of space-time (see MC in Action: Be It Ever so Digital, There's No Place Like HomeNet!) And overall, the research evidence seems to suggest that people can reap positive benefits from interacting with others online, including, but not limited to, increased face-to-face interactions, suggesting that "People are not hooked on gadgets—they are hooked on each other" (Rainie & Wellman, 2012, p. 6).

This is a classic argument in research—the debate between media usage being a social or individual activity—and we wish to make three points about it. First, *nearly every new communication technology that comes along has similar claims made against it*. For example, when the telephone began to spread through American society, there were critics who worried about the breakdown of social order that would come about because people could now talk to their families and friends without physically going to see them. The evidence for the phone, however, seems to support the opposite overall. Second, oftentimes these types of claims

MC IN ACTION

BE IT EVER SO DIGITAL, THERE'S NO PLACE LIKE HOMENET!

Our findings show the variety of ways people are domesticating the Internet—turning a technology invented for scientists and elaborated for electronic commerce into a household feature.

~The HomeNet Project, Carnegie Mellon University

The impact of communication technology on social interaction is a common area of debate in the social sciences, with some arguing that technology separates people while others contending that it brings us closer together. To address some of these concerns from a scientific approach, scientists with Carnegie Mellon University started The HomeNet Project—a unique series of studies in which families were provided with computer equipment and Internet access in exchange for providing CMU researchers with detailed records of how the equipment was used.

Starting in 1995, HomeNet studied families both in the Pittsburgh area (the home of CMU) as well as a nationally representative survey in 2000–2002, and the results from their work have been surprising to many. As varied as Internet usage is for families across the United States, the "killer applications"— those programs that are used the most—are almost entirely based around interpersonal communication and social interaction. Although the first study seemed to suggest that increased Internet usage was related to increased depression and loneliness, later studies seemed to suggest that this was a matter of how the computer was being used. In particular, it seemed to affect people new to the technology, and so over time people were better able to utilize the technology to accomplish their interpersonal goals (recall the discussion of transparent technologies in Chapter 3). Overall, the Internet seemed to be used primarily for communicating with friends and family as well as meeting new people. In fact, the researchers found that one of the best predictors of continued Internet usage was people who use the technology to communicate with each other, such as sending e-mails back and forth. While the last of these studies was done in 2002, research is still ongoing as we enter a new age of social media—programs seemingly custom-made to encourage social interaction.

Recent research has started to look at some of the ways in which using social media can lead to positive or negative outcomes. For example, communication scholar Catalina Toma has found that viewing one's own Facebook profile tends to make one feel better, whereas viewing someone else's profile tends to make one feel worse, perhaps due in part to the positivity bias that tends to permeate Facebook profiles (e.g., Toma, 2013). Another recent study from the Pitt Center for Research on Technology found that the depressive effects of time spent using social media were almost entirely mediated by social media addiction (Shensa, Bowman, Sidani, Marshal, & Primack, 2016). Overall, it seems that how social media are used, rather than simply using these tools, is what leads to outcomes, be they good or bad.

You can read more about Carnegie Mellon University's HomeNet Project at: http://homenet.hcii.cs.cmu.edu/

seem to exist because *people only think about how things have been done, rather than how they can be done*. For example, we would not deny that the telephone or the Internet "changes" society, or at least allows for changes in the way we interact. However, this does not necessarily lead to a breakdown in the overall goals of traditional communication (in fact, if you get nothing else from this book, we hope you get that people seem to use technology to accomplish their already existing goals) nor in their ability to accomplish those goals. Third, we would argue that *both of the preceding situations can be possible*. It is possible that spending a lot of time online can lead to feeling lonelier. It is also possible that it leads to feeling less lonely and can build social capital. It is our contention that these outcomes are not qualities inherent in the technology itself, but are more about how a person uses that technology. The Internet and MC are not magic wands that will serve to alleviate all the problems that exist in communication (and remember, there are many issues with face-to-face communication as well). They are instead tools that can be used socially, unsocially, and antisocially.

Social Network(ing) Sites

One of the very interesting recent developments for social interaction online are sites like Facebook. Social media researchers danah boyd and Nicole Ellison define social network sites (SNS) as "web-based services that allow individuals to (1) construct a public or semi-public profile within a bounded system, (2) articulate a list of other users with whom they share a connection, and (3) view and traverse their list of connections and those made by others within the system."

Social network sites (SNS) Internet-based computer programs that allow users to create profiles and share information with other users.

So, how do they differ from past technology? Social network scholars Nicholas Christakis and James Fowler (2009) suggest several ways. First, we might say that these differ in scope. Social network sites are enormous, and they allow us to stay in touch with far more people than we ever could face-to-face. This enormity allows us to create a sense of communality, because social network sites increase the scale at which we can share information and contribute to collective efforts (think Wikipedia, Chapter 4). We can also find very specific connections with people we normally would not come in contact with, as we can form communities with those we share similarities with regardless of where they live. Finally, using our virtual identities we can alter to some extent how we are perceived—which can help us form more meaningful connections (for better or worse).

Second, and perhaps the biggest qualitative change, is the notion that these types of sites allow for "public displays of connection" (Donath & boyd, 2004). The biggest new change is the ability to broadcast your social network to others publicly and to see others' social networks. In the past, how could you get that information? The effects of these public displays of connection are just starting to be examined.

Online social networking is not just for kids, either. A Pew report in 2015 showed that as of July 2015, 76 percent of all online adults in the United States were on at least one SNS, up from 67% in December 2012. Although earlier studies showed a higher usage of SNS overall by women compared to men, the most recent numbers suggest there is no statistically significant differences between women and men in overall social media usage. Not surprisingly, use of SNS is

skewed toward younger adults, with 92 percent of 18–29-year-old Internet users saying they are on one. However, 56 percent of online adults 65 years and older reported using at least one SNS as well, which might suggest that the social networking "craze" seems to be one that cuts across different age categories. In fact this is unsurprising, as the desire to socially engage others is not conceptually tied to one age group over another.

But why are so many people turning to SNS? Perhaps even more interesting than sheer percentages of people who use them is how they are used. A group of Pew studies have examined this phenomenon (for a rundown, visit: http://pewinternet.org/Commentary/2012/March/Pew-Internet-Social-Networking-full-detail.aspx and http://pewinternet.org/topics/Social-Networking.aspx?type Filter=5). It seems that by and large people use SNS to maintain their social networks. Various Pew studies have found that the average user of SNS has more close ties and is about half as likely to be socially isolated as the average American. Furthermore, SNS users get more social support from their ties, with Facebook users specifically getting the most social support (this will be discussed more in Chapter 8). These findings add more evidence to the idea that we use these tools to help accomplish our social goals and that they are not necessarily a hindrance to positive social relationships.

In short, SNSs such as Facebook have become a major channel of interpersonal communication. The average person has 338 friends on Facebook (as of 2014), and there are people with 500, 1,000, and even 1,500 friends. The notion of what a "friend" is will be addressed somewhat in Chapter 8. However, can a person have too many friends on Facebook? What do you think of a person who has 1,500 friends on Facebook? How about a person who has 50 friends? Researchers associated with Michigan State University (Tong, Van Der Heide, Langwell, & Walther, 2008) found curvilinear effects for the number of friends on Facebook and popularity. This means having too few friends makes you appear more negative, but so does having too many friends. This has been called this the "Goldilocks effect" of social media (Westerman, Spence, & Van Der Heide, 2012) and has been recently found with Twitter and the number of followers a user has as well.

Goldilocks effect A phenomenon that explains how having too few or too many friends or contacts can result in others making negative judgments about the social attractiveness of a SNS user.

Context collapse A situation, common to social networking sites, in which information created for a specific audience is shared with multiple audiences at the same time.

One of the most interesting parts of social networking sites is the public nature of one's social networks. This brings up another question about what happens when all of that information is public and can be seen by others. Does what your friends post on your Facebook change how others perceive you? In short, yes. Research has found that your friends' posts have a big impact on how others perceive you. Posts about being "social" made a person seem more likable, but also more credible, although posts about excessive drinking did the opposite. (Walther, et al., 2008). And, if the pictures of your posters were physically attractive, you were seen as more physically attractive. Other studies (e.g. Vitak, 2012) have proposed the notion of context collapse, or how information posted on social media networks often intended for one group of people (for example, your roommates) can quickly find its way to other unintended groups (such as our parents or professors). So, be careful of the company you keep, even on Facebook (see MC in Action: JK I'm white!).

MC IN ACTION

JK I'm White!

With the push of a button, Justine Sacco sent a message out into the Twitterverse that said she was hoping she wouldn't contract AIDS on her trip before boarding a flight to Cape Town, South Africa. Over the the 11-hour flight, she had lost her job as a public relations professional for IAC, and her life would change forever. By the time she landed, she was the #1 worldwide trend on Twitter. How is this possible given that she only had 170 followers?

It seems that when she tweeted out what she saw as a joke (which many people ended up seeing, and saw as an incredibly insensitive comment), she was not considering how vast of an audience is possible online. She may have only been thinking about her 170 followers, but things like retweets and shares on social media make one's potential audience online much larger than our considered audiences often are. Thus, our contexts often collapse online, and our various worlds come into contact with each other, including friends, family members, co-workers and bosses, and even complete strangers.

More about Justine Sacco's story can be found here: http://www.adweek.com/adfreak/justine-sacco-fired-iac-hope-i-dont-get-aids-tweet-154639 with some later follow-up here: http://www.nytimes.com/2015/02/15/magazine/how-one-stupid-tweet-ruined-justine-saccos-life.html?_r=0

Deceiving Others Online

One issue that is commonly mentioned in popular press coverage of online interaction is deception. Typically, this portrayal suggests that online interactions are full of lies and that lying is more frequent online than offline—particularly in the realm of romance (see MC in Action: Manti and the Catfish Fry). Of course, the first statement could be true without the second one also being true.

Can people lie online? Of course they can, and they have been since the early days of the Internet. Indeed, in what is likely one of the earliest popular accounts of MC, an article called "The Strange Case of the Electronic Lover" in *Ms. Magazine* detailed a story about a male psychologist who pretended to be a female in an electronic chat group (The original article can be found here: http://lindsyvangelder.com/sites/default/files/Plinkers.org%20-%20Electronic%20Lover.htm_.pdf). And the affordances and the limitations make some lies possible that would have been at least very difficult in the past. However, other parts of the channel seem to restrict lying on the whole. So, although catfishing happens, it is probably not as widespread as mediated coverage of it might make it seem to be. In fact, some research suggests that lying is less common online than it is face-to-face. Furthermore, it seems that the kinds of lies that happen online, especially in dating Web sites, are similar to the ones that occur face-to-face (Ellison, Heino, & Gibbs, 2006; Toma, Ellison, & Hancock, 2008). A few pounds here, a couple years there, a few fewer gray hairs, a few dollars more, these lies seem to be things that we might call impression management. We try our best to make ourselves look good. So, we may shave a couple years off of our age, or we may post a picture that only shows us from our good side.

Dating Web sites Web pages that are specifically designed to help users form and sustain romantic connections with other users.

Impression management The act of disclosing and concealing personal information in order to control the impressions that others form of you.

MC IN ACTION

MANTI AND THE CATFISH FRY

During the 2012 NCAA FBS football season, traditional power Notre Dame returned to their glory days, reaching (although ultimately losing) the BCS national championship game. The team was propelled all season by all-American linebacker Manti Te'o and his inspirational story. During the season, in the week leading up to a game against rival Michigan State, Manti's grandmother and his girlfriend Lennay Kekua—who had been dying of complications with leukemia—both passed away within 24 hours of each other. Heartbroken, Manti decided to play in the game against Michigan State and recorded 12 tackles, one sack, and a fumble recovery, leading his team to a 20–3 victory. Part of the reason Manti played in the game rather than returning home to Hawaii were the inspirational words of Kekua, who told him that no matter what happened to her, he should continue playing football.

After the season ended, details began emerging about Manti's girlfriend. It seems she may not have actually died of leukemia as was reported during the season. It also seemed that she may not have actually existed in the first place. Instead, it came to light that Te'o was part of an elaborate hoax (most likely as the victim of the hoax), which was designed to make him believe that Lennay Kekua actually existed, created by Ronaiah Tuiasopo. Pictures of his girlfriend existed, but the actual person who those pictures were of did not know they were being used. And Manti had never met his girlfriend face-to-face.

Known as a "catfish," this is defined on Urban Dictionary as "someone who pretends to be someone they're not using Facebook or other social media to create false identities, particularly to pursue deceptive online romances." The phrase was coined by documentary filmmaker Ariel Schulman, who showed a similar story in the 2010 movie *Catfish* and has worked on a MTV series of the same name. As discussed in Chapter 5, this is just the kind of media coverage that could lead people to think that this is a common phenomnon. But is it?

Online, you can be anyone you want to be because of the restriction of the visual information that would tell you that a person is not who they say they are, right? It is hard to ignore the fact that what happened to Manti Te'o would not have happened face-to-face (or at least would have been incredibly difficult). The lack of nonverbal cues in many online platforms does lead to possibilities for deception that would be hard, if not impossible, to pull off face-to-face. However, as Cornell professor Jeff Hancock has pointed out, social media actually seems to lead to less deception overall, compared to face-to-face interaction. In general, Hancock suggests that the publicness and permanence of online interaction allows people the ability to go back and check on information that would have been ephemeral in the past. Realization of this makes people leery of posting lies, knowing that someone is likely to call you out on a lie, and that people can later check to see what you have said as well.

For video of Dr. Hancock discussing this notion, go to http://www.cnn.com/2013/01/13/opinion/hancock-technology-lying/index.html

Presence: At the Heart of MC?

People use technologies to connect with others. It even seems that at least much of the time, this connection and online interaction lead to very positive outcomes. But how is this possible? We argue that one of the main concepts to understanding this is called social presence, which is a specific form of a larger concept known as telepresence.

Telepresence is a concept that derives from various fields. Simply put, it is an "illusion of non-mediation" (Lombard & Ditton, 1997). In other words, it is using media without realizing or acknowledging its use. In some ways, you can think back to the idea of transparent technology from Chapter 3. The concept of telepresence has some important characteristics. First, it is generally considered as a *continuum*. This means that the feeling of telepresence is not an all or nothing game; you are not simply present or absent. Instead, you can feel more or less present at different times. Second, it is a *psychological state*. This means it is not an inherent quality of any given channel, but instead it can be experienced through any channel, given the right circumstances. For example, some people find books to be the most highly presence-inducing channel. This has been characterized as "the book problem" by presence scholars, as it is a relatively low tech medium, and yet can be incredibly engrossing to people who like reading. Third, it *varies across time*. During an interaction (or any other mediated experience like watching a movie) your level of presence will go up and down throughout the experience.

Generally speaking, we can think of telepresence as a combination of the user expectations of three things: content, channel, and user (Pettey, Bracken, Rubenking, Buncher, & Gress, 2010). Certain types of content are more likely to increase the feeling of presence. Also, although stated previously that presence is not inherent in a channel, there are certain characteristics that make telepresence more likely, like interactivity. Finally, some users are more likely to experience telepresence than others. Most of the time, telepresence occurs because of the right combination of these three. The right user has the right content through the right channel, and then telepresence increases.

So far, we have only mentioned telepresence as a general category, but scholars suggest there are different types of it (e.g., Lee, 2002b). The one we will focus on in this chapter is social presence, which can simply be thought of as the experience of feeling connected to another person, or feeling like an interaction is "real," while using some sort of communication technology.

Is this feeling of "realness" strange? We argue that not only is the feeling not at all strange but it is in fact quite natural and, under the right circumstances, a fairly common occurrence. In a book called *The Media Equation*, Reeves and Nass (1996) highlighted their research program that can help us understand why this experience may be so natural and easy to feel. They suggest that the media equation is that "media equals real life," and as such, we tend to interact with mediated objects and people (or both) in the same way as we do real ones (see MC in Action: The Death of Clippy). This does not necessarily mean that the content shown on television, for example, presents an accurate depiction of real life. Instead, it means that we respond to media as we do real life. Reeves and Nass present a program of research showing this. What they do is take an established finding from interpersonal and social psychology research, and replace one of the

Social presence When using communication technology, a feeling that one is engaging another person in a nonmediated way.

Telepresence When using communication technology, a feeling that one is interacting in a mediated environment without consciously thinking about this mediation.

MC IN ACTION

THE DEATH OF CLIPPY

Depending on how old you are, you may remember the Office Assistant known as "Clippy," who would pop up at times while you were working in Microsoft Word, for example. Clippy would come on the screen and ask "useful" questions like "It looks like you are writing a letter. Would you like help?" This assistant was pretty much universally panned by users and critics alike. Even Microsoft has come to realize how bad Clippy was, parodying the Death of Clippy in a recent "trailer" for the release of Microsoft 2010, which can be seen here: http://www.youtube.com/watch?feature=player_embedded& v=VUawhjxLS2I#! (For a list of various parodies of Clippy, please see the Wikipedia page on Office Assistant at http://en.wikipedia.org/wiki/Clippy)

What was wrong with Clippy? Microsoft attempted to provide more cues for this Office Assistant, by offering it as a paper clip agent. However, this story might suggest that more cues are not always associated with increased social presence. We might also suggest that the types of questions Clippy asked seemed unnatural and unhelpful, which served as a reminder that Clippy was not a good agent, and thus left users without a connection to this character. In short, Clippy did not act very human, and so we may have been left feeling rather inhumane toward it.

people with a computer, and consistently find similar results as the study using two people. They find this despite also finding that people suggest that they know this is a ridiculous thing to do.

If you think this is strange, consider watching movies. Have you ever cried or seen a friend cry during a movie? Most likely. And yet, why would this happen? You know that the people on the screen are actors, so it seems kind of ridiculous to cry at movies (unless you are crying because you know how much the actor was paid). And of course, if you stop to think about it, it is ridiculous, and people will articulate it. However, much of our human responses occur without thinking about them.

The human species evolved over a long period, and it evolved to rise to meet a variety of specific challenges (Lee, 2002a). One of those challenges was not communication media, which are incredibly new. For tens of thousands of years, if a person saw something that looked like another person and, maybe more importantly, behaved like another person, it was another person, not a representation of one on a screen and not a robot or video game character. Thus, we likely evolved to respond to these presentations as human, and if something walks, talks, and acts human, we will respond to it as a human (see MC in Action: Virtual Morality).

This is because technological evolution outpaces biological evolution. For most of human existence, responding humanly to something because it behaved humanly served us well (you can even consider the way we respond to animals).

MC IN ACTION

VIRTUAL MORALITY

If it is the case that most individuals respond to media portrayals as if they are real, then how might this influence the way in which we understand our virtual actions. This was the central question of research by media researchers Sven Joeckel and Leyla Dogruel as well as one of the authors of this book (Joeckel, Bowman, & Dogruel, 2012).

In a study on German and U.S. computer users (both children and adults), participants were asked to play a video game that presented them with a variety of different moral dilemmas dealing with issues of harm, fairness, and loyalty, among others. Each person's in-game decisions were recorded, and then the researchers examined the relationship between each user's real-world moral orientations and the decisions they made in the game related to each moral dilemma. The researchers found when individuals were confronted with a moral scenario related to an issue of great importance to their real lives (such as a person who does not like violence) that they would avoid committing a moral violation when given the opportunity. However, when individuals were confronted with a moral scenario that was not so important to them, the chances of them committing a moral violation were no greater than a coin flip! In other words, gamers seem to make gut decisions when faced with issues of importance to their real lives, but made game decisions when faced with issues that are not particularly important. Put another way, it seems that a video game player's moral decisions in the virtual world are very similar to their decisions in the real world—that is, there does not seem to be a separate virtual morality.

Yet, it is important to note that the video game in this study was one that did not reward or punish moral violations (see social learning theory, Chapter 6). What do you think? Have you ever been bothered by the content of a video game? Have you ever done something in a video game that you would not otherwise do in real life? How might a video game that seems to glorify moral violations change the findings of the preceding study?

Share your thoughts with us on Facebook at https://www.facebook.com/groups/234255823447372/ or on Twitter, using the #MediaAsTools hashtag.

More about this study can be found at: http://www.tandfonline.com/doi/abs/10.1080/15213269.2012.727218#preview

Our brains have not adapted as fast as technology. Thus, it is our default to respond humanly to something that seems human, and social presence (as well as other kinds) is probably both easy and a natural state because of it. It takes something weird (like a bad acting performance) to start you thinking and get you realizing that this is not "real."

Why So Much Interaction?

Based upon these concepts of telepresence, social presence, and the notions set forth in *The Media Equation*, we might suggest two main reasons that so much social interaction occurs online. First, as we have said before, humans are an inherently social species, and as such the creation and maintenance of relationships is

one of our main reasons for communicating in general. We strive to interact with one another as social creatures, and we are rewarded for this interaction in the form of meaningful relationships with others. Second, as has also been said at other points in this book, the Internet (and internet technology in general) is a communication tool that provides many affordances for social interaction, including the ability for social presence. So, when we have a goal (relationships) and a tool allows us to accomplish that goal (a vast network of social others wanting to interact and form relationships), we are likely to use the tool for the goal.

Moreover, we suggest that the Internet specifically and communication technologies in general are neither inherently good nor bad for relationships. Instead, it and they provide us a tool to use for interaction—and a particularly well-suited tool for fostering interaction at that. In the end, it is the quality of the interaction between two people rather than the manner in which that interaction takes place that is the strongest predictor of the quality of a given relationship. Consider the following passage from Christakis and Fowler (2009).

"Yet, new technologies—whether massively multiplayer online games such as *World of Warcraft* or *Second Life*; social network websites such as Facebook or MySpace; collective information sites like YouTube, Wikipedia, or eBay; or dating sites like Match.com or eHarmony—just realize our ancient propensity to connect to other humans, albeit with electrons flowing through cyberspace rather than conversation drifting through the air. While the social networks formed online may be abstract, large, complex and supermodern, they also reflect universal and fundamental human tendencies that emerged in our prehistoric past when we told stories to one another around campfires in the African savanna. **Even astonishing advances in communication technology like the printing press, the telephone, and the Internet do not take us away from this past; they draw us closer to it.**" (p. 257, emphasis added)

Key Terms

Para-social relationship (pg 111)
ARPAnet (pg 112)
E-mail (pg 112)
Social interactions (pg 113)
Social network site (SNS) (pg 115)
Goldilocks effect (pg 116)
Context collapse (pg 116)
Dating Web sites (pg 117)
Impression management (pg 117)
Social presence (pg 119)
Telepresence (pg 119)

References

Boyd, d. m., & Ellison, N. B. (2007). Social network sites: Definition, history, and scholarship. *Journal of Computer-Mediated Communication, 13*(1), article 11. http://jcmc.indiana.edu/vol13/issue1/boyd.ellison.html

Christaikis, N. A., & Fowler, J. H. (2009). *Connected: The surprising power of our social networks and how they shape our lives.* New York: Little, Brown and Company.

Deci, E. L., & Ryan, R. M. (1985). *Intrinsic motivation and self-determination in human behavior.* New York: Plenum Publishing Co.

Donath, J., & boyd, d. (2004). Public displays of connection. *BT Technology Journal, 22,* 71–82.

Ellison, N., Heino, R., & Gibbs, J. (2006). Managing impressions online: Self-presentation processes in the online dating environment. *Journal of Computer-Mediated Communication, 11* (2), article 2. http://jcmc.indiana.edu/vol11/issue2/ellison.html

Joeckel, S., Bowman, N. D., & Dogruel, L. (2012). Gut or game: The influence of moral intuitions on decisions in virtual environments. *Media Psychology, 15*(4), 460–485.

Lee, K. M. (2004a). Why presence occurs: Evolutionary psychology, media equation, and presence. *Presence, 13,* 494–505.

Lee, K. M. (2004b). Presence, explicated. *Communication Theory, 14,* 27–50.

Lombard, M., & Ditton, T. (1997). At the heart of it all: The concept of presence. *Journal of Computer-Mediated Communication, 3*(2), article 4. http://jcmc.indiana.edu/vol3/issue2/lombard.html

Pettey, G., Bracken, C. C., Rubenking, B., Buncher, M., & Gress, E. (2010). Telepresence, soundscapes and technological expectation: Putting the observer into the equation. *Virtual Reality, 14,* 15–25.

Putnam, R. (1999). *Bowling alone: The collapse and revival of American community.* New York: Simon & Schuster.

Rainie, L., & Wellman, B. (2012). Networked: The news social operating system. Cambridge, MA: MIT Press.

Reeves, B., & Nass, C. (1996). *The media equation: How people treat computers, television, and new media like real people and places.* Stanford, CA: CSLI Publications.

Sherry, J. L., & Bowman, N. D. (2008). History of the Internet. In H. Bidgoli (Ed.), *The handbook of computer networks: Vol. I. Key concepts, data transmission, digital and optical networks.* Hoboken, NJ: John Wiley & Sons.

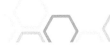

Toma, C. (2013). Feeling better but doing worse: Effects of Facebook self-presentation on implicit self-esteem and cognitive task performance. *Media Psychology, 16,* 199–220.

Toma, C., Hancock, J., & Ellison, N. (2008). Separating fact from fiction: An examination of deceptive self-presentation in online dating profiles. *Personality and Social Psychology Bulletin 34,* 1023–1036.

Tong, S. T., Van Der Heide, B., Langwell, L., & Walther, J. B. (2008). Too much of a good thing? The relationship between number of friends and interpersonal impressions on Facebook. *Journal of Computer-Mediated Communication, 13*(3), 531–549.

Vitak, J. (2012). The impact of context collapse and privacy on social network site disclosures. *Journal of Broadcasting and Electronic Media, 56,* 451–470.

Walther, J. B., Van Der Heide, B., Kim, S., Westerman, D., & Tong, S. T. (2008). The role of friends' behavior on evaluations of individuals' Facebook profiles: Are we known by the company we keep? *Human Communication Research, 34,* 28–49.

Wellman, B., Haase, A. Q., Witte, J., & Hampton, K. (2001). Does the Internet increase, decrease, or supplement social capital?: Social networks, participation, and community commitment. *American Behavioral Scientist, 45,* 436–455.

Westerman, D., Spence, P. R., & Van Der Heide, B. (2012). A social network as information: The effect of system generated reports of connectedness of credibility on Twitter. *Computers in Human Behavior, 28,* 199–206.

CHAPTER 8

Falling in Love (or Like) Through Technology

When we are trying to form a relationship with somebody, which do you think is better: talking to them online or talking with them off-line?

Maybe you think the answer seems obvious: off-line. If you are like many people, you might argue that online relationships are not as good as off-line, face-to-face (FtF), "real" relationships. After all, online communication usually lacks nonverbal cues—especially touch—which seem crucial for delivering emotionally charged interpersonal messages that are so crucial to a relationship. For example, there are times when you just want a hug from your boyfriend or girlfriend, and one is hard-pressed to replicate such an action online.

But perhaps you answered that using various communication technologies can be better. It might be the case that you like being able to interact more frequently with your partner—such as sending text messages during a quick break between classes or being able to visit your partner's Facebook page and share information with them when they are not available. Both allow you to overcome space-time barriers. Maybe you have even found yourself in a relationship that moved very quickly online, and you felt it would not have moved that quickly FtF.

We will answer the question in a way that might be very unsatisfying to many of you reading this, but in a way that we believe more accurately reflects what we know from research: it depends. It depends on the goals of the communicators individually as well as their goals for the relationship. The rest of this chapter will explain these dimensions and suggest that both are desirable and functional.

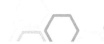

Questions to think about while reading this chapter:

- How important is physical touch to a relationship?
- What is meant by the concept of social capital?
- What is the distinction between weak and strong ties, and why is it important when studying communication technology?

Do We Want to Touch Everyone We See?

When we ask students about the lack of nonverbal cues that often exist online and how that impacts relationships, there is often a suggestion that the lack of non-verbal cues impedes relationships. Usually this discussion centers on touch and how the lack of it is problematic. Indeed, touch is likely a very important part of close relationships. A classic study by psychologist Harry Harlow demonstrated the power of touch using rhesus monkeys (see MC in Action: Monkey Lovin'). He found that when baby monkeys were presented with two monkey "mothers," the babies would choose to spend most of their time with stuffed monkeys that were soft and cuddly, only visiting the wire monkeys that delivered food to eat. This study suggests that haptic communication is an important part of how we share information with each other and how we accomplish our goals and that without such haptics we are diminished in our ability to stimulate meaning.

Touch is a very useful and powerful nonverbal cue. But is the lack of touch a death sentence for relationships? We might suggest that this depends on the kind of relationship you are thinking about and what your goals are for that relationship. For example, it is very likely that if your relationship with your professor does not include touch that you are perfectly okay with this. We do not expect to touch or be touched by our supervisors at work, campus administrators, or our favorite barista, and yet we have perfectly good relationships with each of these people (see MC in Action: Robot Touch). In fact, in some of these situations, touch might be considered inappropriate and could even damage the relationship, as touch in each case might be an expectancy violation (Burgoon, 1978). However, the kind of relationship that comes to mind most quickly as one in which touch is integral is probably a romantic relationship. Indeed, we largely agree that for most long-term romantic relationships a lack of touch is something that likely will be problematic over the long haul. This is because there are some things that cannot likely be replicated in romantic relationships without actual physical touch . . . yet (see MC in Action: Reach Out and Really(?) Touch Someone). But, going back to the functional approach that this book is founded upon, are there some things that people can do online that lead to similar outcomes as touch does FtF? Might we even be able to do some of them better sometimes?

But again, there are many instances FtF when we do not want nonverbal cues, as they may interfere with accomplishing our goals. For example, if you walk into your local fast-food restaurant to get a quick meal, you probably do not want the person behind the counter to touch you. Rather, you just want them to take your order and give you your cheeseburger as fast as possible. Touch, and likely many

Haptic communication Sending meaning through the use of nonverbal cues associated with touch.

Expectancy violation A situation in which our assumptions about anticipations of another's thoughts, actions, or behavior are not met.

other nonverbal cues, will likely just get in the way of accomplishing those goals. For example, the person behind the counter might be in a bad mood (anyone who has ever worked in the food industry can likely empathize and sympathize), and you may be distracted by their negative nonverbal cues. Such a situation is what MC scholar Joe Walther refers to as an impersonal interaction, one that is more about the task at hand than the people involved in the task. We will not focus on this kind of interaction in this chapter, but bring it up to make an important point: there are different kinds of rela-

There are some things that cannot likely be replicated in romantic relationships without actual physical touch.

tionships one might have with another person—both FtF and using MC—and not all of them require or even desire a full range of social cues. We will discuss two such relationship types in more depth: weak ties and strong ties.

MC IN ACTION

MONKEY LOVIN'

Before you start reading this section, please know that you may find it upsetting. At best, much of the research that Harry Harlow conducted with monkeys was ethically questionable. At worst, there are no questions; it is just wrong.

Harlow conducted many experiments using monkeys. The goal was to study attachment and love. In the classic study, Harlow would put a baby monkey into a room with two surrogate "monkeys." One surrogate was a wire monkey that had a bottle attached to it to provide food. The other surrogate was a cloth monkey with no food. What Harlow noticed was that most monkeys would only spend time with the wire monkey long enough to get nourishment and then would dart over to the comfort of the cloth monkey. Another study would frighten baby monkeys, and Harlow

noticed that many of the scared babies would seek refuge with the cloth monkey.

Another group of studies Harlow conducted would isolate baby monkeys from other monkeys. Some would be totally isolated from any contact with other monkeys. Some would be "partially" isolated; they could see, smell, and hear other monkeys, but they were caged so they could not touch other monkeys. Not surprisingly, the totally isolated monkeys, who were kept that way for up to two years, were severely psychologically disturbed and were nearly impossible to reintegrate back with normal monkeys. However, the monkeys who were raised without touch also were very disturbed, with some even going as far as to engage in self-mutilation. Thus, it seems that touch is very powerful indeed.

If you would like to read the original source, it was published in a 1958 issue of American Psychologist (see reference section at the end of this chapter). There are also many videos available on YouTube about these studies. One showing Harry Harlow discussing and showing examples of some of his experiments can be found here: https://www.youtube.com/watch?v=OrNBEhzjg8I

© Wavebreakmedia/Shutterstock.com

MC IN ACTION

ROBOT TOUCH

Imagine you were asked to touch someone. That might be kind of weird for you, depending on who that person is. Now imagine you were asked to touch someone you didn't know in an intimate area. This would almost assuredly weird you out, and with good reason. Finally, imagine you are asked to touch a robot in the robot's intimate areas. How would this make you feel?

Researchers at Stanford University recently conducted a small-scale study to address this question. These researchers found that we respond to touching a robot in similar ways as we would to touching a human. It seems that we have longer reaction times and find it emotionally distressing/arousing when asked to touch a robot in its intimate areas when compared to its more public areas (like a hand). This is very much in line with the computers as social actors perspective mentioned in the last chapter, but applied to robots as well. Indeed, human-robot interaction is likely to dramatically increase in the future, and so studies documenting how we communicate with robots (and how robots communicate with each other and with us) become increasingly important.

To watch a video and see pictures of the study, including people touching the robot, please go to: http://www.huffingtonpost.com/entry/robot-private-parts-study_us_5703d07be4b083f5c608de6c?

Building Bridges and Creating Bonds

Have you ever heard of Lois Weisberg? Chances are that you have not. Lois lives in Chicago, smokes, is a grandmother, and is not particularly charismatic. In all of this she seems like a relatively normal and unremarkable person. But journalist Malcolm Gladwell suggests that she might run the world (you can read the Gladwell article about Lois Weisberg from *The New Yorker* here: http://www.gladwell.com/1999/1999_01_11_a_weisberg.htm).

Homophily The extent to which two people (or two things) are similar to one another.

Lois has a particular knack for doing something that many people do not seem to do. Consider that most people follow the principle of homophily when creating their social circles. That is, we tend to like and talk to people who are similar to us. Thus, our social circles end up looking a lot like us. However, Lois does things a little differently. Throughout her life, she has reached out and made connections across a wide variety of people. In short, "She's the type of person who seems to know everybody, and this type can be found in every walk of life" (from the article).

So, why would someone like Lois be called out for potentially running the world? To answer this question more fully, it will take some more detail about the structure and power of social networks found throughout the rest of this chapter. Lois is a type—a relatively uncommon and extraordinary type, but a type nonetheless. In short, it is because Lois is a connector. She seems to know everybody, or at least people know people who know her. She acts as a bridge, connecting people across various, differing groups. Thus, although you may not know Lois yourself, it would not be terribly surprising if you someday come to realize that someone you know knows her. It seems that Lois is a master of social networking, whether she tries to be or not.

MC IN ACTION

REACH OUT AND REALLY(?) TOUCH SOMEONE

While it can be debated as to whether or not haptics are a necessary part of the communication process, there have been several advances in the early 21ˢᵗ century (and even before) to replicate touch when using communication technologies. For example, many video game controllers such as the Nintendo Wii feature force-feedback systems that vibrate and shake the controller to simulate pushing a button or switch or even the resistance of a bow and arrow.

But can we actually touch another person?

Virtual reality researcher Jeremy Bailenson and his colleagues at Stanford University's Virtual Human Interaction Lab are among a growing group of researchers who believe we can and that it might help us better communicate in virtual environments. His laboratory has conducted research suggesting that a computer joystick clamped to a laboratory table could successfully "communicate" a variety of feelings such as disgust, anger, sadness, joy, fear, interest, and surprise with a reliability significantly different than chance. While live handshakes were still better overall, the joystick apparatus was still successful at giving people a sense of the emotions of the "person" with whom they were shaking hands.

Of course, we might not always want to shake hands with a joystick, but perhaps improvements in the technology might make it possible for individuals separated for a variety of reasons—such as romantic partners missing the touch of a partner or hiring managers teleinterviewing a graduating college senior and wanting to make a "handshake deal"—to overcome perceived nonverbal barriers in communication technology.

For more information about Jeremy Bailenson and the Virtual Human Interaction Lab, including other research about haptics in virtual environments (VHIL), visit http://vhil.stanford.edu/

What Is Social Networking?

Like most of the things discussed in this book, social networking is not something that was created by the Internet. But if you are similar to many of the students we have worked with, you may equate the idea of social networking with the Internet, especially social media—after all, the terms are often discussed synonymously. However, we are quick to remind our students that the general concept of social networking is a basic human idea and something we have been doing for a very long time. Once again, the Internet has allowed us to step up our social networking, with potentially very positive and negative outcomes.

So if not invented by the Internet, then what is social networking? Christakis and Fowler (2009) suggested that networks are organized sets of people made up of two things: individuals and their connections. The people part is easy; each individual is a node in some social network(s). But the connections among these nodes are the truly interesting part of a social network. It is the way in which individuals are intertwined and the ties that exist among people in a group that really make social networks interesting and sometimes difficult to study. These connections are also what give social networks, and people like Lois Weisberg, their power.

Node In social networking, it is the basic unit of analysis—usually any given person in a larger network of people.

Social Network Structures

Bucket brigades A type of social network in which one person communicates or interacts with only one other person in a linear fashion, passing information from one to one.

Telephone tree A type of social network in which one person is responsible for contacting a set number of people who in turn contact a set number of people "below" them.

There are many ways that these types of social networks can be structured. Christakis and Fowler (2009) pointed out some such as bucket brigades, where each person in a line is connected to two other people except for the person at each end of the line, who is only connected to one person. Imagine a line of people handing sandbags to each other one at a time to build a wall. Each person hands off the heavy bag of sand so that nobody has to carry the heavy bag for a long distance, saving the group's energy. Another type of organizing is the telephone tree, which exhibits spreading linearity, where each person would be responsible for contacting two or some other number of people except those at the end of the tree. Such an example of this would be a chain letter in which one person is asked to send the message to ten (or more, or fewer) people, who are in turn asked to send to ten more. In this system, information is able to spread quickly across many different groups. In both cases, the systems have neat and clean structures.

First, although both of these network structures have their usefulness, they also have issues. For example, with a bucket brigade, if one person in the line drops their bag or moves slowly, it slows the progress of the entire network. Telephone trees have issues with information only flowing in one direction. Furthermore, most naturally occurring social networks are a lot messier. In networks that we see out "in the wild," there will be certain individuals who are more centrally located with many connections. There will also be those individuals who have fewer connections and thus are more fringe members of a particular network. There are also some people who are densely interconnected within a specific group, but some people who have ties into many groups, although they may only be fringe members of each of those groups. Just as the Internet has no written rules for behavior, neither do the social networks that form using the Internet.

Rules of Social Networks

Another very interesting way to think about our social networks—and we will argue that each of us exists within at least one (if not multiple) social network—is that they seem to follow five general rules of thumb (Christakis & Fowler, 2009).

1. **We shape our networks** To a large extent, we choose what groups we want to be part of, and we also choose how many connections to have within and between these groups. In this way, we have a great deal of influence over how our social networks end up being shaped. Much of our choice is this matter is governed by the concept of homophily. The Internet makes it even easier to find people with whom we share similarities, as we no longer are as restricted by space constraints in determining whom we talk to. We do not only have to interact with the people who are physically located in the same place as us: in our neighborhood, school, etc. We can seek out people whom we are similar to from around the world.

2. **Our network shapes us** Your position in a social network has a big impact on your life. A person with no close contacts has a very different life from those with many. This is likely one idea you have thought about before. However, a person with few acquaintances also has a very different life

from those with many. This is an idea that you may have never given much thought to, as closeness is often considered an inherent good (Parks, 1982); but, as will be discussed in more detail, acquaintances provide some interesting and important benefits as well.

3. **Our friends affect us** This probably is not too surprising, but the people you associate with have a big impact on your life. If you ever heard your parents say that they did not want you hanging out with another kid because that kid was "trouble," they understood this principle in ways that scientists are really just starting to uncover. Your network has impacts on a whole host of things, including your happiness, weight, drinking behaviors, and so on. Things that spread through networks can be positive (social support) or negative (gossip), but this spread impacts us.

4. **Our friends' friends' friends affect us** This one is more interesting because it suggests that people you may not even know may have some impact on your life. Again, it may not be much of a surprise that your friends influence you. But who influences them? Their friends do, some of whom you might know, but some of whom you might not. And who influences those people? Their friends. So that spread means you may be influenced by people you do not know, which means there is some hidden power lurking within social networks.

5. **The network has a life of its own** Finally—and as discussed earlier when talking about network structures—it is important to realize that networks have emergent properties; that is, networks tend to shrink, grow, and change based on how they are being used, and not just by one person but by every individual person in the network. This means you cannot understand them simply by looking at each individual part, but also need to look at each network as a whole. This is one of the toughest parts of studying social networks.

Connection versus Influence

Some of you may be familiar with the game "Six Degrees of Kevin Bacon," or the idea that you can link any actor or actress to Kevin Bacon in six steps or fewer. The goal is to get to from someone to Bacon by thinking of movies that people have been in together in as few steps as possible. For example, if you want to get from Kevin Bacon to Samuel L. Jackson, you get there through one person: An actor named Don Whatley. Bacon was in *My One and Only* in 2009 with Whatley, and Whatley was in *xXx: State of the Union* in 2005 with Samuel L. Jackson. There are few actors or actresses not connected to Bacon in six connections or fewer.

Many have heard this idea, but do you realize where it comes from? It was popularized by a classic research study (Travers & Milgram, 1969). The researchers gave letters to a few hundred people in Nebraska that were addressed to someone in Boston whom they did not know. They asked each person to send it to someone they knew who was more likely to know the person in Boston (or at least more likely to know someone else who might). They tracked how many times it took for the letter to get to the person in Boston, and on average, it took six steps.

Now how does this happen? It turns out that about three people were the main people who ended up getting the letter to its final destination in Boston. In other words, almost all of the letters that got to the final person came through one of three people (Gladwell, 1999). These people are interesting because it suggests that they know a lot of other people and specifically they know a lot of different kinds of people. It is the same with the six degrees of separation game with Kevin Bacon. Bacon is an interesting actor for this game because he has been in many different kinds of movies. And the aforementioned Lois Weisberg becomes such a powerful person because she knows a lot of people from various walks of life and can thus bridge across different groups of people.

However, just because we might be connected to people through six degrees, does not mean we influence that far out. What Christakis and Fowler have found in a variety of contexts is that we do have an impact on our friends, our friends' friends, and our friends' friends' friends. Of course, this influence gets smaller at each step but still is a sizable enough one at that third degree to matter. After this, influences tend to shrink as the people four degrees out and beyond often have little in common with each other, or the message might have changed so much from degree to degree that its core content is lost (think about playing the telephone game in elementary school, where one student tells another student a message—for instance, "mountaineers have big beards and no fears," continuing this process until the student at the end of the telephone line hears something like "scary ears go with beards").

What does all of this say for MC? First, it suggests a major reason why SNS are so popular. We like to keep up with our acquaintances, which is why we are told to network in the first place. Prior to SNS, this could be difficult to do. Sites like Facebook have made it much easier to maintain a larger number of these types of relationships. Stephanie Tong and Joe Walther have referred to these as "lightweight" tools. Tong and Walther (2011) pointed out that maybe the biggest potential benefit (and likely a big use) of SNS is for relational maintenance—or helping us both form and sustain our relationships with others. After all, they are social "networking" sites, and people likely use them to network and to manage a number of relationships that in the past would have been difficult, if not outright impossible. They seem to be a way to keep track of previously made acquaintances and help make it so no one has "long lost" friends anymore. Anecdotally, high school reunions seem to be on the way out. You do not need to get together with people ten years later to see what they have been up to. You never lose touch with them in the first place.

It also suggests that the number, and possibly the power, of weak ties (Granovetter, 1973) can be greatly magnified here. If people have impact on us out to three degrees FtF and you have 100 friends and acquaintances, who each have 100 more friends and acquaintances (who in turn have 100 more friends and acquaintances), then we are talking about potentially one million people who might have some impact on you. If we up that to 300 friends and acquaintances for each "degree" on Facebook, that substantially increases the number of people who can influence you (and in turn, whom you might influence) to 27 million people. (See also, Using the long tail, Chapter 2). Some of the changes for MC involve scope, as mentioned in Chapter 7.

Do the technologies, such as Facebook and other social media, allow for an increased ability to maintain acquaintances and act as a bridge? Work by MC scholar Nicole Ellison and her colleagues has extensively examined bridging social capital and social network sites like Facebook and suggested that it may be a powerful use of these kinds of technologies. Repeatedly, they find that those who use Facebook report more social capital—in particular, bridging capital.

Bridging social capital, like the kind that Lois Weisberg seems to display, is incredibly important and is sometimes overlooked when we think about relationships online. However, users of social network sites also report greater levels of bonding social capital, which is probably what most people tend to think of when they think of relationships. Again, we see that users of social network sites are able to utilize the channels to accomplish their relational goals overall. One of the ways in which they might do that is called networked individualism.

Networked Individualism

Rainie and Wellman present networked individualism as the "new social operating system." Instead of a decrease in social communication, what they suggest is that people are largely changing how we socially communicate. As they say, "people function more as connected individuals and less as embedded group members" (p. 12). But we still communicate with others, and in fact, evidence suggests we communicate with others even more than in the past.

These changes have been long in the making (and happening) and have been brought about by what Rainie and Wellman refer to as the triple revolution. Changes in how we network (such as an increased mobility brought about by the automobile, among other things), changes in the technology available to us (the Internet), and changes to how we can access the Internet (especially in regard to mobility) have all led to an increased ability to network and communicate with others at any time from any place, and with any one.

There are many positives to networked individualism. The biggest is that we can get our goals accomplished more completely as we are not bound to communicate only with those in our embedded groups, who may not be able or willing to help us meet our needs and goals. However, there are also negatives. Networked individualism puts the onus on YOU to network and communicate, and so it requires a lot of effort if you can no longer simply rely on embedded group memberships for networking. There are also increased potential privacy issues from the need to communicate more.

So, is this all good or bad for society? We will leave you with their answer to this question: "both and more" (p. 18). Technology is a tool, capable of good and bad uses and effects, and as a powerful tool, these impacts can be "more." As McEwan (2015) has also pointed out, "However, while communication technologies are sure to adapt, evolve, and change over time—barring some catastrophic event—we will not be returning to the days before the internet. Thus, academics, pundits, and the general public must move away from either/or, good/bad style arguments in order to really delve into how people adapt technology to their interpersonal communication purposes" (p. 160).

Networked Individualism A "social operating system" that suggests people operate and interact more as individuals connected to various groups rather than embedded members of groups.

Building Closeness Online

People use the Internet for communicating with other people. This is not a really controversial statement, as most of you have likely used some technology to interact with people in a very social way. You may even be doing it while reading this section of the book. However, some early theories about online communication suggested that online communication would not be social. Maybe it is because originally computers were only in large organizations and were designed and used primarily for business functions, such as storing and processing data—they were not intended to foster or even facilitate human-to-human interaction. These theories suggest that people would not, or could not, use MC to form or manage relationships, as this was something seemingly outside the scope of the technology.

One such theory is known as media (or information) richness theory (MRT). This theory suggests a rather intuitive idea that some channels are better for some messages. Specifically, MRT argues that an optimal match between the channel used for a message and the equivocality of the message exists. When a message has higher equivocality (it has more than one potential meaning or interpretation), using a richer channel leads to greater efficiency because a richer channel is thought to provide more communication information. When equivocality is low, a leaner channel is more efficient because the extra information provided in a rich channel is unnecessary (see MC in Action: It's Not You, It's Me. <Send>).

Media richness theory A theory in MC research that suggests that communication channels can be understood in terms of the number of social cues they provide the user, and there is an optimal matching of communication goal and communication channel based on which cues are desired.

Equivocality Information that has more than one potential meaning or interpretation.

MC IN ACTION

IT'S NOT YOU, IT'S ME. <SEND>

Breaking off a romantic relationship can be hard to do because of the often-intense emotions involved in the process. Many of us can remember the somber moment when somebody says "it's not you, it's me" as eyes swell with tears, emotions run hot and cold, and couples (at least, some of them) find a private area to break up so as not to have an emotional outburst in front of family, friends, or strangers.

So, why not just send a text?

Sending a text message communicates a lack of desire to interact while allowing both parties to read the same "it's not you, it's me" message without having to read and respond to the other's nonverbal signals. After all, if one has already made up their mind about the dissolution of the relationship, then what can be gained by further interaction?

Of course, many of you (ourselves included) recognize that the preceding suggestion is remarkably cold and impersonal. But we might ask you to think: Is not a breakup in fact cold and impersonal?

What is your reaction to this suggestion? Using notions of relationships and technology, share your feelings with your class, as well as on our Facebook at https://www.facebook.com/groups/234255823447372/ or on Twitter, using the #MediaAsTools hashtag.

One issue with MRT is the distinction between lean and rich channels. In general, a channel can be said to have four characteristics: bandwidth, immediacy of feedback, message personalization, and natural language. Overall, a rich channel allows a lot of these (that is, it is "rich" in the number of cues available for communication), and a lean channel allows fewer (that is, it is "lean" in the number of cues available for communication). In some cases, this dichotomy can be rather straightforward. If we compared a FtF meeting with one's boss to a written letter from the boss's desk sent to the entire organization, we can likely understand the former being far more "rich" than the latter. The FtF conversation utilizes all of our senses and so has high bandwidth, allows for immediate interaction between myself and my boss, is likely a personalized discussion as we are the only two people in the interaction, and uses our natural spoken language to interact with each other. By contrast, the letter has low bandwidth because it lacks nonverbal information, allows for no direct method of response, is written for all members of an organization, and is likely typed out in a very formal language style expected of company memos. However, these distinctions might be much less clear when dealing with many of the technologies popular today (and likely to be popular tomorrow). Although MC is often thought of as being rather lean—let us consider e-mail as an example (Daft, Lengel, & Trevino, 1987), is it truly? E-mail might only allow limited bandwidth and is not particularly immediate, but it does allow for natural language and a great deal of message personalization. And when considering a technology such as Facebook, this becomes even murkier. How these four characteristics interplay in terms of "richness" has not been fully articulated.

The evidence for MRT seems to suggest that there may be something to the approach. When people are asked what channels they would use, they tend to answer in accordance with MRT: by suggesting they would use richer channels for more equivocal messages. However, when actual channel choice is examined, the picture is much less clear. People are often able to use very lean channels rather effectively for incredibly interpersonal messages—such as the love e-mails that helped spread the ILOVEYOU computer virus (see Chapter 2). How is this possible? Newer theories have since been proposed to help address this phenomenon.

Social Information Processing Theory

"As we continued to talk, going through the motions of getting to know each other, I realized that we already did know each other, as well as any two people could. We'd known each other for years, in the most intimate way possible. We'd connected on a purely mental level. I understood her, trusted her, and loved her as a dear friend. None of that had changed, or could be changed by anything as inconsequential as her gender, or skin color, or sexual orientation."

Could you know someone you've never met face-to-face? The above quote, from page 321 of Ernest Cline's novel *Ready Player One*, is a thought that occurs to the main character, Wade Watts, as he interacts with someone he had only met in the OASIS, (the novel's version of a virtual reality world similar to *Second Life*) prior to this face-to-face meeting. Wade also realizes that he has gotten to know his friend very well, even if he has never seen her before.

In addressing some of the conceptual issues with MRT, Walther (1992) offered an alternate perspective to understanding some of the issues with MRT. His social information processing theory seeks to explain interpersonal processes online and suggests that people can form deep and meaningful relationships online, even using the leanest of channels.

Social information processing theory (SIPT) begins with the assumption that people have the same reasons for communicating with each other no matter the channel they use. People seek to reduce and manage uncertainty, form impressions of others, develop affinity, feel social presence, and so on. These are basic human desires of relatedness (see Chapter 7) and ones we come to find ways to address, even through lean channels that lack nonverbal cues. More recent evidence suggests that more skilled communicators might be better able to accomplish their goals online (Walther & Bazarova, 2008).

So, how are people able to overcome limitations such as a lack of nonverbals online to do interpersonal things? First, it is important to note that time plays an important part in this process. MC takes longer than FtF. Limits on bandwidth mean that less information gets through at any one given time. Second, it takes more time to type and read than to speak and listen (and look). A useful metaphor is that MC is like sipping from a straw, and FtF is like gulping from a cup. If information is like the water in the cup, a person can get all of that water (information) using either the straw or gulping. It is just that sipping takes longer.

Another thing that people can use while interacting through MC is circumventions. Although MC may offer reduced nonverbal cues, they still seem to be able to utilize what is provided through the channel. For example, people utilize chronemics online to send e-mails (Walther & Tidwell, 1995) or post a Facebook message when a friend is away from their computer or engage in more or less rapid Twitter conversations much in the same style they would FtF (more rapid responses in a conversation could indicate more interest in the conversation, for example). People may also use emoticons to show their emotions, such as smiley faces "=)" or sad faces "=(" and any number of other keystroke combinations to represent different emotional states (see MC in Action: I <3 U). People have been shown in research to ask more and deeper questions and self-disclose more and with more depth when they interact with strangers online (Tidwell & Walther, 2002). In addition, online channels allow individuals to lurk online—that is, they can seek out someone by Googling them (Ramirez, Walther, Burgoon, & Sunnafrank, 2002) or by looking at a social media user's profile and read through different conversations and posts without actually interacting and without anyone knowing about it (something much more difficult in real-world interactions, when lurking in on a stranger's conversations is not widely accepted).

Taking the time to effectively interact through MC and navigating the circumventions necessary to do so takes a good deal of effort. People have to be both willing and able to put forth this effort in order to have relationships online, but it can be done. One motivating factor is the anticipation of future interaction. If you think you will be interacting with a person again (or at the very least, if you want to), you are more likely to put in this effort. In and of itself, it is possible that this increased effort leads to more positive outcomes in relationships started/maintained online.

Social information processing theory A theory positing that humans use information to reduce uncertainty in order to forge relationships, and that the medium they use can subsequently impact how those relationships form. But they can and do form.

Chronemics Using a sense of time, such as response latency or pausing during a conversation, to communicate nonverbally.

Emoticons Using combinations of keyboard symbols to represent facial expressions.

I <3 U

How do you put emotion into the written/typed word? Of course, one way to do this is by choosing specific words. No doubt, poets have been using emotional language likely since there has been language to use.

More recently, people have begun to use emoticons, short for emotional icons, to help infuse their words with more emotion. How recently? A 2009 New York Times article suggests an emoticon may have appeared in the written copy of a speech given by Abraham Lincoln in 1862 (although it may just be a typo). See http://cityroom.blogs.nytimes.com/2009/01/19/hfo-emoticon/

Scott Fahlman is credited as being the first person to send a digital emoticon :-) when he posted a message to the computer science general electronic bulletin board at Carnegie Mellon University in 1982. (A reproduction of the thread can be found here: http://www.cs.cmu.edu/~sef/Orig-Smiley.htm).

Today, there exist a whole lot of emoticons, way more than "Honest Abe" or Scott Fahlman likely ever dreamed. Some are pretty elaborate, being way more than a simple ;) or :-) from the past. There are many (incomplete) lists of emoticons that can be found online, including one here: http://www.cs.cmu.edu/~sef/Orig-Smiley.htm

One of the main notions of SIPT is that impressions and relationships can be formed online, but they just take longer than they do FtF. But how many of you know someone who felt like they had known someone forever even after interacting online? This would go against the ideas of SIPT. To help account for these experiences, Walther (1996) suggested the notion of hyperpersonal relationships: ones that become more personal through MC than they would FtF. To account for how this happens, he suggested that the limitations of the channel, rather than leading to less personal relationships, could actually sometimes lead to this "hyper" personalness. To explain how this happens, Walther goes back to the classic communication model and looks at each of the four parts.

> **Hyperpersonal relationships** Relationships that develop online more than they would FtF.

1. First, hyperpersonal happens because of sender effects. Sources of messages online can sometimes use the lack of nonverbals in order to better selectively self-present (put their best foot forward) (Walther, 2007).

2. Second, hyperpersonal happens because of receiver effects. When senders are selectively self-presenting themselves and the cues about the sender are limited, receivers may be better able to idealize the sender. This may be especially likely to happen if the receiver is deliberately seeking new relational partners or if they only have selected information on which to judge them (i.e., they both belong to the same Facebook group, so they have something in common).

3. Third, channel effects come into play for hyperpersonal. Channel allows for greater control (in general) over message construction than FtF. For example, you can pause to think and edit before sending a message (although certainly not everybody takes advantage of this). You also do not have to attend to as many distracting cues (one's own physical back channeling, etc.) This disentrainment (freedom from the rules of FtF interactions) frees one up to pay even more attention to selective self-presentation, and so on.

4. Finally, and perhaps most interestingly, feedback effects come into play. As idealizing receivers send selective messages back to the source, it can lead to behavioral confirmation, where the original source starts to behave more like the partner's idealized expectation of them (a sort of other-fulfilling prophecy). For example, if a person sends a message to a receiver and the receiver really likes the source, the receiver may think the source is really outgoing and fun and will respond positively to that person. As this continues to happen, the source gains confidence and actually starts behaving as more outgoing and fun.

Now throw all four of these things together, and you have a recipe for relationships that take off way faster than they might otherwise do. Are such hyperpersonal relationships common? Maybe at some level, but even at their fullest level, probably not. As Joe Walther has said about people falling in love with others whom they have only met online, "It probably doesn't happen to a large percentage of people, but it happens occasionally, and it's very intense" (http://www.livescience.com/26378-teo-scandal-real-online-love.html).

Think back to Sal 9000 . . . is this what he is experiencing at some level? A hyperpersonal "relationship"? And might this hyperpersonal notion also help explain what happened to Manti Te'o as well?

Hyperpersonal relationships tend to carry a negative connotation, at least from talking about them with our students. But can aspects of the process lead to more "positive" outcomes? Going back to the notion of beyond being there (Hollan & Stornetta, 1992), it is important to remember that FtF is not inherently the gold standard. Thinking of things as such and building systems to try to replicate FtF forgets that FtF has its own issues. MC offers affordances that can help overcome the limitations of FtF in some situations (for example, the ability to overcome space and time restrictions). However, do you sometimes even use the limitations of a channel to your advantage in accomplishing your goals? In other words, is the lack of nonverbals always a limitation? Can nonverbals actually get in the way of effective interpersonal communication? Walther (2008) suggested at least one way in which the lack of nonverbals provided online might be the only way for interpersonal communication to take place. He suggests that sometimes seeing the other person may remind you of negative prejudices you hold toward the other person. Using the example of Arab-Israeli relations, he suggests that just maybe MC is the only chance for many members across these groups to have true, interpersonal communication. That is quite a thought . . . that MC may help bridge the gap for peace in a war-torn area.

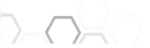

Key Terms

Haptic communication (pg 126)
Expectancy violation (pg 126)
Homophily (pg 128)
Node (pg 129)
Bucket brigades (pg 130)
Telephone tree (pg 130)
Networked individualism (pg 133)
Media richness theory (pg 134)
Equivocality (pg 134)
Social information processing theory (pg 136)
Chronemics (pg 136)
Emoticons (pg 136)
Hyperpersonal relationships (pg 137)

References

Burgoon, J. K. (1978). A communication model of personal space violation: Explication and an initial test. *Human Communication Research, 4,* 129–142.

Christakis, N. A., & Fowler, J. H. (2009). *Connected: The surprising power of our social networks and how they shape our lives.* New York: Little, Brown & Co.

Daft, R. L., Lengel, R. H., & Trevino, L. K. (1987). Message equivocality, media selection, and manager performance: Implications for information systems. *MIS Quarterly, 11,* 355–366.

Ellison, N. B., Steinfield, C., & Lampe, C. (2007). The benefits of Facebook "friends:" Social capital and college students' use of online social network sites. *Journal of Computer-Mediated Communication, 12*(4), article 1. http://jcmc.indiana.edu/vol12/issue4/ellison.html

Granovetter, M. S. (1973). The strength of weak ties. *American Journal of Sociology, 78,* 1360–1380.

Harlow, H. (1958). The nature of love. *American Psychologist, 13,* 673–685.

Hollan, J., & Stornetta, S. (1992). Beyond being there. *Proceedings of the ACM CHI'92 Conference on Computer-Human Interaction,* 119–125.

McEwan, B. (2015). *Navigating new media networks: Understanding and managing communication challenges in a networked society.* New York: Lexington Books.

Parks, M. R. (1982). Ideology in interpersonal communication: Off the couch and into the world. In M. Burgoon (Ed.), *Communication Yearbook 5* (pp. 79–107). New Brunswick, NJ: Transaction Books.

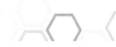

Rainie, L., & Wellman, B. (2012). *Networked: The new social operating system.* Cambridge, MA: MIT Press.

Ramirez, Jr. A., Walther, J. B., Burgoon, J. K., & Sunnafrank, M. (2002). Information seeking strategies, uncertainty, and computer-mediated communication: Toward a conceptual model. *Human Communication Research, 28,* 213–228.

Tidwell, L. C., & Walther, J. B. (2002). Computer-mediated communication effects on disclosure, impressions, and interpersonal evaluations: Getting to know one another a bit at a time. *Human Communication Research, 28,* 317–348.

Tong, S. T., & Walther, J. B. (2011). Relational maintenance and computer-mediated communication. In K. B. Wright & L. M. Webb (Eds.), *Computer-mediated communication in personal relationships* (pp. 98–118). New York: Peter Lang Publishing.

Travers, J., & Milgram, S. (1969). An experimental study of the small world problem. *Sociometry, 32,* 425–443.

Walther, J. B. (1992). Interpersonal effects in computer-mediated interaction: A relational perspective. *Communication Research, 19,* 52–90.

Walther, J. B. (1996). Computer-mediated communication: Impersonal, interpersonal, and hyperpersonal interaction. *Communication Research, 23,* 3–43.

Walther, J. B. (2007). Selective self-presentation in computer-mediated communication: Hyperpersonal dimensions of technology, language, and cognition. *Computers in Human Behavior, 23,* 2538–2557.

Walther, J. B. (2009). Computer-mediated communication and virtual groups: Applications to interethnic conflict. *Journal of Applied Communication Research, 37,* 225–238.

Walther, J. B., & Bazarova, N. (2008). Validation and application of electronic propinquity theory to computer-mediated communication in groups. *Communication Research, 35,* 622–645.

Walther, J. B., & Parks, M. R. (2002). Cues filtered out, cues filtered in: Computer-mediated communication and relationships. In M. L. Knapp & J. A. Daly (Eds.), *Handbook of interpersonal communication* (3rd ed., pp. 529–563). Thousand Oaks, CA: Sage.

Walther, J. B., & Tidwell, L. C. (1995). Nonverbal cues in computer-mediated communication, and the effect of chronemics on relational communication. *Journal of Organizational Computing, 5,* 355–378.

CHAPTER 9

Persuasion

By this stage you probably have a pretty good idea of how new media technologies are used. Back in Chapters 3 and 4, we examined the use of media as a tool to negotiate everyday life, we explored the concept of digital literacy, and we addressed the problems that can arise when there are discrepancies across populations in terms of their ability to access and use new media technology.

Let us think about media from a business perspective. Media technologies are enormous economic engines, and their utility in advertising and social marketing cannot be ignored. In 2015, worldwide spending on digital advertising was estimated at $170 billion (U.S.). The continual proliferation of media technologies, including the recent explosion in social media, has not only provided users with new ways to create and publish their own content, but it has also presented advertisers and social marketers with a new frontier of outlets for advocating for consumer products, health choices, and ideologies.

Social marketers Advertising and marketing professionals who use new media technologies, specifically social media, to attempt to influence audiences.

The range of available outlets also poses great challenges. As we have discussed earlier, primitive conceptualizations of mass media were based on the assumption of one-way communication: from an organization to a mass audience. By now you should have figured out that the technological advances of the last thirty years have led us to break from this mold. Contemporary conceptualizations of media use and effects assume that we actively seek the information we desire, and then use that information to navigate everyday decisions. The assumptions relied upon by advertisers since at least the time of Gutenberg and his printing press—merely placing persuasive messages in public places—have been thrown into disarray.

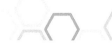

This has forced a steep learning curve in terms of how to identify target audiences for a product or concept, locate the information in appropriate media and content, and craft an effective persuasive message. Furthermore, as these advances in technology drive us toward becoming more media literate, our ability to discern useful and secondary information improves; this makes capturing the attention of an otherwise disinterested individual very difficult.

In Chapters 9, 10, and 11, we will address some of the issues revolving around new media and persuasion, including the ways in which we understand the psychology of persuasion and the ways in which this understanding can be used across a variety of media platforms. Chapter 9 will provide a broad overview of contemporary persuasion theories that have may be applied in different ways in different mediated contexts.

Think about the following as we begin this chapter:

- What theories explain how we are persuaded by media? How have new media technologies altered our view of these technologies?
- Are we more easily persuaded by substance or by style? Does it matter?
- Do you have to believe that you can do something in order to be persuaded to do it?
- Do emotional appeals affect us, and how can these appeals be made more powerful by new media?

Dual Process Models

Think about a typical 30-second television commercial for a car, the kind you might find between quarters as you watch your favorite football team on television. What kind of information do you find in these ads? Specifics on gas mileage, displacement, and torque? Estimated resale value in five years? Cubic feet and cargo capacity?

Chances are, no. You are far more likely to see and hear loud music, see quick cuts of the car performing, and maybe hear Matthew McConaughey say something weird . . . but little to no actual information about the car. Yet, millions of people buy cars every year. One possible explanation lies in a body of research that can be categorized broadly as the dual process approach.

Elaboration likelihood model A model of human perception that states that we take in information in two separate ways: central, or factual arguments, and peripheral, or secondary stimuli.

Dual process theorizing began with the work of Petty and Cacioppo and was further advanced by Cialdini and colleagues. The Elaboration Likelihood Model (ELM), in basic terms, says that we take in information in one of two ways. First is the central route. This is where we weigh factual information and logical arguments. On the other hand, we have the peripheral route. The peripheral route is where we process everything else—lights, sound, setting, and even secondary arguments. An example of this might be listening to a political debate in which audience members might focus on the candidates' answers or the candidates' appearance, such as was the case when Richard Nixon debated John F. Kennedy in the first televised presidential debate in U.S. history (see MC in Action: Nixon Won, Kennedy Won).

MC IN ACTION

NIXON WON, KENNEDY WON

On the evening of September 26, 1960—less than a month away from the 1960 presidential election—over 70 million Americans turned on their television sets to watch the first televised presidential debate in U.S. history. In that debate, incumbent Vice President Richard Nixon, an elder statesman with a known political pedigree, was squared off against Democratic challenger and relative political unknown Senator John F. Kennedy, a young candidate with little in the way of legislative or executive expertise.

For many viewing the debate, they saw more than a Republican debating a Democrat on the domestic issues of the day. Rather, they saw a sweaty, clammy, and uncomfortable Nixon debating a tanned, thin, and charismatic Kennedy on a national stage, and this was enough to convince the television audience that Kennedy was more fit to be president than Nixon. After all, how could a person be president of the United States if they could not even feel confident on camera? Later reports suggested Nixon to have been ill the day of the debates, and perhaps even more interesting, the majority of radio audiences reported that Nixon had indeed won the debate—these audiences were focusing only on the content of the debate topics rather than the appearance of the candidates. Nonetheless, Kennedy would go on to be elected as the 35th president . . . although Nixon would eventually be elected as the 37th president eight years later.

The first of four great debates, the night has been showcased as an example of the power of television and for communication scholars a great example of peripheral processing.

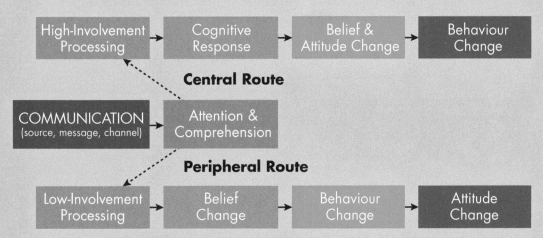

You can watch a video of the famous debate on YouTube at: http://www.youtube.com/watch?v=gbrcRKqLSRw and *Time's* Kayla Webley wrote a piece on the impact of this debate on modern-day politicking at: http://content.time.com/time/nation/article/0,8599,2021078,00.html. You can also view the elaboration likelihood model at: http://343f11.pbworks.com/f/1322630408/ELMdiagram.gif.

In his groundbreaking work on peripheral cues, Cialdini identifies what he calls the "weapons of influence," a number of elements that can be added to persuasive messages in order to gain compliance without actually focusing on the message content itself—that is, Cialdini suggested that many times peripheral processing could lead to rather strong persuasive effects. Called fixed-action patterns, or click-whirr responses, these weapons rely on patterns that are strongly ingrained into our culture and ourselves. They simply require some sort of trigger feature to set the process in motion, and get people complying without critically analyzing messages, and sometimes, without even being aware they are complying. These weapons of influence include reciprocity (the notion that someone is doing you a favor, and so you feel like you should do something for that person), social proof (a feeling that everyone is doing it, and so you should as well), liking (the spokesperson is attractive or admired), scarcity (the product will not be around much longer, and so you had better act now), authority (someone with expertise vouches for the product), and consistency (staying true to your commitments) (see MC in Action: Keys to Persuasion). These are especially powerful weapons because typically these are things we want people to do. For example, we do not like people who do not repay what they owe. In fact, people tend to feel very bad when they owe somebody something and thus try to quickly repay favors when they can. However, a skilled persuader or "profiteer" can utilize this notion of reciprocity to their advantage.

Think about late-night infomercials. How often do you hear words to the effect of "act now while supplies last." That is scarcity at work. Ever see an ad for a bizarre, possibly unhealthy diet plan, followed by a testimonial from a guy wearing a lab coat and a stethoscope? That is authority (since you presume he is a doctor, as opposed to an actor wearing a lab coat). How about a statement telling you that "5 million Americans can't be wrong" when describing how many people have already tried the product? This is social proof in action. It makes sense that

MC IN ACTION

KEYS TO PERSUASION

Do you recognize Cialdini's persuasion keys (listed below) from your own experiences? For more about each of the six processes, take a look at: https://www.youtube.com/watch?v=cFdCzN7RYbw Then, spend an hour or two watching infomercials or at the mall, and provide examples of the following, including the name of the product/place:

- Reciprocity
- Social proof
- Liking
- Scarcity
- Authority
- Consistency

late-night advertising would rely heavily on peripheral cues, since not only are you not heavily invested in these products, but you are likely sleepy and not doing a whole lot of active processing.

Eagly and Chaiken offer a similar dual process approach, which they term the Heuristic Systematic Model. They offer that whether someone processes persuasive information systematically (for example, centrally) or heuristically (for example, peripherally) is dependent upon the cognitive resources they have available and their motivation to use these resources. In other words, thinking about logical arguments requires effort, and if we either cannot or do not want to expend that effort, we are more likely to respond to heuristics (notice again that it comes back to being willing and able). They add that attitudes formed by heuristics are less stable and easier to change with counter information.

In either approach, someone's level of involvement is critical because it will affect how they process the information. If we have a standing interest in a product, for example, we probably want factual information and logical arguments about it. On the other hand, if we have little or no interest or if we are completely unaware of the product, we will respond better to heuristics or peripheral information. Historically, advertisers have thought of mass audiences as being largely uninvolved and thus have relied mostly on peripheral cues.

The issue involvement argument makes sense if you think about it. Let us return to our car ad example from above. Car ads often feature a whole host of secondary, heuristic content, from flashing lights, to attractive women, to dancing hamsters. These are likely effective at drawing your attention to a product you may not have been aware of and are likely to at least get you to pay attention and retain the name of the car.

But what happens when you actually decide to buy the car? Chances are you do not rely on the dancing hamsters (and if you do, we have some land in Florida we would like to sell you). Now you want data, factual information concerning miles-per-gallon, cost, performance, ratings, and so on. Now you will turn to a variety of different sources because you are already involved in the message. You are prepared to devote a certain amount of time and effort to a purchasing process to which you are more or less committed, and to do so you need systematic information that will help you make a good choice. In fact, if presented with poor arguments or negative information at this point, you may decide not to purchase the vehicle.

Our understanding of how we use issue relevant and issue irrelevant information has been somewhat challenged by our motivations for using interactive media technologies. If we are seeking information online—through social media, blogs, the Web, and so on—then by definition we have already made a decision to be involved. As we will see in Chapter 10, advertisers have had a very different problem in new media circles. Since people are consuming media with very specific goals, how do you make them aware of new products and services? If people are already online with specific informational needs, they are engaging in systematic processing (see MC in Action: Yelp!). Advertisers and marketers are faced with a new challenge—distracting people from their intended goals to focus on something else.

Heuristic systematic model A similar model to ELM, but one that argues we are more likely to use peripheral information if we cannot or do not want to expend energy on processing a message.

Heuristics Cognitive shortcuts that we use to process information very quickly.

YELP!

Advertisers have long known the power of word-of-mouth promotions. Indeed, much of the research on persuasion—in particular, media persuasion—focuses on the importance of influencing opinion leaders rather than influencing audiences directly. People seek out the opinions of their friends when making purchasing decisions, from a cup of coffee to a sports coupe, and understanding this influence is key to any advertising campaign.

In here, we see social media platforms playing an increasingly prominent role—perhaps, the most prominent example being Yelp (NYSE: YELP; www.yelp.com). Launched in October 2004, the Web site was designed to be a digital platform where users could ask others for product and service recommendations via e-mail. The service worked by asking users to complete a Web form, answering "I'm looking for a (blank)" and "near (blank city, state, or zip code)." Users would enter in a short description of what they were looking for and a few of their friends' e-mail addresses and wait for responses.

The service became very popular with smaller businesses such as local restaurants, many of which traditionally relied on word-of-mouth advertising and had very meager (if any) advertising budgets. These businesses began throwing Yelp parties to attract customers and encourage them to share their experiences with others, and the program's reputation as a powerful electronic word-of-mouth platform exploded—generating nearly $138 million dollars in advertising revenues as of 2012. Yelp's customer recommendations are published for anyone with Web access to read and share, and mobile users are even able to filter recommendations based on their physical location using their smartphone's geo-positioning software.

And Yelp reviews matter. Researchers from the University of California at Berkeley (Anderson & Magruder, 2012) have found that increasing a restaurant's rating by only one-half of a star (out of a five-star system) can help them sell out nearly 33 percent more frequently. In fact, their findings have led many to question the honesty of many Yelp reviews as businesses have been known to post fake reviews and in extreme cases harass customers who post negative reviews. Of course, as Yelp is a user-generated site, the quality of the reviews is dependent on the people writing them.

So, the next time you hear somebody asking for Yelp, it is likely that they are okay . . . they just want a recommendation for a good brew or burger.

Have you ever used Yelp! to find a restaurant in your hometown, or while on vacation? Perhaps you've written a Yelp! review yourself. Let's talk about your experiences with these programs, both on Facebook at https://www.facebook.com/groups/234255823447372/ and on Twitter, using the #MediaAsTools hashtag.

Opinion leaders People who influence others through word of mouth.

Geo-positioning software Software programs that use satellite relay to determine the position of a person, place, or object on Earth.

Behavioral Intention Approaches

If people are committed and are making decisions based on factual arguments, another approach that makes a lot of sense can be found in the communication and psychology research: the theory of reasoned action (Ajzen & Fishbein, 1980). Ajzen and Fishbein conducted a series of studies in the 1970s and 1980s in an attempt to determine the individual decision processes that lead someone from information to action. For years, persuasion research had proven good at predicting attitude changes, but not necessarily actual behavior. For example, people may report that they feel less positively about drinking and driving, but still don't do anything to change their behavior when planning a night out. Ajzen and Fishbein came to the conclusion that there are things other than just message design and placement that are going to play a role in how likely someone is to comply. Most importantly, they identified *behavioral intentions* as an essential step in the persuasion process that had been overlooked. In simplest terms, the theory of reasoned action argues that attitudes do not directly change people's behavior. Rather, they change what people intend to do, which might or might not lead to a change in behavior (although there is strong evidence that typically we do what we intend to do, given the proper conditions). Think about health campaigns that try to get people to quit smoking. They might be very effective in getting someone to change their opinion on smoking, but they may not actually quit. You will probably also notice that television ads for smoking cessation offer links to Web sites with more information. Why?

> **Theory of reasoned action** A model of persuasion that offers that messages influence attitudes and subjective norms, which influence behavioral intentions, which then may or may not lead to behavior change.

This is where behavioral intentions come in. If someone has not only changed their attitude, but has made a decision to quit smoking, they will likely seek out information on how to quit. The persuasion process then becomes one in which the audience member is actively involved, and their likelihood of complying becomes even greater. Of course, there are still things that could go wrong. After seeking out this information, the person might decide that quitting is too difficult, too time-consuming, or will not provide any kind of positive benefit. They might think that they are incapable of actually quitting or simply are not motivated to do so.

> **Behavioral intentions** Expressed desire to modify a behavior in the future.

As Ajzen and Fishbein continued to tweak and refine their conceptualization of how rational arguments impact persuasion, they determined that something else was important: whether or not people think they can get it done. Ajzen and Fishbein began referring to this as "behavioral control." A behavior such as smoking might not actually be under a person's control (this is why it is an addiction). When they put all the pieces together, they concluded that persuasive messages drive attitude changes, attitudes drive intentions, and intentions drive behavior, assuming people actually buy into the idea that they can perform the behavior in question. That presents a number of steps where things can go wrong, but it also helps explain why social marketing campaigns are so challenging. As we will see in Chapter 10, unlike consumer products, people have very strong opinions when it comes to their behaviors.

Connecting this to our smoking example, antismoking advertisements may be very successful in getting a person to have a less positive attitude toward smoking and may lead to the person even intending to stop smoking. However, these changes will only lead to a behavioral change if the individual actually *believes* that they can quit—that is, that they have the ability to quit. On the other hand,

someone who has been smoking for decades may have given up on the idea of quitting, and even if they develop a negative view of their habit, they probably will not try to quit.

The addition of behavior control (sometimes called "self-efficacy") led Ajzen and Fishbein to rename this theory the theory of planned behavior (Ajzen, 1991). It has been used to inform health campaign designs across a wide range of behaviors, including smoking, drinking, signing up for treatment programs, using contraceptives, dieting, wearing seatbelts or safety helmets, exercising regularly, voting, and even breast-feeding (Fishbein, Middlestadt, & Hitchcock, 1994). In fact, it is often the case that self-efficacy is often forgotten in persuasion, as many campaigns tell us about something we need to change, yet fail to teach us how to change it or how their product or service will help us actually change it (see Chapter 11's discussion of fear appeals; Witte, 1992).

Theory of planned behavior A model similar to the theory of reasoned action, but with the added argument that self-efficacy moderates the process.

Fear appeals A campaign strategy that attempts to get people to change their behaviors by instilling fear regarding the behavior in question.

Modeling Approaches

Self-efficacy is a key component in another way of thinking about how advertising influences people: behavioral modeling. In his work on social cognitive theory (see Chapter 6), Bandura provides us with a means of understanding the influence of advertising through the observation of others and some of the features of behavioral models that make them more or less influential.

The concept of vicarious modeling revolves around the assumption that we learn behaviors and when to perform these behaviors through the observation of others. Before a behavior takes place, we observe it in others and determine the steps that are necessary to do it, the conditions under which the behavior should take place, and any rewards that might be associated with it. This allows us to figure out how things work ahead of time, so that we can avoid errors and pitfalls that may be associated with not knowing how to do something, doing it incorrectly, or doing it at an inappropriate time. Thus, learning is for the most part a surrogate process as opposed to a direct experience. Bandura himself offers that vicarious learning (see Chapter 6) is the observation of a model through which "an individual forms an idea of how response components must be combined and sequenced to produce the new behavior. In other words people guide their actions by prior notions rather than by relying on outcomes to tell them what they must do" (1977, p. 35).

Like reasoned action and planned behavior, modeling approaches are most commonly used when considering health campaigning, as opposed to marketing consumer products or political candidates. This is because, like the theory of reasoned action and the theory of planned behavior, social cognitive approaches emphasize empowering audience members to believe that they can accomplish some kind of goal or successfully perform some kind of behavior. Through the observation of others, audience members may acquire what is known as self-efficacy; this is the belief that one can perform the behavior in question. A number

Theory of planned behavior A model similar to the theory of reasoned action, but with the added argument that self-efficacy moderates the process.

Fear appeals A campaign strategy that attempts to get people to change their behaviors by instilling fear regarding the behavior in question.

Self-efficacy Our beliefs in our ability to do something.

of moderating factors can influence this, such as perceived similarity; if you see someone with whom you identify learning the behavior in question and enacting that behavior to a positive outcome, you may believe that you can do it too. If someone then believes they are capable of doing something, they will likely devote greater effort to it. Further, one's ideas of the outcome associated with that behavior might be more favorable if they experience a lot of self-efficacy.

In his work on behavioral modeling, Bandura outlined four components of vicarious learning: attention, retention, motor reproduction, and motivation. First, a persuasive message must grab the attention of the observer; this is not as simple as it seems. There are many things taking place around us at all times that we devote no attention to, since they are relatively unimportant to us. As you read this, you are likely unaware of the hum of the fluorescent light above your head, or the footsteps of someone fifty feet from your window. We engage in similar passive processing with media. Thinking back to our discussion of ELM, consider how much media we consume passively, whether it is the radio in the car or the television in the background as we work. Further, standing beliefs and worldview may influence what we choose to devote our attention to, since we tend to filter out information that is not consistent with these beliefs (Nathan & Kovoor-Misra, 2002). This has an influence on our thinking regarding message placement (as we will see in Chapter 11).

Attention Focusing on a stimulus.

The second step in this process is retention, or the ways in which we place the behavior in our memory and retain it for future use. These mental models then act as heuristics that allow us to recall information about situations, objects, or their environment (Nathan & Kovoor-Misra, 2002). In social marketing circles, the accurate retention of information is the key, since you are likely advocating for a specific, highly detailed behavior (think smoking cessation, HIV testing, not drinking and driving, and so on.). This is also part of the reason that social marketers provide information for additional resources, such as a link to a Web site with further information. It may be impossible to explain complex health phenomena in thirty seconds, but if the ad raises interest it may drive people toward seeking information on their own that they can in fact retain and act upon.

Retention Placing information in our memory for future use.

The third step is motor reproduction, the ability of the observer to reproduce the behavior (Bandura, 1977). Again, self-efficacy is the key here; one must not only be capable of the behavior, but must know that he or she is capable. Think of the appeals that are often used in social marketing. They typically include some kind of message assuring the audience member that they do it and that there are resources available to help.

Motor reproduction The ability of someone to reproduce a behavior they have observed and retained.

The final step is motivation, or the perception of potential positive and negative outcomes that will follow the behavior (Bandura, 1977). If someone thinks they will be subsequently rewarded, they will engage in the behavior. They will also do so if they perceive some kind of negative outcome associated with not performing it. Health campaigns encouraging women to get HPV vaccinations, for example, discuss negative health outcomes that can be avoided if one gets immunized. Likewise, anti-drunk driving interventions often discuss the loss of life and legal liabilities that are associated with that unfortunate behavior. Behaviors that are presented as leading to positive outcomes are likely to be adopted, while those leading to negative outcomes will be avoided.

Motivation The perception of positive or negative outcomes that will follow a behavior.

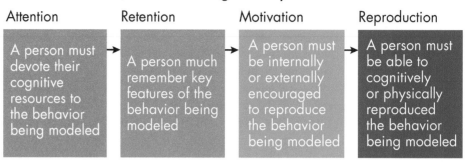

Social Learning Theory model

Attention
A person must devote their cognitive resources to the behavior being modeled

Retention
A person much remember key features of the behavior being modeled

Motivation
A person must be internally or externally encouraged to reproduce the behavior being modeled

Reproduction
A person must be able to cognitively or physically reproduced the behavior being modeled

Bandura adds that there are a number of contextual features that might make a behavioral model more effective. Of course, reward is important—if we see a behavioral model receiving some kind of reward for his or her actions, we will want to model our behavior off of that person. We are also more likely to model behavior off of those whom we perceive (rightly or wrongly) to be similar to ourselves. By creating messages assuring that people like you can change their behaviors, social marketers can engender a sense of self-efficacy while exemplifying the behavior change in question.

Exemplification

Exemplification theory (Zillmann, 1999; Zillmann & Brosius, 2000) offers us a particularly useful means of understanding the persuasive effects of interactive media. As we saw back in Chapter 5, exemplification theory argues that mediated portrayals of objects and individuals drive judgments and reactions to real-world encounters. Based on a number of evolutionary assumptions, exemplification theory argues that exemplars that are iconic and arousing will influence perceptions more than those that are not (Zillmann, 2002). Those that are easy to remember and recall are more likely to influence social perceptions, and this influence may carry over into persuasive processes. Essentially, we are better at extrapolating from individual exemplars to groups of people and behaviors than we are at drawing inferences about individuals from group patterns and data; needless to say this is found troubling by scientists and statisticians alike.

However, when used responsibly, exemplification approaches may be fruitful in encouraging prosocial behavior. While most studies concerning exemplification have revolved around news and information, this knowledge can be extended into our consideration of persuasion, particularly when it comes to new media. Past research has found that emotionally arousing and extremely detailed exemplars are more effective at forming and driving people's judgments than are base-rate or passive messages (Aust & Zillmann, 1996; Gibson & Zillmann, 1994). This research also suggests that level of involvement is likely to influence judgments. If we are actively seeking information about some kind of health issue—for example, using WebMD to find information about the flu—then it is likely that we

are devoting a great deal of cognitive energy toward this information and that emotionally arousing and highly detailed information should be effective in the persuasion process.

Given the highly interactive nature of new media technologies, it makes sense that emotionally arousing exemplars would be particularly effective, given that we will allocate a lot of cognitive energy to them (as we would in our preceding high involvement example) because we have to interact with them. Much like the modeling and planned behavior approaches, exemplification may have particular utility for new media practitioners in terms of social marketing. In terms of public health judgments, information concerning risk may be especially influenced by exemplars. Some studies have found that the use of emotional exemplars can persuade people to understand the threats posed by food contamination (Aust & Zillmann, 1996) or mechanical accidents (Zillmann, Gibson, & Sargent, 1999). Zillmann (2006) also argued that exemplars that are emotionally arousing can get people to take action in response to perceived threats.

MC IN ACTION

Darfur Is Dying

Since 2003, the Darfur region of Sudan has been the site of nearly 500,000 deaths and over 2.8 million displaced people fleeing civil unrest stemming from conflicts between several warring ethnic and tribal factions in Africa's third-largest nation.

From April 2006 to April 2007, over 1.2 million individuals relived the conflict—or at least, a virtual version of it—nearly 2.4 million times.

Referenced in Chapter 6, *Darfur Is Dying* is a particular type of video game—a serious game—designed to expose players to some of the details of the war in Darfur. In the game, players assume the role of a displaced refugee family that must fetch fresh water from a distant well and then bring the water back to help keep a refugee camp watered for seven days. In the meantime, players must avoid militia and armed security forces, and if they do get caught, the player is given a narrative account of how Janjaweed forces have been reported to treat their captives.

While the game has been criticized for doing little to actually impact the ongoing civil war, many critics suggested that it brought awareness to a conflict that had previously received little attention in international media. While it remains to be seen if *Darfur Is Dying* really provided a meaningful exemplar of the refugee experience in the Sudan, such games provide promise that we can learn and hopefully act on a number of social concerns not normally part of our daily lives.

When you have a moment, play the game yourself. Share your experiences with us on Facebook at https://www.facebook.com/groups/234255823447372/ or on Twitter, using the #MediaAsTools hashtag

In 2006, NPR's Michelle Norris sat down for an interview with Susana Ruiz, the game's creator and, at the time, a graduate student at the University of Southern California. The complete interview is available at: http://www.npr.org/templates/story/story.php?storyId=5386745.

Taken together, exemplification approaches would argue that people make judgments (especially concerning risks) based on concrete, emotional, and attentionally favored exemplars. While most of this research looks at message characteristics that will impact their effectiveness, less research has considered how exemplification will vary from medium to medium. Further, less research has approached the impact that involvement with the medium will have on persuasion and subsequent social judgments.

When we think about interactive media and the notions of telepresence we discussed in Chapter 7, some have suggested that different types of telepresence may make exemplars more or less effective in persuading people. Spatial presence, or the feeling that one is physically located in a virtual environment, may be especially important in inducing compliance. If people feel as if they are immersed in a virtual environment and experience places and objects as though they are real, they might be expected to have stronger memories associated with these exemplars, experience more emotional arousal from them, and be better able to recall information from these memories (see MC in Action: *Darfur Is Dying*). This should lead to greater compliance with the messages in question, especially if those messages are related to public health campaigns describing some kind of health threat that should be avoided.

Conclusions

As you can see, there are numerous ways that we can think about persuasion in mediated contexts. This is only a short overview of a vast range of persuasion research that has attempted to determine the reasons why people comply with certain messages. In terms of delivery through new media technologies, our assumptions regarding the level of involvement on the part of the user likely changes. The concept of the mass audience—a large, passive mass of individuals who can be easily duped with little effort—is for the most part antiquated. By simply using interactive media, we are indicating that we are both actively processing information and that we have very specific interests to which advertisers must appeal.

To this point, we have examined the theoretical reasons and research exploring how advertising might get us to buy something—be it a product, a behavior, an ideology, or a political candidate. In Chapters 10 and 11 we will take things a step further, exploring the ways in which advertisers and social marketers actually use this knowledge. We will next look at the ways in which advertisers typically push their products, using multimedia campaigns bridging traditional and innovative approaches to marketing.

Key Terms

Social marketers (pg 141)
Elaboration likelihood model (pg 142)
Heuristic systematic model (pg 145)
Heuristics (pg 145)
Opinion leaders (pg 146)
Geo-positioning software (pg 146)

References

Ajzen, I. (1991). The theory of planned behavior. *Organizational Behavior and Human Decision Processes, 50,* 179–211.

Ajzen, I., & Fishbein, M. (1980). *Understanding attitudes and predicting social behavior.* Englewood Cliffs, NJ: Prentice-Hall.

Anderson, M., & Magruder, J. (2012). Learning from the crowd: Regression discontinuity estimates of the effects of an online review database. *The Economic Journal, 122,* 957–989.

Aust, C. F., & Zillmann, D. (1996). Effects of victim exemplification in television news on viewer perception of social issues. *Communication Quarterly, 73,* 787–803.

Bandura, A. (1977). Self-efficacy: Toward a unifying theory of behavioral change. *Psychological Review, 84,* 191–215.

Fishbein, M., Middlestadt, S. E., & Hitchcock, P. J. (1991). Using information to change sexually transmitted disease-related behaviors: An analysis based on the theory of reasoned action. In J. N. Wasserheit, S. O. Aral, & K. K. Holmes (Eds.), *Research issues in human behavior and sexually transmitted diseases in the AIDS era* (pp. 243–257). Washington, DC: American Society for Microbiology.

Gibson, R., & Zillmann, D. (1994). Exaggerated versus representative exemplification in news reports: Perception of issues and personal consequences. *Communication Research, 21,* 603–624.

Nathan, M. L., & Kovoor-Misra, S. (2002). No pain, yet gain: Vicarious organizational learning from crises in an inter-organizational field. *Journal of Applied Behavioral Science, 38,* 245–266.

Witte, K. (1992). Putting the fear back into fear appeals: The extended parallel process model. *Communication Monographs, 59,* 329–349.

Zillmann, D. (1999). Exemplification theory: Judging the whole by some of its parts. *Media Psychology, 1,* 69–94.

Zillmann, D. (2002). Exemplification theory of media influence. In J. Bryant & D. Zillmann (Eds.), *Media effects: Advances in theory and research* (2nd ed., pp. 213–245). Mahwah, NJ: LEA.

Zillmann, D. (2006). Exemplification effects in the promotion of safety and health. *Journal of Communication, 56,* S221–S237.

Zillmann, D., & Brosius, H.-B. (2000). *Exemplification in communication: The influence of case reports on the perception of issues.* Mahwah, NJ: Lawrence Erlbaum Associates.

Zillmann, D., Gibson, R., & Sargent, S. L. (1999). Effects of photographs in news-magazine reports on issue perception. *Media Psychology, 1,* 207–228.

CHAPTER 10

Advertising

Imagine it is March 2015 and you are in Austin, Texas for the annual convention/party known as South by Southwest (SxSW). While you have some downtime, you check out Tinder, and you come across a beautiful 25-year-old named Ava nearby. Eager to make more of a connection with her, you quickly swipe right. Luckily for you, so does she, and you are off and chatting. She requests to ask you some questions, you answer, and finally Ava tells you that you have passed her test, and asks you to go to her Instagram account to see if she passes your test. You think this might be your lucky day, and so you happily check this out.

Does this story sound too good to be true? What do you think was at Ava's Instagram account? For the many people who swiped right on Ava's Tinder account in Austin, they were brought to an Instagram account promoting the movie *Ex Machina*, a film about a human-ish robot, which debuted at SxSW. "Ava," the name of the robot in the film, was a chatbot that used a photo of Alicia Vikander, the actress who played Ava in the film. So, in all, this was a clever, catfishing advertisement for the movie, in that it played on some of the same themes of the film (For more details on this story, check out http://mashable.com/2015/03/16/ex-machina-tinder-marketing/#YZcKMWCzGPqg http://hellogiggles.com/tinder-profile-sxsw/

Advertising has changed considerably over the course of the last few years. While the use of persuasive messages to encourage consumers to buy products has a long history in American culture, norms and assumptions we hold concerning the ways in which advertising takes place are being irreversibly shaped by the explosion in available media platforms that has occurred in recent years. The current chapter will discuss conventions

that have historically been associated with advertising, including some of the basic economic principles on which the industry is built. It will go on to discuss the ways in which both the Internet and social media presented challenges to advertising professionals and consumers alike. The chapter concludes by discussing the ways in which modern advertising agencies use multiplatform marketing in order to reach consumers with different attitudes and levels of commitment toward their products.

Things to think about:

- Where do our norms come from in advertising? How did the industry evolve to where it is now?
- What historical events have been critical in the development of advertising?
- What did advertisers not grasp during the early days of the Internet?
- Where does most online ad revenue now come from?

Traditional Advertising Conventions

Handbills Short announcements or advertisements, typically printed on a single sheet, handed out in public areas.

While we often think of advertising as a phenomenon associated with electronic media, this is an incomplete description that ignores a long history of non-electronic advertising and the norms that developed over that long period. There is evidence of basic advertising in the form of handbills and placards as early as ancient Greece; these often contained basic information concerning the availability of products, from whom, and at what price. The ancient Romans were known to use similar methods for publicizing not only the availability of goods and services, but also the deliberations and decisions of the Roman Senate. Throughout the Middle Ages, handbills were frequently utilized in order to promote basic goods and services. Naturally, the development of the printing press in the 15th century led to more handbills being printed and distributed, eventually precipitating early newspaper advertising.

However, we really begin to see the rise of advertising as an economic force during the middle part of the 19th century. Industrialization and steam-powered presses allowed advertisers to produce large quantities of handbills, and later led to the mass production of broadsheet newspapers. More importantly, however, is the impact industrialization had on the creation of goods and services and on media itself. First, we were able to produce consumer goods and products at a rate never before been seen in human history. Shortly after the American Civil War, our nation had for the first time a surplus of economic goods; that is, we were mass-producing more consumer products than we actually use, and thus our supply outweighed demand. At this time in our history, advertising became less about informing and more about persuading. The focus in advertising shifted from informing consumers about the availability and price of products, to convincing consumers that they ought to buy one product instead of another.

With this shift in mass production came a shift in the economic structure of media. As is often documented, Benjamin Day's *New York Sun* became the first of what was known as the penny press newspapers (see Chapter 5). Day and his colleagues developed a brilliant economic model. Since newspapers could print tens of thousands of copies of their product in a single day, it drove the price per copy down to almost nothing. Recovering the cost of producing the physical paper itself through its purchase price became irrelevant. Instead, the economic focus shifted away from purchase of the media itself, and toward revenue generated by those purchasing advertising space in the media. The more people who read the newspaper, the more money a publisher could charge advertisers to purchase space. Day was the first to use the term "news hole," in which the advertising is typeset first and the news and information is edited accordingly to fit in the leftover space. In this way, the news content was actually just used as filler to legitimize the selling of advertising space. Indeed, Day and his contemporaries knew they could generate more revenue by selling ad space to businesses than they could by selling newspapers to the general public.

This economic model was co-opted by magazines, and eventually by radio and television. Of course, it was expanded and perfected in electronic media during the first part of the 20th century. Radio became an enormously profitable means of advertising consumer products. From the 1920s until the 1950s, entire radio shows were typically underwritten by one sponsor. Thus, listeners of extremely popular shows such as *Texaco Star Theater* or *The Lone Ranger* would hear the same product mentioned dozens of times (see MC in Action: Quiz Show Scandal). This often took the form of a long form advertisement, where the stars or hosts of the shows themselves would go off on ten to twelve-minute sidebars about the products made by the company underwriting the show. Furthermore, the newfound ability to provide an audio track allowed advertisers to develop sophisticated means of differentiating their products from otherwise identical products. Through the use of stories, vignettes, and jingles, advertisers were able to paint a more complete picture of the benefits their products provided as well as provide more heuristic cues (see Chapter 9). They were also able to reach millions of people simultaneously, and were able to repeat the same message over and over again to a relatively captive audience. While this notion seems strange to us now, radio advertising was largely embraced by the general public. In the early days of commercial radio, there was some confusion and debate about the best way to monetize the medium. Some proposed licensing fees for owning radio sets, or charging extravagant taxes on their purchase. Early radio listeners were aware of this debate, and advertising was seen as a means of keeping radio free for anyone who had purchased a set. Listeners would gladly endure a ten-minute commercial considering the alternative.

Radio faced a major limitation in that it could not show pictures of the product or brand logos in the way that magazine advertising could. Therefore, despite the potential impact of radio on interested consumers, advertisers often relied on campaigns that utilized both print display ads and radio audio ads to raise awareness of the product to a large base of consumers. Almost one hundred years later, we are returning to multiplatform marketing and working to identify what media works best with which consumers.

Penny press A term referring to cheap, mass-produced newspapers of the late 19th century that made their profits from ad sales rather than sales of the paper itself.

News hole The space that is left for content once the advertising has been placed.

MC IN ACTION

QUIZ SHOW SCANDAL

During the 1950s, quiz shows were phenomenally popular on American television. In 1956, the show *Twenty-One* came under fire for being rigged; sponsors had trained contestants by giving them the answers ahead of time. Sponsors wanted smart, attractive people associated with their products. Given that the shows had a single underwriter, any given quiz show was largely associated with that product.

The entire affair was found so unsavory by the American public that it led to a congressional hearing held by the House Committee on Legislative Oversight. Contestants from several game shows testified to having been coached, and while no one went to jail over the hoax, it was seen by many as an act of betrayal toward the American public.

Out of this congressional hearing came eventual legislation changing the format of advertising on network television. Advertisers were no longer permitted to sponsor an entire program, but rather advertising sponsorship had to be shared across multiple products. The intent here was to prevent any one company or organization from having undue influence on the nature of the content.

Sixty years later, we still find ourselves in a situation where a very small number of organizations have a great deal of influence over content—only this time on the Internet. Google, for example, has become the largest resource for advertisers who wish to buy sponsored links; yet online advertisers are almost entirely dependent on Google NetRatings to evaluate their Web traffic and their effectiveness in reaching large yet highly specified audiences. An entire cottage industry—search engine optimization (SEO)—has developed around the use of Google metrics and maximizing the chances that one's Web site will appear in Google searches. SEO professionals use a variety of code writing, placement, and partnering strategies to build sites that have a stronger chances of appearing in Web searches that are conducted in certain places along certain keywords. Google also offers sponsored links, where companies can pay to have links to their Web sites appear at the top of a search, sometimes alongside large font contact information and/or maps to their brick and mortar locations.

What do you think? Is the reliance on Google and a small number of other Web products for sponsored links problematic? Are we entering an age when a small number of companies will have an alarming influence over the industry? Or is the business of new media so different that we cannot even draw these comparisons? Give this some thought. Share your thoughts with us on Facebook at https://www.facebook.com/groups/234255823447372/ or on Twitter, using the #MediaAsTools hashtag.

Of course, between the 1950s and early 2000s—that period between radio's popularity and today's Internet-dominated media scene—advertising in the United States was almost completely dominated by television. After the establishment of national television networks in the late 1940s, television diffused faster than any medium in our history. In 1950, fewer than 10 percent of American households owned a television; by the end of the decade, that number was well over 90 percent.

Television combined the reach of radio with the visual representations that were possible in print to reach an increasingly large audience with textual, audio, and now visually appealing content. Following the quiz show scandal, the FCC imposed a new format for advertising both in television and radio. Since the line between advertisers and producers was becoming blurred, the regulatory agency mandated that the media move away from having entire programs underwritten by one sponsor to the model we still see in place today where multiple sponsors purchase 30- to 60-second spots during designated ad breaks. While limiting some of the direct influence of advertisers, this also allowed for greater advertising revenues, as now multiple sponsors could pay for ad time placed within wildly popular shows.

This may sound bizarre to many of you reading this book, but between 1948 and the mid-1980s many television markets only had three network stations; Fox showed up as the "fourth network" in 1986. For most of that time period there was no cable or Internet television, and as a result many argued that advertisers had a stranglehold on the American public. After all, audiences had become dependent on television as a primary source of news and entertainment (see Chapter 13), and with only three real channel options—American Broadcasting Company (ABC), CBS Broadcasting Inc. (formerly the Columbia Broadcasting System, the world's second-largest broadcast company), and National Broadcasting Company (NBC)—the cost of advertising was at its highest in history, adjusted for inflation. American advertisers went from spending nothing to spending over $120 million in television advertising between 1940 and 1952.

This boom in television advertising also led to the development of many conventions that we associate with modern advertising. For example, advertising mogul Rosser Reeves and others developed what they called unique selling proposition or USP. With USPs, advertisers highlight one aspect of the product in the attempt to separate it from other identical products that serve the exact same purpose. For example, peanut butter is pretty much peanut butter; however, one peanut butter manufacturer bills itself as the one that "choosy moms choose." Since we can presume that most parents like to think of themselves as somewhat discriminating when it comes to what they choose to feed their child, this statement separates this brand from others. Unique selling propositions are often utilized in hard-sell advertising, in which this simple defining characteristic is repeated over and over and over again in order to create a quick heuristic for the consumer—after all, many of you reading this now likely know what candy melts in your mouth not in your hand. If the candy does melt in your hand, you probably know what paper towel is the quicker picker upper (see MC in Action: They Don't Melt, But How Do They Taste?)

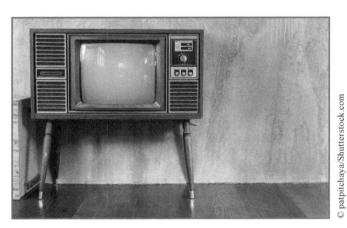

© patpitchaya/Shutterstock.com

Television opened up a new world for advertisers to showcase their products.

MC IN ACTION

THEY DON'T MELT, BUT HOW DO THEY TASTE?

Sold in nearly 100 different countries, Mars Incorporated's M&M candies have been manufactured for nearly 80 years, with the first run of candies being produced in Newark, New Jersey, in 1941. While certainly not the first chocolate candy to be mass-produced in the United States, their patented candy shell preserved the milk chocolate inside, protecting it from melting when being transported or carried around.

In 1954, following a post-World War II surge in the candy's popularity due to stories about U.S. troops praising them as an easy candy to carry around in the trenches of the European and Pacific theatres, marketing executives with Mars created the now-famous "melts in your mouth, not in your hand" slogan.

© Roman Samokhin/Shutterstock.com

In this example, the USP is the candy shell. But let us look closer and think about our reasons for wanting candy. Portability is likely important to us—nobody wants a pocketful of melted chocolate—but what about the taste of the candy, or the quality and flavor of the chocolate or the shell? Also, M&Ms usually cost a bit more than other generic chocolate candy brands on your average store shelf that also encase chocolate inside of candy, cookie, or any number of other edible shells. These candies also do not melt in your hand, but the M&Ms heuristic is so attached to the brand itself that M&Ms is one of the best-selling and most-recognized brands in the world today.

Reach The number of people exposed to an advertisement.

This continued emphasis on advertising also drove the development and expansion of the media research industry. Organizations like Nielsen, Arbitron, and eventually Google NetRatings developed services for advertisers increasingly concerned with the reach—or the number of people exposed to a particular product. Nielsen ratings were developed for the purpose of negotiating the cost of advertising space on network television. Other more specified research agencies, such as AC Nielsen and Roper Starch, evolved to make specific determinations regarding audience needs and responses. These agencies eventually concerned themselves not so much with the number of people who are being reached, but with determining target demographics, aspects of the product that were appreciated, and the ideal means of promoting those products to those interested.

Facebook and Social Media Advertising

While many of the conventions found in modern advertising trace their roots to television and radio, the development and proliferation of the Internet in the 1990s had a dramatic impact on how advertisers thought about doing business. First, advertisers saw the Internet as yet another medium that could be exploited for advertising purposes using the same techniques that are so successful in radio and television. The problem was they had no idea what they were doing exactly. Many were (and still are) thinking about the Internet as a mass medium only. While they have been somewhat true in a Web 1.0 world, it almost assuredly is not as true in a Web 2.0 world. Given the interactive nature of the medium, advertisers believed they could simply place banner ads alongside popular Web sites or in pop-ups and could reach viewers accordingly.

It did not exactly work. As advertisers began developing other metrics such as click-through rate to evaluate the popularity of different sites and the actual number of times that consumers would click on an ad, media research agencies began discovering that people clicked on less than 1 percent of all banner ads. In recent years, they have developed more sophisticated means of reaching consumers.

Click-through rate A measure of the effectiveness of an online ad based on the number of hits it receives.

Increasingly, Internet advertising has become dependent on sponsored links. A sponsored link is, for example, a link that will appear among the first hits in Google's search engine results. Advertisers typically attempt to outbid each other for sponsored links that will be associated with search terms they believe are germane to their product. These terms could include the product name itself, attributes of the product, locations associated with the product, or physical descriptions of the product. In these instances, advertisers negotiate the cost of the ad space based on the click-through rate associated with these links. In other words, in modern Internet advertising, advertisers pay a fixed amount for every individual who clicks on a sponsored link coming off of Google search. This has quickly made Google one of the most powerful advertising outlets in the world, with annual revenue in excess of $50 billion.

Sponsored links A type of advertising in which companies pay search engines to list their products or services first when certain key words are used in searches.

Furthermore, the rise in popularity of social networking sites has played a significant role in how advertising has changed. Social networking sites such as Facebook also allow advertisers to reach highly specified, narrowcast audiences. When someone indicates that they "like" a particular person, good, or service on Facebook, this provides advertisers with a wealth of data concerning their product preferences, lifestyle, age, location, demographics, and personal interests. It also allows advertisers to utilize an electronic version of the classic word-of-mouth advertising, as these likes and comments are then seen by a person's social network. With this highly specified information, advertisers can use Facebook to expose users to ads for products that are likely suited to their wants and desires and can utilize the power of social networking (as discussed in Chapter 8).

Social Media and Big Data

The vast quantities of data that can now be exchanged through a variety of media have also impacted direct marketing. Retailers and manufacturers often retain our product purchase information, including our telephone numbers and e-mail

MC IN ACTION

SURPRISE, YOU'RE PREGNANT!

"My daughter got this in the mail!" he said. "She's still in high school, and you're sending her coupons for baby clothes and cribs? Are you trying to encourage her to get pregnant?"

~Concerned father, Minneapolis

Picture for a moment that you have a teenage daughter (or imagine your own father). Moving through high school, you have concerns about her as she begins dating, and you are a bit slow on having the sex talk with her. One day you check your mailbox, and you find the standard fare: bills, a community newspaper, and a stack of advertisements and coupons.

As you go through the stack to filter the important mail from the junk mail, you notice a mailer from Target with your daughter's name on it—and the content of the mailer is a bit peculiar: diaper coupons. How would you feel about this?

Well, this is precisely what happened to a father in Minnesota. The father was enraged at the thought that Target was selling his daughter inappropriate products—not breaking the law, but crossing decency boundaries—and when he asked about the campaign, he learned something about big data. Target "targeted" his daughter with baby ads because they had been tracking her purchases over the prior several weeks.

Using an industry-secret "Guest ID" method (usually shoppers who use store credit cards or loyalty cards are easiest to track), Target followed as the young woman bought products such as lotions and vitamins as well as her other normal shopping routine. Comparing her shopping habits with those of other Target customers, statisticians were able to suggest that she was buying many of the same products as one might expect a pregnant woman to purchase. Target had a great volume of data on her purchasing behaviors while in the store, they have the tools in place to gather diverse data (shopping, demographic profiles, and so on.) and process it quickly, and they had the people in place to give them trust in their calculations.

As for the daughter? It turns out she was pregnant. Weeks after the father's complaints to the company, he found out that his daughter was due in August of that year. *Time*'s Keith Wagstaff covered the story of Target's targeted advertising at: http://techland.time.com/2012/02/17/how-target-knew-a-high-school-girl-was-pregnant-before-her-parents/.

addresses, and sell this data to advertisers and marketers who may believe that you are someone they want to reach. Every time you apply for a credit card, give your e-mail address for "updates and sales" at the store, or buy something online, you are giving away information that may be used to identify you as part of a target demographic. Triangulating these data allows marketers to create a very specific and sophisticated profile of your interests, product preferences, and spending habits. All of these data can be used to determine which product you may be interested in and to contact you directly concerning it.

This focus on collecting and analyzing large quantities of data concerning highly specific information about individuals is often referred to as a focus on big data. According to IBM, each day people generate somewhere in the magnitude of 2.3 million terabytes of data (the equivalent of nine million laptop hard drives by 2013 standards). These data come from everything from weather balloons and interspace telescopes to individual text messages and Facebook status updates. IBM further breaks down the big data concept into four sub-dimensions: volume, which refers to the sheer amount of data produced by network users; velocity, which refers to the speed at which we are able to collect and analyze data; variety, which refers to the many different types of data; and veracity, which refers to our ability to trust the inferences we are able to make from the data we collect. Indeed, advertisers have begun to employ statisticians and social scientists to help them make sense of these big data and use them to reach out to new customers, even when those customers do not know they need a product yet (see MC in Action: Surprise, You're Pregnant!)

Big data The increasing focus on the electronic amalgamation of enormous amounts of consumer data in order to target consumers.

MC IN ACTION

PLEASE ROB ME

Many social networking platforms allow users to "check in" to physical locations, using the GPS devices embedded in a phone or tablet to tell their social media friends and followers their whereabouts. While this might be a neat way of keeping your public informed of your daily routine (at least one of this book's authors is a particularly heavy social media user), we might suggest that notifying others of your entire timeline, for example, that you are at an ATM at 2:00 am or that you are coming home from the mall with hundreds of dollars' worth of jewelry after a shopping spree, might not be the best idea in terms of your personal safety. In fact, it may draw direct attention to those who might want to do you harm.

Regardless of where you are when you check in, if you are checking in there is somewhere you are definitely not—at home. Recognizing the problems that might be tied to this, the Web site www.pleaserobme. com was launched in the year 2010. The site aggregates check-in information from Twitter and FourSquare and allows site visitors to search by location and identify people who are not at home. If the information is posted on a public timeline, pleaserobme. com can ping back users with a message warning them that the entire world can tell that they are not currently in their house.

According to the site developers, the goal is not to put people in danger, but "to raise some awareness on this issue and have people think about how they use services like Foursquare, Brightkite [now defunct], Google Buzz, and so on." You might want to give pleaserobme.com a look and then think about the information you choose to broadcast concerning your whereabouts.

Have you ever had concerns that your social media feed might be a bit too public? Share your thoughts with us (with caution, of course) on Facebook at https://www.face-book.com/groups/234255823447372/ or on Twitter, using the #MediaAsTools hashtag.

It does not just end with your Facebook page or your e-mail address either. Increasingly, your smartphone is becoming a tool that is used by advertisers to track your preferences. Think about it. Most smartphones now contain some kind of Web browser, which can be enabled with the same data-harvesting software that you might find on your laptop. The difference is that many smartphones also feature GPS and navigation technology on board. Advertisers are not only able to figure out what it is you like, and what your spending patterns typically entail, but can *figure out where you are* (see MC in Action: Please Rob Me). At this time, advertisers are still developing more efficient ways of utilizing this geographic information (such as the Yelp program discussed in Chapter 9), for example, to target consumers directly with advertisements based on their physical location. In this way, we have seen communication technology alter the advertising model from one in which the consumer brings themselves to an ad to one in which an ad is delivered—in a highly customized and personalized way—directly to the consumer.

Multimedia Campaigning

The availability of Web advertising, sponsored links, social network advertising, and database marketing has given advertisers a host of new means of grabbing your attention. The academic study of media has, on several occasions throughout history, erroneously assumed what was sometimes called the replacement hypothesis. In the replacement hypothesis, one assumes that, as we only have so much time and attention to devote to any given activity, we cannot adopt a new medium without sacrificing time devoted to another.

Of course, as we have found out time and time again, this simply is not true. We did not stop reading magazines and newspapers when the radio became available. We did not stop listening to the radio just as television became popular. We have not turned off our radios or stopped watching television just because the Internet and mobile telephony are available. Communication scholar John Dimmick coined the theory of media niche (Dimmick, 1984; 2002) to explain that, historically, media channels rarely cease to exist but are rather repurposed to fit a particular use for an individual. A common example is the evolution of radio from a primary form of entertainment and information (it was not uncommon for folks to gather around older radio sets in the 1930s) to a supplemental form of media that we use while doing something else (such as listening to music or news while we drive, exercise, or clean our rooms). We are better multitaskers—or at least, multimedia users—than we are often given credit for in academic circles.

How many times do you watch television while you stream another video feed on your laptop or tablet? How many times do you listen to the radio while you are checking your e-mail? How many times do you have multiple screens up on your computer, for example, your Facebook profile, your Twitter feed, and a set of Google search results? If you are like most adopters of new media chances are quite often. Now more than ever, advertisers rely on what is known as integrated marketing communication, or IMC. In principle IMC uses as many media channels as possible to market a specific product to interested individuals. Think back to Chapter 9 when we discussed how important involvement is in the persuasion

Replacement hypothesis The notion that as new media are introduced they replace the time we spent with older media.

Theory of media niche A theory of media that suggests that media channels rarely disappear but instead are repurposed to fit the evolving needs of audience members.

Integrated marketing communication Using as many media channels as possible to promote a product.

process. This should tell you something about the different techniques that advertisers can use to reach audiences who may be more or less aware of a product and its purpose. For instance, one can conduct a campaign in which television and radio are used to raise awareness of a new product. Since we know that Internet use is a relatively active process, we would want to first introduce some product awareness before directing consumers toward the specified information on a Web site. Of course with the use of aggregated data or information drawn from social networking sites, we could figure out who would likely be interested in the product based on their affiliation with other products and services. In either case an advertiser would have to raise awareness of the product first and provide a means by which the consumer could obtain more information.

Another reason why IMC has become so critical is the sheer abundance of information we receive. In order to cut through ad clutter and deliver a persuasive message to audiences that will retain and act upon information, you simply have to place your ad in many locations.

Conclusions

Clearly, new media technologies have changed the ways in which we think about advertising and, to an extent, the economic model of the industry. It appears as though finally, after almost two decades, advertisers have found efficient and highly profitable means of selling their products. Of course, not everyone in marketing is in the business of selling products—some sell ideas, behaviors, or politicians. The persuasion process under these circumstances is quite different, as is the way the business operates. Chapter 11 will go on to explore campaigning, and health campaigning in particular, along with the ways in which new media is changing the landscape of social marketing.

Key Terms

Handbills (pg 156)
Penny press (pg 157)
News hole (pg 157)
Quiz show scandal (pg 159)
Television markets (pg 159)
Unique selling proposition (pg 159)
Reach (pg 160)
Click-through rate (pg 161)
Sponsored links (pg 161)
Big data (pg 163)
Replacement hypothesis (pg 164)
Theory of media niche (pg 164)
Integrated marketing communication (pg 164)

References

Dimmick, J. (2002). *Media competition and coexistence: The theory of the niche*. Mahwah, NJ: LEA.

Dimmick, J. & Rothenbuhler, E. (1984). The theory of the niche: Quantifying competition among media industries. *Journal of Communication, 34*(1), 103–119.

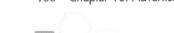

CHAPTER 11

Campaigning

They forgot to add mold as the secret ingredient.

~"Ben," a disgruntled yogurt customer posting on the company's Facebook page in response to a recent scandal involving tainted yogurt sold in stores.

As you have read, technology has changed the ways in which we market goods and services and has had a dramatic impact on the economic structure of the advertising industry. Of course, we know that persuasive media is not limited to goods and services. In a similar vein, the Internet and social media have changed the ways in which we think about marketing behaviors and ideas. Although the notion of social marketing is a newer concept than that of traditional advertising, its norms and practices have been no less influenced by the development of media technology. This chapter will discuss the practice of social marketing in general terms and then go on to discuss the ways in which social marketers have utilized new media technologies to improve their effectiveness, and will offer some potential pitfalls as well (as evidenced by the Facebook post that begins this chapter).

Things to think about:

- What public health issues are you concerned about? How did you find out about them? How did you respond to this information?
- Where did social marketing come from? Why did people decide that they could sell behavior like they sell products?

- What are some of the challenges that come along with social marketing? Can you think of a time that you tuned out an ad asking you to change your behavior? Why?
- What should social marketers do in terms of placing these messages?

Campaigns

There is a lengthy history of using media in attempts to influence social behaviors. Existing evidence suggests individual reformers were using pamphlets and other channels before the founding of the United States as a sovereign nation. For example, infamous Puritan minister Cotton Mather used pamphlets and public addresses to promote inoculation against smallpox in Boston in 1721. Other early American campaigns were designed to gain favor for the abolition of slavery, women's suffrage, and the temperance movement (the abolition of alcohol)—each of these campaigns was eventually successful in influencing public perception in favor of their respective causes and (perhaps with the exception of the temperance movement) these influences are felt even today. Indeed, there is a long history of using media to promote social changes.

But what, by definition, is a campaign? Communication scholars Ronald Rice and Charles Atkin define public communication campaigns as "purposive attempts to inform or influence behaviors in large audiences within a specified time period using an organized set of communication activities and featuring an array of mediated messages in multiple channels generally to produce noncommercial benefits to individuals and society" (2013, p. 3). In their work, Rice and Atkin suggested 10 principles for successful campaigns in 1994 that still hold true over 20 years later. They are:

1. Understand historical and conceptual dimensions, which suggests that campaigners need to know the past and present situations surrounding their campaign. For example (and we will carry this example throughout the chapter), an anti-smoking campaign in a small town might need to understand past campaigns in the area as well as general perceptions about smoking.

2. Apply and extend relevant theory, such as understanding the role of fear appeals in a campaign aimed at using scare tactics to prevent smoking (see Chapter 9's discussion on fear appeals, also addressed later in this chapter).

3. Understand theoretical implications and interactions of campaign components, such as knowing how audiences might attend to different aspects of the same campaign. Using the anti-smoking campaign as an example, one would want to understand how graphic images of smoking's negative health effects might contrast or complement detailed pamphlets that discuss ways to counter those effects.

4. Plan the campaign: match objectives to individual cost-benefits. In order to ensure that a campaign can be most effective, it is important to make sure that the goals being sought are matched with an equal amount of resources. While one might assume that campaigns most often suffer from

underfunding or understaffing, it is just as important that campaign managers are careful not to overfund or overstaff an issue—especially when using public funds.

5. Apply formative evaluation. In education, an important principle of the teaching process is to measure student learning during a lesson and not just at the end of the semester; this way, teachers can adjust their teaching according to the progress being made by their students. The same principle should be applied to good campaigns—successful campaigners have a handle on the progress of a campaign so that they can make alterations accordingly.

6. Analyze and understand the audience. As will be explored in Chapters 12 and 13, different audiences select and attend to campaign information in very different ways, and it is important for successful campaigners to know the demographics and psychographics (beliefs) of the individuals they hope to reach.

7. Analyze and understand media choices. Assuming that we are talking about media campaigns, one would be wise to know which channels target audiences would use in a given campaign. For example, knowing that college students tend to watch very little prime time television would be useful for an anti-smoking campaign aimed at college students as it would suggest that purchasing expensive television commercials would be an ineffective strategy.

8. Mix multiple media and interpersonal channels when cost-effective. As a basic principle of communication, media persuasion is often not as strong as interpersonal persuasion so it is a good idea when possible to include grassroots conversations along with media messages. Returning to the anti-smoking campaign as an example, many of these campaigns encourage one to speak with a family member or loved one about their smoking addiction—this is an effort to engage interpersonal conversation around a campaign topic.

9. Understand uses and contradictions of mass media. Similar to their seventh point, at this stage in a campaign one must consider how the campaign messages fit with the media they are being shared through. For example, describing a vivid illness resulting from smoking might not work as well as showing images of the illness and, thus, a radio channel would not be as effective as a television commercial for this message. Also, running an anti-smoking commercial during a television program in which the main character and protagonist is a smoker (who does not seem to suffer any adverse effects as a result) would be a contradiction.

10. Identify reasonable criteria for campaign success, and use summative evaluation to assess both theory and program success. Any campaign must have clearly defined goals from the onset, and steps should be taken to measure these goals. An anti-smoking campaign should be influential in changing public opinion about smoking as an unhealthy activity, but it should also likely result in a decrease of cigarette sales in a given target region.

Considering this text is primarily concerned with mediated communication, we are going to focus primarily on the second, seventh, and ninth steps in their model—though we will touch on other areas throughout the writing.

Public Health and Social Marketing

Social marketing was born, in a sense, out of traditional advertising. During World War II, a number of advertising executives formed what was known as the War Advertising Council (WAC), later changed to just the Ad Council. At the time, radio had exploded in popularity, and marketers recognized its effectiveness in selling consumer products. Given how good radio marketing was at selling toothpaste, industry leaders convened to see if there was a way they could use their talents to help the war effort. What emerged from that collaboration was a series of advertising campaigns aimed at selling war bonds and at conserving materials

MC IN ACTION

HOLD THE BACON FAT!

Fats make glycerin, and glycerin makes explosives. Every year 2 billion pounds of waste kitchen fats are thrown away, enough glycerin for 10 billion rapid fire cannon shells. A belt 150 K miles long, six times around the Earth. A skillet of bacon grease is a little munitions factory.

~Narrator from *Out of the Frying Pan and into the Firing Line* (Disney, 1942)

World War II saw perhaps the birth of widespread use of campaigning to encourage Americans at home to support the war efforts of Allied soldiers in both the European and Pacific Theatres. Although many of these campaigns were controversial in that they tended to show bigoted and racist images of German and Japanese people, many others were more educational in nature—showing Americans wishing to support the war abroad ways in which they could contribute.

The above quote is from Disney's *Out of the Frying Pan and into the Firing Line*, and was designed to teach families (targeting housewives specifically) how to recycle bacon grease and other kitchen fats. In the video, Minnie Mouse is shown how to pour her meat drippings into metal containers, chill them and deliver them to a local butcher. The butcher purchases the

drippings and sends them off to a processing facility in order to be manufactured into glycerin, which is used in the manufacture of ammunition that is sent to the battlefront. Indeed, a disappointed Pluto—who had hoped to eat the meat drippings—eventually comes around to understand the importance of recycling for the war effort and offers to deliver the fats himself.

Such videos were influential in persuading Americans to aid the war effort by making simple lifestyle changes to conserve goods—other videos approached the recycling of metal and rubber, both integral in manufacturing tanks and other war equipment. You can view the entire video with Minnie Mouse and Pluto courtesy of the Prelinger Archives (www.prelinger.com) at: http://www.youtube.com/watch?v=pS2Tgkmo5-w.

that could aid the war effort (keep in mind that the notion of recycling was, at the time, largely unheard of (see MC in Action: Hold the Bacon Fat!).

The campaigns were remarkably effective, and the results may look surprising to you in the context of today's polarized political climate. By the end of the war, over 85 million Americans (well over half of the population) had purchased war bonds, and the U.S. government had raised over $180 million to aid in the war effort (about $2.3 billion in 2016 dollars). Though the end of the war brought an end to this campaign, it became clear that marketing efforts could be used to sell something other than soap. They could be used to sell ideas, behaviors, concepts, and values. The stunning effectiveness of the war bonds campaign led the Ad Council to consider the possibilities associated with social marketing.

The Ad Council began partnering with other government agencies and nonprofit organizations to create campaigns aimed at encouraging responsible, healthy, or otherwise pro-social behaviors. You may be familiar with their first project, a 1947 partnership with the U.S. Forest Service that featured a bear named Smokey reminding people to be careful and not start forest fires. You have probably seen at least a few of the many other campaigns they have developed over the decades too, like those for the United Negro College Fund, National Crime Prevention Council, and USAID.

During the late 1960s and 1970s, other government agencies, nonprofits, and nongovernmental agencies (NGOs) began to consider the power of social marketing. Soon organizations like the American Lung Association, UNICEF, and Mothers Against Drug Driving (MADD) were flooding the airwaves, with some degree of success. The ongoing MADD campaign against drunk driving, for example, has been heralded as one of the more successful campaigns in history; since 1980, DUI fatalities in the United States have been almost cut in half. Of equal note, there is evidence that the campaign has been effective in creating a social stigma against drunk driving that did not exist a generation ago. A similar campaign in the early 2000s was the Truth campaign against smoking, which pushed individuals to learn more about the tobacco industry; this campaign rested on the notion that people may be inclined to quit smoking if they believe they are helping to fund corrupt businesses. While correlation does not imply causation, a number of sources document a downturn in youth smoking after the implementation of the Truth campaign

Relative Effectiveness

Of course, we also need to examine what we mean by "success" in the context of a public health campaign. Social marketers face a number of obstacles in trying to get people to change their behaviors. There are several factors that inhibit the ability of these campaigns to change behavior, regardless of their appeal or the strength of the message.

These barriers are especially problematic when it comes to health behaviors. First, the results or improvements that come along with a behavior change may take a long time to manifest. Consider a campaign aimed at getting people to stop smoking. If you smoke, you should quit because smoking causes cancer and will eventually kill you. However, if you smoke and become short of breath when you

climb a set of stairs, that will not stop the day after you quit. It may take several weeks before you notice a difference in your cardiovascular health, and you may even feel worse for a period of time (jittery, overeating, etc.). Since quitting is difficult to begin with and the benefits might not be immediately visible, it might be difficult to retain this behavioral change.

Social marketers also need to deliver complex messages in a very short amount of time, at least in traditional media. Radio and television spot ads are usually 28 seconds in length, sometimes 58 seconds. How much information can you deliver in 28 seconds, particularly if it is a health threat or issue with which the listener is unfamiliar? If you need to offer resources for further information, how do you squeeze that into the space while still effectively motivating the audience to action?

Social Marketing Works When You Are (Kind of) Scared

A large body of research examining the effectiveness of social marketing has looked at fear appeals. This literature suggests that for any given health message, audiences must be adequately motivated to change their behavior, but not so scared as to respond in an antisocial manner, block out important factual content, or experience hopelessness and give up. High fear can be effective, but people need to feel that they can do something that will work. Social marketing using fear appeals is most effective when it also provides some sort of behavioral recommendation. In other words, now that we have your attention, here is what you should do next.

This also presents challenges for the social marketer. The right level of fear is an elusive concept, and this level is likely to vary from health outcome to health outcome. A great deal of research has explored the use of fear appeals in anti-smoking, HIV prevention, and anti-DUI campaigns, with a fair degree of success. There is also likely to be variability from person to person in terms of the level of fear they can handle. For instance, someone may be able to look at a picture of a car wreck stemming from a drunk driving incident, internalize the message, and consider their behaviors. But to the same person, a picture of a human lung, ridden with cancer from smoking, may cause repulsion and they then block out the rest of the message. Nevertheless, it seems as though every time a new health crisis raises its head, a new evaluation of the ideal levels of both fear and factual knowledge becomes necessary.

Social marketing is really effective at two outcomes, neither of which is converting the stubborn. First, we have research evidence that health campaigns and other social marketing campaigns are very effective at agenda setting (see Chapter 5). For many of us, there are societal ills or health threats that we learn about through social marketing. Had you heard of the HPV virus before seeing an ad advising women to get vaccinated? Were you aware of the synthetic drug called "bath salts" before seeing a campaign that mentioned it? Perhaps not. Social marketing campaigns are remarkably effective at raising awareness of previously unknown issues (see MC in Action: Bath Salts).

MC IN ACTION

BATH SALTS

On May 26, 2012, Rudy Eugene of Miami, Florida, committed a vicious assault on a homeless man that was captured on film. Eugene, who was naked at the time, held his victim in various chokeholds and wrestling positions, while biting off parts of the man's face. By the time all was said and done, Eugene had been shot by a Miami police officer, and his victim was left blind and severely disfigured.

The harrowing footage of this assault quickly went viral and became known as the "Miami Cannibal Attack." Shortly after the incident, Miami Police speculated that the synthetic drugs known as "bath salts" may have been involved, since Eugene's behavior was consistent with the violent, delusional behavior associated with its abuse. The drugs were, at the time, completely legal and available on the Internet. Though the toxicology report on Eugene actually failed to reveal evidence of the use of bath salts, the incident set off a nationwide interest in these drugs,

their addictiveness, and the consequences of their use.

Almost overnight, social marketing campaigns began appearing on billboards, television ads, and Web sites regarding bath salts and the risks associated with their use. Bath salts became a central concern in health programs and interventions conducted by health centers in high schools and colleges. As news agencies jumped on the story, it became clear that bath salts were linked to numerous unprovoked assaults across the country and that the drug was highly addictive and extremely dangerous. The event generated so much buzz that President Obama eventually signed the Synthetic Drug Abuse Prevention Act, which banned the legal sale of mephedrone (the key ingredient in bath salts) and numerous other synthetic drugs. While the reporting was graphic and rather disturbing, the viral nature of its distribution set off a larger conversation that eventually led to policy changes.

Once you know about a threat that you were previously unaware of, you might look for more information. Even if you are aware of the behavior in question, if you are seriously considering modifying your behavior you may want to look for more information on the first steps you should take. We also know that social marketing campaigns can accomplish this: providing leads through which those who are interested can find out more. Think about any PSA you have seen in the last 10 years; chances are it includes a link to a Web site or a reference to a Twitter handle. In modern social marketing, we are aware that we cannot convert those who are completely unwilling to be converted, and we may face tremendous obstacles in persuading people to change their behavior. But if a conversation can germinate and resources can be provided for those who are already thinking about adopting the behavior change, we can maybe make a difference.

This is where the Internet and social media come into play. For those already considering a behavior change, new media technologies provide resources for both information and support that can be actively consumed by the audience. Given the importance of self-efficacy in the persuasion process, it is likely that this person has already decided that they can quit smoking, get tested, or stop driving drunk. Now they need to know how and to feel as though they are not alone.

Narrowcasting for Those Interested

Although we know more about traditional media from an impact standpoint, there is some preliminary evidence that interactive media technologies can be fairly successful in shifting opinions toward health behaviors. As we saw with advertising in Chapter 10, social marketing in new media environments seems to work best when it is used alongside other outlets in some kind of multimedia campaign. Abrams, Schiavo, and Lefebvre (2008) reported that public health campaigns using varying types of social media typically use a standard Web site, organizational profiles on multiple social networking sites, and a blog or vlog. These new media elements are almost always combined with television and print advertising.

In some ways, this is not too different than integrated marketing and our earlier lessons concerning level of involvement, in that we may respond better to messages in different media depending on our interest in the matter at hand. If we are largely unaware of or ambivalent toward a particular issue, we will need to be informed or alerted to its existence. In this case, the agenda setting function discussed previously comes into play. We need to be reminded that this is something we should concern ourselves with before receiving directions on where to go next.

Most social marketing experts and researchers would agree that for most, this is where it ends. Cutting through the noise of our mediated world to draw attention to a specific or perhaps unknown behavior or health issue is very difficult, and those who will attend to this information may have contradictory attitudes. For example, a person with an unhealthy diet may recognize and devote attention to messages concerning heart disease, but if they are fully committed to their current diet, they will likely ignore the message. Worse, if their attitudes are polar enough, they may experience reactance and emotional stress and as result eat an entire box of donuts as part of an emotional control.

However, there is a small portion of the population that is both interested and already considering the changes that are being advocated. In this case, successful social marketing can use new media to inform and provide tangible, behavioral recommendations. Keep in mind that as we discussed earlier, self-efficacy is an important part of the persuasion process. It is unlikely that someone will follow the leads provided by traditional media and seek out additional information if they do not believe they can do it. If we can get people to use social media to obtain more information, we are already halfway there.

Social media sites and profiles may be able to provide individuals with both information concerning a health behavior and a sense of community. Take for example the "Quit Smoking Today" group on Facebook. This forum provides medical information, tips for those who want to quit, and detailed accounts of individuals' stories from those who have quit in the past. It also provides the chance for group members to post and to "like" the posts of others, thereby creating as organic sense of community. At this writing, this group has over 90,000 "likes" on Facebook. Someone redirected to this Facebook page would likely sense that they were part of a larger community of people who are facing the same challenges but are equally (if not more so) committed to the change. In this way, social proof (see Chapter 9) may also be a contributing factor, as the belief that many others are taking on a difficult challenge may make it more appealing.

Twitter feeds provide a similar opportunity for community building and providing opportunities for social reinforcement. A simple search for related hashtags will bring back an even wider range of microblog accounts of individual experiences, struggles, and hope. A search for the hashtags #quitsmokingnow or #stopsmoking brings back dozens of tweets from people making the same choices and, of course, the occasional spam tweet that hyperlinks to a Web page advertising a smoking cessation aid. Regardless, it provides another opportunity for those who are somewhat committed to obtain information and commiserate with others.

Inducing Fear, But Controlling Danger

As referenced in Chapter 9, one particularly popular method of campaigning for public health and safety issues is the use of fear appeals—messages intended to frighten or scare viewers enough to pay attention to a message and motivate them to take protective action against that fear. Specifically with health campaigns, fear appeal ads often contain gruesome images of the consequences of engaging in unhealthy behaviors, such as former smokers giving testimonials through synthesized voice boxes as the result of tracheotomy procedures or teenagers speaking about the dangers of texting while driving in reference to severely injured or deceased friends. The thought behind these messages is that inducing fear is a good way to get an individual's attention so that they will pay more careful attention to the message content (the central processing route reference in Chapter 9). However, evidence on fear appeal effectiveness had been mixed in research for decades—it seemed that campaigners and researchers were having difficulty finding the "sweet spot" of sorts as to how much fear to induce before it became counterproductive.

In the early 1990s, campaign researcher Kim Witte drafted an early version of her extended parallel process model that synthesized many earlier perspectives of fear-based campaigns to help identify the elements of an effective one. Her main contribution to the research was identifying the distinction between danger controls and fear controls. The argument is that when an individual is scared, this creates a high state of cognitive dissonance—a mismatch between one's beliefs and their actions—that requires attention. For example, a smoker who receives an anti-smoking campaign might experience dissonance from the fact that he or she is indeed a smoker (behavior), but is now scared about the long-term effects of their smoking as a lifestyle choice (belief). To reduce this unpleasurable dissonance, individuals have two choices: they can either stop the behavior (danger control) or change the negative feelings they now have about it (fear control). Campaign managers are often hoping for audiences to engage in danger controls, but all too often they engage in fear controls. Thus, we know that fear appeals can be a powerful method of getting audience attention and under some circumstances can result in real behavior change, but they are complicated and require more than mere fright. A good fear appeal also requires a call to action, and requires the target to feel that they can both do the action and that the action will work to help overcome the threat. Another theory related to fear appeals is the terror management theory (TMT; Greenberg, Pyszczynski, & Solomon, 1986). This theory

Extended parallel process model A model of persuasion common in social marketing that suggests that fear can be a motivating factor to behavior change, especially when people feel they can do the behavior and it will work.

Cognitive dissonance A mismatch between one's beliefs and one's actions.

Terror management theory A theory suggesting that the induction of fear of death can lead to compliance with health messages.

looks at a particular type of fear—the fear of death. TMT looks at how individuals cope with an increased sense of mortality salience, which can be difficult to both induce and control (MC in Action: The Only Thing to Fear Is Fear!).

Future of Campaigns

Some campaigns, such as the large-scale public health and safety campaigns mentioned in this chapter, may not be as overtly manipulative as traditional public relations or advertising efforts mentioned in Chapter 10. In fact, some research has suggested that a growing number of people do not trust PR practitioners. For example, in one public opinion study, not a single respondent gave PR practitioners "high marks" for honesty and ethical standards, and when asked about the most credible source for information, only 5 percent listed a PR officer (compared to 55 percent listing a company's CEO (see Judd, 1989 & Pratt, 1991). Finally, in a study of Public Relations Society of America (PRSA) members, top corporate managers were rated as more ethical than PR practitioners; that is, PR practitioners were indicating that they did not trust their own peers! Unfortunately, many of the campaigns mentioned in this chapter use the same PR practitioners listed above, and if public trust in PR is weakening, we might wonder if future public health and safety campaigns will suffer as a result.

To help address this issue, PR scholars David M. Dozier, Larissa A. Grunig, and James E. Grunig have introduced a new model called two-way symmetrical public relations.

First, symmetrical campaigns are delineated from asymmetrical campaigns. Two-way asymmetrical PR is what many people think of when they think about PR, and this might be a major reason why PR practitioners are not trusted. This model is the one introduced into the field largely by infamous PR innovator Edward Bernays in the beginning of the 20th century, and is often characterized by persuasion tactics that are customized using audience analysis data such as demographics and opinion surveys and polls. Many political campaigns can be characterized as two-way asymmetrical PR—candidates conduct public opinion polls to get quick data about an audience's beliefs and adapt their persuasive campaigns to win votes by speaking to those beliefs. Some might simply call this "good old fashioned" manipulation. In contrast, two-way symmetrical models utilize principles of negotiation and dispute resolution in order to come to solutions that are mutually beneficial to multiple stakeholders—what some might call a "win-win situation." The two-way symmetrical model advocates for engaging in a dialogue *with* an audience, rather than only talking *at* them, and working to gain a better understanding of the needs and concerns of each audience as an ongoing part of the campaign. Returning to a political example, one might consider the classic town hall meeting as an example of two-way symmetrical PR—from time to time, politicians will meet in person with large groups of their constituents in an open-question format, usually taking note of concerns expressed and working those concerns into their own policy initiatives.

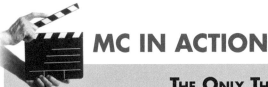

MC IN ACTION

THE ONLY THING TO FEAR IS FEAR!

One of the most difficult aspects of the persuasion process is capturing an individual's attention. Many individuals are resistant to persuasion when they recognize it, and as has been discussed already, it can be difficult for individuals to overcome their own heuristics in order to process a message carefully (of course, not all persuasion requires careful processing).

To combat this and attract attention, many advertisers and campaign managers have turned to using fear appeals to grab individuals' attention. The logic behind fear appeals suggests that frightening people should get them to pay attention to a message so that they can better protect themselves, as fear is a particularly strong motivator for human response.

But is fear enough? Communication and persuasion scholar Kim Witte developed the extended parallel processing model to suggest that merely scaring audiences is not in itself enough to suggest behavioral change. After all, fear might get us to pay attention to a message, but if a message scares us too much, we are just as likely to go into a state of fear control where we work to manage our emotions, for example, by discrediting the message or being repulsed by and then ignoring it. Such a campaign might be a memorable one, but likely does little to persuade us toward any sort of action.

Have you ever watched or listened to a fear campaign? If so, what was the campaign about, and where did you see or hear it? Did you think it was effective? Share your thoughts with us (with caution, of course) on Facebook at https://www.facebook.com/groups/234255823447372/ or on Twitter, using the #MediaAsTools hashtag.

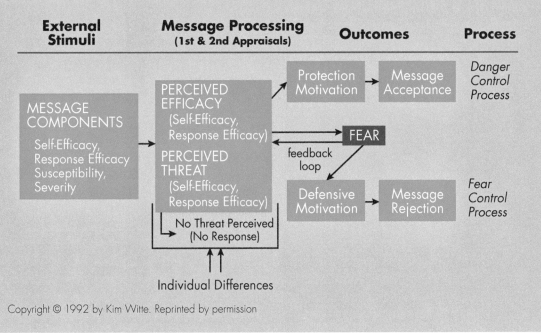

MC IN ACTION

THEY FORGOT TO ADD MOLD AS THE SECRET INGREDIENT!

In August and September of 2013, the prominent yogurt brand Chobani was having issues with their products. Reports came in from several places of yogurt containers expanding while sitting on store shelves (or in people's cupboards), and people opening containers of yogurt at home were finding discolored substances with a faint odor to them. On August 31, the company posted on their Facebook wall that their main concern is the quality of their products, and they were voluntarily removing and replacing some products that did not meet their quality standards.

For more information, please read here: http://cho.ba/17v8RMp

Almost immediately following the posting, a customer showed his displeasure at the statement's lack of precision—many customers were bothered that Chobani did not issue an official recall (which would have included manufacturing dates, serial numbers and shipping areas with affected product).

Following their statement, Chobani returned to normal marketing-type posts, including a September 1 post showing a picture of key lime yogurt and another post a few days later advertising a yogurt popsicle. Both of these posts garnered less-than-positive reactions from audience members.

Finally on September 5, a post was made (with a picture of the CEO and founder of Chobani) stating that Chobani wanted to apologize to its friends and customers, saying that if they had any Chobani products with the code 16-012, they should be discarded and to contact the Chobani Customer Loyalty Team for help at *http://chobani.com/care*.

This final apology post received 1,930 comments, of which most are positive.

What could Chobani have done differently and better, if anything? Or, did they handle this as well as could be expected? Share your thoughts with us (with caution, of course) on Facebook at https://www.facebook.com/groups/234255823447372/ or on Twitter, using the #MediaAsTools hashtag.

One benefit of using two-way symmetrical models is that they provide an avenue for alternate approaches when an initial approach fails—as the campaign is constantly evolving with audience feedback, practitioners are able to make adjustments and develop new approaches based on the feedback from an initial approach. Indeed, one of Bernays' greatest "successes" was convincing women to start smoking (a success for the tobacco industry, but likely not one celebrated by public health officials). At the time of this campaign (late 1920s), encouraging women to smoke was considered a social good, as it was seen as giving women the right to choose what they wanted to do (in general, women were discouraged from smoking in public at the time). However, as we have come to find out more about the negative health risks of smoking, most people would no longer consider this a social good. In fact, one might wonder if practitioners and those running campaigns always know what is best for a given public. Moreover, some even wonder if symmetrical campaigns always result in achieving goals. As Dozier,

Grunig, and Grunig (2001) pointed out, "The more righteous and noble sounding the reform, the more asymmetrical such campaigns are likely to become" (p. 242). This might be because campaigns that see themselves as more righteous are less likely to seek input from target audiences who are seen as in need of correction—the equivalent of a parent "knowing what's best" for their children.

Yet, two-way symmetrical models have proven useful. It seems as if engaging with an audience to hear what they have to say can be a very useful and important part of a campaign, and this is where communication technologies such as social media come into play. It is key that we keep in mind the fact that these are "social" media. Utilizing them in the same manner as other traditional mass communication channels (similar to two-way asymmetrical models) seems to go against what the audience expects and wants from social media (See MC in Action: They Forgot to Add Mold as the Secret Ingredient!). As has been mentioned before, Web 2.0 is a social place, and so campaign planners should recognize this and utilize it to their advantage. Thinking about two-way symmetrical models of campaigns can help with this, and using social media as social tools rather than marketing tools can go a long way in achieving this goal.

Conclusion

Of course, this all brings us back to integrated marketing, and to Abrams, Schiavo, and Lefebvre's (2008) observation that social media campaigns are universally done in conjunction with traditional media campaigns. Given the extra importance of self-efficacy in social marketing, perhaps it is the case that social media be reserved only for those who have already made up their mind to consider the behavior that is being advocated. Campaigns aimed at modifying behavior would be wise to use television and print to alert people to the issue and provide enough information to pique interest and then redirect them toward new media resources that can both inform and persuade. If and when the individuals they reach are both motivated and have time to search through the information and the personal accounts, social media is potentially a very useful and effective tool in advocating for healthy behavioral changes.

Key Terms

Social marketing (pg 170)
Ad Council (pg 170)
Extended parallel process model (pg 175)
Cognitive dissonance (pg 175)
Terror management theory (pg 175)
Mortality salience (pg 176)
Two-way symmetrical public relations (pg 176)

References

Abrams, L., Schiavo, R., & Lefebvre, C. (2008). New media cases. *Cases in Public Health Communication and Marketing, 11*, 3–10.

Dozier, D. M., Grunig, L. A., & Grunig, J. E. (2001). Public relations as communication campaign. In R. E. Rice and C. K. Atkin (Eds.), *Public communication campaigns* (3rd ed., pp. 231–248). Thousand Oaks, CA: Sage.

Greenberg, J., Pyszczynski, T., & Solomon, S. (1986). The causes and consequences of a need for self-esteem: A terror management theory. In R. F. Baumeister (Ed.), *Public self and private self* (pp. 189–212). New York: Springer-Verlag.

Judd, L. R. (1989). Credibility, public relations and social responsibility. *Public Relations Review, 15*, 34–40.

Pratt, C. B. (1991). Public relations: The empirical research on practitioner ethics. *Journal of Business Ethics. 10*(3), 229–236.

Rice, R. E., & Atkin, C. K. (2013). *Public communication campaigns* (4th ed.). Los Angeles: Sage.

Sharpsteen, B. (1942). *Out of the frying pan, into the firing line*. [Motion picture short]. USA: Disney.

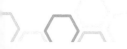

CHAPTER 12

Entertainment in the Digital Age

It is Friday night. It has been a long week at school, but now you finally have a chance to relax. All you want to do is sit down on the couch and watch a movie.

If this was 1995, you probably would have hopped in the car and driven down to a local movie rental store. You would have walked in, checked out what they still had left on the shelves (Friday nights usually left one with very few options), picked up a VHS cassette, brought it home, popped it into your VCR (assuming the last person who used the video rewound the cassette properly and that your VCR heads had been cleaned recently to properly read the magnetic tape from the cassette), and sat back and watched the movie you just rented.

How many of you would do this today? How many of you have ever done this? Today, a quick visit an online streaming video service such as Amazon Prime, Hulu, or Netflix has you sampling from thousands of films and television shows, ready to be viewed within seconds and without the need to rewind or clean—even viewing from your mobile phone (as the authors of this book have done several times when traveling, and we promise never during faculty meetings). The technology has allowed for entertainment that is truly on-demand: wherever and whenever you want it.

In the past, media audiences have been conceptualized as passive receivers of static content. Yet, as media technology has become increasingly interactive, our understanding of the audience has shifted from one of passivity

to one of agency. As early as the 1960s, media critic Marshall McLuhan (1964) distinguished between hot media (those media that require our active engagement and attention; also called "lean forward" media) and cool media (those media that allow us to relax and disengage; also called "lean back" media). But as we have discussed throughout this text, media is no longer viewed, but rather it is used and participated in. Media is a tool used by individuals to accomplish goals, and in the following chapters, we will talk about one of the most popular, economically successful, and controversial areas of media use: entertainment. In particular, Chapter 12 will define the notion of entertainment, and Chapter 13 will explore in more detail the uses and effects of entertainment media.

> Questions to consider when reading this chapter:

- What is entertainment? Is entertainment more than just enjoyment?
- How did entertainment come to be so important to society?
- What is digitization, and why is it important to understanding how media is used?
- How did file sharing challenge our understanding of intellectual property?
- Has on-demand content altered our expectations about delivery? If so, how?

What Is Entertainment?

As a concept, media entertainment is surprisingly difficult to define. At the most basic level, entertainment is a media effect that is characterized by positive thoughts and feelings. To be entertained is to feel genuinely and generally good about an experience, all things considered. Clapping at the conclusion of a Broadway musical, cheering at the end of an action-packed Hollywood blockbuster, or even nodding your head to the beats of the latest Top 40 single streaming through your laptop are all examples of common entertainment media experiences. Each of these can best be classified as hedonic experiences—they are immediately positive and pleasant. Such experiences are typically understood as enjoyment reactions to entertainment media, the sort of "man, that was fun" reaction we often think about when we are being entertained: it is fun to laugh at a cartoon, or to beat our favorite video game, or to listen to a good song.

Indeed, enjoyment from media entertainment is one of the most compelling reasons that we engage it. Movies and video games allow us to escape reality for a few hours at a time, letting us forget any troubles or stress and involve ourselves in a fantasy story (compare Sherry, Lucas, Greenberg, & Lachlan, 2008, for a discussion of this in respect to video games). Such activities can be important to relieve stress and help us feel revitalized and energized toward work and other organized activities. In fact, media psychologist Leonard Reinecke and his colleagues (e.g., Reinecke, 2009) have conducted several studies showing that video game play can result in stress release and increased productivity at work—so not only do we feel

Hot media Those media that require our active engagement and attention in order to be used.

Cool media Those media that can be used without active engagement and attention.

Media effect Something that happens as a result of using media. Effects can usually be understood as being cognitive (influencing our thoughts), affective (influencing our feelings), or behavioral (influencing our behaviors).

Hedonic/hedonism A "pleasure of the flesh" usually characterized by immediate positive feelings.

Enjoyment An entertainment media effect characterized by hedonic reactions to content.

better after playing games, but we also work harder! Fun and play have also been suggested as important elements of human development, particularly for children who often learn the very basics of decision-making and abstract thought when engaging their peers on the playground or at the city park (covered in a recent *New York Times* article: http://www.nytimes.com/2013/04/23/science/zeal-for-play-may-have-propelled-human-evolution.html?smid=tw-share&_r=3&).

Of course, one might question whether or not all entertainment experiences are enjoyable. For example, movies such as *Schindler's List* (Universal Pictures, 1993), *The Boy in the Striped Pajamas* (Miramax Films, 2008), and *Requiem for a Dream* (Artisan Entertainment, 2000) are gripping tales of humanity that often cause a wide range of emotional experiences within audiences members, and the film noir (roughly, "dark film" in French) movement of the 1940s was specifically and critically noted for its reliance on creating intense negative emotions in audience members—stress, fear, and suspense among them. Any fan of Alfred Hitchcock can relate to the intense anxiety that films such as *The Birds* (Universal Pictures, 1963), *Psycho* (Paramount Pictures, 1960), and *Rear Window* (Paramount Pictures, 1954) brought about in the audience (see MC in Action: Terrified Actors Make Terrified Audiences). Television docudramas, sad love songs, and even newer forms of video games (such as the *Final Fantasy* series and the critically acclaimed *Heavy Rain*) have all been especially noted for their ability to cause a number of emotional reactions in audience members—many of which seem conceptually opposite of enjoyment (Oliver, 2006). Indeed, the earliest forms of Greek drama were classified simply as comedy or tragedy, with the genres distinguishable as much by an audience's responses of laughter and sorrow as they are by the content inherent to each.

Why would audiences want to have these more somber experiences? Communication scholars Mary Beth Oliver and Art Raney (2011) argued that these emotions cultivate a sense of self-reflection in audience members—a eudaimonic experience by which we contemplate our humanity and ourselves. These effects lead to more meaningful media experiences that allow us to cope with aspects of our personal and social lives, beyond merely distracting us from boredom or making us laugh. That is, they result in a greater appreciation for the social world around us. For example, a spouse dealing with the death of his or her partner in a war might find similar stories about coping with death and war to be useful in making sense of his or her situation. It may also be the case that the experience of tragedy makes audiences reflect upon their emotional responses, and under less dire circumstances experience some degree of gratification from the knowledge that they were able to have an emotional reaction (Oliver, Weaver, & Sargent, 2000). In fact, such logic might explain how media users can experience pro-social results from decidedly antisocial media content—a phenomenon that will be discussed in Chapter 13.

Does this mean that video games can be considered on par with famous Greek tragedy? Possibly. Although in Chapter 13 we will present a few specific examples of video games that are far more serious than they are fun (such as the critically acclaimed third-person shooter-cum-war commentary that was *Spec Ops: The Line*), we can also highlight recent research by the aforementioned Oliver and colleagues (2015) that was among the first to attempt to quantify the prevalence of appreciation among video game players. They found that while nearly all

Eudaimonic/ eudaimonia
A "pleasure of the mind" usually characterized by deliberation and insightfulness.

Appreciation An entertainment media effect characterized by eudaimonic reactions to content.

MC IN ACTION

TERRIFIED ACTORS MAKE TERRIFIED AUDIENCES

No doubt even the casual movie-goer is familiar with the name Sir Alfred Hitchcock. Perhaps the most critically acclaimed director of the film noir movement of the 1940s, the British-born director developed many modern film editing techniques meant to create anxiety in the audience members and involve them in the space of the film itself with first-person camera perspectives that seemed to mimic a person's gaze. For many Hitchcock fans, watching one of his films feels almost voyeuristic —one often feels as if one is spying on the trials and tribulations of unassuming others (often facing some sort of immediate danger). A great example of his methods can be found in the film *Rear Window* (1954) in which a disabled Jefferies (Jimmy Stewart) is forced to watch through his high-powered camera lens the potential assault on his lover Lisa Fremont (Grace Kelly) while she snoops around his neighbor's apartment to find evidence of a potential murder. In one particular scene, the camera switches between third-person close-ups of Jefferies' facial expressions of fear and helplessness and first-person angles of Fremont through Jefferies' camera lens—or rather, Fremont in one frame of the shot and a shadowy figure in the other.

However, in at least one instance it was not only the audience that was terrified by the film experience, but the actors themselves. In a bit of Hollywood lore, during the filming of *The Birds* (1963) Hitchcock was attempting to get more genuine fright reactions from his leading actress Tippi Hedren. In a pivotal scene, Hedren's character Melanie Daniels is attacked by a menacing flock of wild birds as an ambiguous and ominous warning (we do not wish to spoil the movie for you, so go watch it). In filming the scene, Hitchcock ordered his staff of bird handlers to don heavy protective gear . . . and hurl the live birds directly at Hedren while on set! It was widely reported that after several minutes of filming Hedren appeared visibly shaken and scared by the birds, one of which had cut her eyelid so deeply that there were fears that she had suffered actual damage to her eye; she was eventually removed from the set in tears. Although she was awarded a Golden Globe for her performance in the film, one might wonder if she was acting or if she was genuinely frightened by the birds.

Voyeuristic/voyeurism Watching intimate events between people from a distance.

gamers surveyed were able to report on their "most enjoyable video game experience" when prompted, a surprisingly 72 percent (nearly three-fourths) were also able to report and recall a "most meaningful video game experience." In fact, follow-up analyses found that while many of the same games appear in both recollections, it was the player's evaluation of more specific elements of those games that mattered most: enjoyment was a feature of evaluations of gameplay mechanics, while appreciation was a feature of evaluations of game narrative. Their study was featured in Reddit.com's Ask Me Anything series—an online forum organized by the /r/science sub-reddit that invites Reddit users to directly ask researchers questions about studies of particular interest—and a discussion with the study authors (both Oliver and Nick Bowman, one of the authors of this textbook) has been archived at https://www.reddit.com/r/science/comments/340qvj/science_ama_series_we_are_dr_mary_beth_oliver/.

It is important to understand entertainment as both enjoyable and meaningful, because this speaks to the many goals that we all have for using media. Just as we have argued for the strategic use of media to help us find information, form relationships, and engage in persuasion (either as the persuader or the persuaded) throughout this book, the experience of being entertained is also a purposive and goal-driven pursuit that is part of our daily social lives.

History of (Mediated) Entertainment
The end of labor is to gain leisure.

~Aristotle

The relationship between entertainment and society is a compelling one. Although it might be easy to assume that entertainment and leisure activities are frivolous (especially if we only focus on enjoyment and fun), much research has suggested entertainment—both fun and meaningful—to be an important aspect of advances in entertainment that can be linked to advances in social organization. Tracing back the social evolution of humans, media psychologists Dolf Zillmann and Peter Vorderer (2001) suggested that some of the earliest forms of leisure activity such as ritual ceremonies and organized meals can be connected with advances in hunting technology (such as tracking animal herds, developing weapons to kill more efficiently, and organizing hunting and gathering roles for different members of a tribe) as well as the use of fire in preparing food (cooking meat), illumination (allowing early humans to function after sunset), and safety (as a weapon or protective barrier). Their argument is that prior to these early innovations, life was little more than a constant perilous pursuit of sustenance. That is, early humans had little time to ponder life as they were far too busy surviving it.

However, as these earliest technologies made life comparatively easier to live, humans found themselves with time on their hands that did not have to be devoted to satisfying survival and security needs (see Maslow, Chapter 3). Some of the earliest forms of musical instruments—primarily animal-skin drums and carved bone flutes—have been dated to the Neolithic Era (commonly referred to as the New Stone Age, a time spanning from BCE 10,200 to BCE 2000). What is so compelling about the world's oldest drum set? These were the first tools discovered by explorers and scientists that had no immediate and functional survival purpose. That is, they were not tools for hunting or shelter, but rather tools for creating sound. For a species to advance to the point in which it can devote both time and scarce resources to something as seemingly frivolous as music suggests it to have been a culturally significant experience. Harkening back to Aristotle's quote as well as his thoughts on eudaimonia as those activities that are good for the (human) spirit (covered extensively in his *Nicomachean Ethics*), we see here a birth of what we might think of as modern humanity—a celebration of our social lives rather than just our survival. To early humans, music was such an important part of their society that they devoted time and resources away from hunting in order to celebrate their accomplishments and, over time, study their futures. Such activities were likely pleasurable and fun, but they also spoke to a newfound spiritual meaningfulness. More evidence of this dedication of resources to leisure and celebration can be found in the Altamira cave paintings in Cantabria, Spain (see MC in Action: That's No Bull, It's Our Deity!). These paintings, having been dated back to BC 40,000, are perhaps the most concrete representation of the culture of our prehistoric ancestors.

From these early ritual practices and leisure activities, we can trace the development of more modern-style entertainment practices. While art and music still occupy prominent roles in our entertainment environment, we now have myriad ways to express our culture and society. Hollywood movies highlight important social lessons, but they also give us something to cheer and jeer. Video games are an increasingly sophisticated form of entertainment with roots in chess and checkers (basically, games of challenge and skill) that are fast evolving into complex narrative devices to tell stories in which the audience is placed inside the world of the game itself (such as was found by Oliver et al., 2015). Even much of the user-generated content of social media platforms seems to span both enjoyment and appreciation-based content. In all of these, we see both enjoyment and appreciation playing important roles in entertainment and advances in communication technology allowing for both to happen.

Digitization and New Media

Perhaps, the most distinguishing feature that differentiates old from new media is the role of digitization—hence the name Digital Age. Older, more traditional forms of media were reliant on physical media in order to retain and transmit content. These analog media—such as vinyl records, movie reels, and printed newspaper—are expensive to produce, and their quality degrades over time (see MC in Action: The Production of a Vinyl Record). An analog medium usually required

Digital Age An age of mass media characterized by using digital methods for message creation and transmission.

Analog A storage medium that uses a physical device to store information for retrieval.

MC IN ACTION

THAT'S NO BULL, IT'S OUR DEITY!

On an afternoon excursion in 1876 with his daughter Maria, amateur archeologist Marcelino Sanz de Sautuola was exploring a series of caves on his land when the duo discovered perhaps one of the most important relics of ancient humans. In the cave, named Altamira ("high view"), they saw by the flickering of their lanterns what seemed to be an outline of horned animals on the cave ceiling. Looking closer, paintings of deer, bison, and other game animals were found covering the walls and ceiling, leading many to refer to the site as the "Sistine Chapel of Prehistoric Art." In fact, the quality of the artwork and the preservation—the latter likely the result of having been unmolested in a semi-sealed cave for nearly 40 millennia—led some to claim the works as a forgery, although the scientific community eventually came to recognize the authenticity of the works. In September 1940, a similar discovery was made in the Lascaux Cave of central France, when a group of teenagers stumbled into a small cave that contained vivid images of horses, stags, and cattle—as well as a few humans. One of the largest paintings in this cave can be found in The Great Hall of Bulls, a 17-foot image of a bull charging.

Besides being very neat paintings, these findings can tell us a great deal about early humans. Recall from Chapter 5 the normative functions of media according to Harold Lasswell. Beyond the surveillance and correlation roles of media, Lasswell also saw media messages as a powerful method of transmitting cultural heritage—literally,

teaching us about ourselves. While several interpretations of these cave paintings exist, leading theories suggest that the images represented rituals associated with hunting as well as chronicles of past hunting successes. Others have also acknowledged the strategic placement of the images appear to line up with major constellations (suggesting a form of celestial worship and viewing the animals as deities), and some have further argued that the images might have been the result of hallucinations brought on by ritual trance-dancing (explained by the overlap of abstract images on the animals themselves).

As a whole, it is clear that the images were a substantial part of the prehistoric culture of the region. Particularly in the French cave, there is other evidence to bear out this conclusion: tiny rear end-shaped divots in the hardened mud and rock suggest the presence of students, who might have gazed upon the fantastic paintings while a village elder regaled them with tales of the hunt, the stars, and the village ancestors. Here, the past and current uses of the cave paintings would have been the same—to preserve and share cultural heritage.

Ancient artwork found in the Altamira cave.

dedicated equipment in order to be used, and storing the product is a cumbersome and consuming process. In contrast, digital technologies (see Chapter 1) overcome many of these limitations due to their lack of a physical medium. Their ephemerality allows them to "exist" in small spaces, to be translated across different formats, and allows them to be accessed from anywhere a network connection can be found. While these changes are not restricted to entertainment media, we can turn to entertainment to see several examples as to how digital technology has made it possible for us to have fun and meaningful interactions in a variety of spaces and ways. Specifically, we can look at a framework of the Three Cs borrowed from media scholars Jennings Bryant and his colleagues (compare, Bryant, Thompson, & Finklea, 2012).

Digital A storage medium that encodes information in binary code to be decoded upon request by a computer processor.

Ephemerality (ephemera) The concept of objects being transitory, or existing only briefly.

Compression

The amount of information that one person can remember is astounding. It has been estimated that the human brain can store between 500 and 1000 terabytes of information. Consider that your average laptop computer can store around 250 gigabytes (as of 2013 . . . so we are positive that this size is grown by the time you read this sentence), so the human brain can store about 400,000 times as much information as your laptop—but this gap is closing at a faster and faster rate. Traditionally, libraries were the foci of information storage and retrieval for societies, as these buildings served as cultural, relational, informational, and entertainment warehouses for our analog medium. Indeed, the destruction of the Library of Alexandria in Egypt was thought to have destroyed nearly all the collected knowledge of our world at the time. Even on the smaller scale, collectors of books and music have often been restricted by the number of items they can physically store—in terms of space, analog media are greedy.

Moore's law From computer science, a prediction that advances in technology allow for more and more digital information to be stored in smaller spaces.

Yet, Moore's law predicts that the capacity of the typical computer microprocessor is expected to double approximately every 18 months. This law, really more of a commentary on Moore's views of the digital revolution than a scientific theory, is compelling. Today, it is not uncommon for the typical college student to carry the entire contents of a library collection on a standard USB data drive with enough memory left over for videos, photos, and music. Digital technology has allowed us to store more information in smaller places.

Conversion

Digital technology has allowed us to transfer information between and throughout data networks with few encumbrances or barriers to access. The earliest forms of media were stored on physical devices and required a special device in order to use them. A good example of this would be music, which was traditionally stored on wax cylinders, then vinyl records, then magnetic tape, and finally pitted laser

MC IN ACTION

THE PRODUCTION OF A VINYL RECORD

In 2011, *The Economist* magazine reported that vinyl record sales were up nearly 400 percent from the same point in 2001, with an estimated four million "33s" being pressed and sold to market by contemporary artists. In 2016, *AdWeek* reported that vinyl sales had increased every year for 10 straight years, with 12 million total units sold in 2015, accounting for 24% of all music revenue. And these numbers did not include any sales for vintage records, which can often be found in garage sales, antique stores, and on eBay for anywhere from a few cents to a few thousand dollars for rare cuts. It seems that reports on the death of vinyl (e.g., Rogers, 2003) have been greatly exaggerated.

The vinyl record is perhaps the best example of analog technology we can think of. If you run your fingers across these records, you will feel a series of pits and grooves on the record's surface. These grooves are near-exact replicas from a "master cut"—a metal-coated lacquer disk that has physical grooves and pits cut into it from a vibrating stylus (needle). The stylus vibrates in reaction to sound waves from the artist's music (usually prerecorded and transmitted electronically, although early recording devices required artists to play music directly into a device that would hold a vibrating stylus). In short, the pits and grooves you are feeling with your fingers are physical representations of sound waves—look at them under a microscope, and they almost look like what you might imagine a wave of sound to look like!

Of course, like any analog technology, vinyl records have their limitations. First, they are remarkably more expensive to produce than digitally pressing CDs. Second, their sound quality can degrade with usage. To play a record, you must place it on a turntable and spin it (full albums generally spun at 33⅓ revolutions per minute, hence the nickname "33s") under a needle that produces vibrations as it traces the pits and grooves of the record. Over time, this needle will wear out the record . . . or worse, you can scratch a vinyl record if you are not careful. Third, vinyl records are large—usually 16 inches in diameter—which makes them difficult to store and transport.

So, why such a resurgence in old technology? Besides the famous (or infamous) album art and artist information printed on classic vinyl "jackets" (the cardboard holders for the records themselves), many music aficionados argue that the analog sound is much smoother and warmer than digital sound because vinyl records are physical reproductions of an artist's sound waves. In contrast, digital reproductions require sound engineers to digitally compress sound waves into a series of "on" and "off" commands for a computer—as you cannot make a curve with straight lines, digital sound can sometimes sound muffled to trained musical ears. Thus, purists argue that analog sound quality is far superior . . . so long as you do not scratch the record!

© mike mols/Shutterstock.com

discs. In each case, a special device is needed to access the information stored on the different media (in order, an Edison phonograph, a record player, a tape deck, and a compact disc player). An infamous example of this can be found in a scene from *Austin Powers: Man of Mystery* (New Line Cinema, 1997) which shows Austin Powers (Mike Myers) attempting to play a compact disc on an old record machine and cringing at the cacophony of sound resulting from the noncompatibility between medium and device.

While not a problem limited to analog media—indeed different digital files can contain lines of programming code that make them incompatible with certain devices, such as the .m4p format used by Apple's popular iTunes programs—the use of digital files has allowed for greater conversion of data from one device to the next. Regardless of manufacturer or components, computers speak a universal binary language that facilitates the sharing of information across devices.

Binary The language of computing technology; this is the storing of information in electrical circuits using a series of "1" and "0" commands to represent "on" or "off."

Convergence

Digital technology has allowed us to access several forms of media from the same device in the same space and at the same time. Consider the many different devices mentioned previously to listen to music, and couple this with a separate device for making a telephone call, watching television, and finally reading a book or newspaper (perhaps separate printed media for each). One can quickly see that a proliferation of media content in the analog system leads to a proliferation of devices to play this content—an impractical and inconvenient system for the modern consumer. In stark contrast is Apple's iPad tablet computer. Weighing less than 1.5 pounds and with dimensions slightly smaller than a standard 80-page legal notepad, the newest generation of iPad comes equipped with a high-definition video display, onboard stereo speakers, an integrated video camera with microphone, Bluetooth and high-speed Wi-Fi antennas, and a touch-sensitive display. By having so many different options on one device, iPad users are able to access text, audio, and video that is stored on the device's onboard memory (as much as 64 GB) or accessed through a network connection. In a sense, the iPad can replace one's need for printed books and newspapers, a radio receiver, and a television set—and with newer technologies focusing on VoIP telephony, even the telephone is no longer required of iPad users. Consumer demand for converged technology such as the iPad has not slowed, with over 84.1 million units selling in the period April 2010 to March 2012, despite price tags that consistently hover around the USD $500 point (in contrast, an entry-level desktop computer could be bought in most department stores for as little as USD $200 during the same time period). While Apple did not invent the so-called "tablet PC" (indeed, Microsoft revealed a similar technology as far back as 2002), the company has been successful at introducing this example of converged technology at a mass level in the form of their popular iPad. Computing has become so inexpensive that the economic barriers to ownership continue to shrink (see MC in Action: One Laptop per Child), as discussed in Chapter 4.

MC IN ACTION

ONE LAPTOP PER CHILD

As a general principle of the economics of innovation, the longer and more widespread a product's adoption time frame is, the cheaper that technology becomes to produce and market. For computer scientist Nicholas Negroponte, the trajectory of laptop and tablet computing—as with many of the innovations before it, marked by rapid technological advancement and decreasing pricing—inspired his vision for One Laptop per Child, a nonprofit charity founded in January 2005 with the expressed goal of bringing computing technology to children around the world. We've already covered the notion of the digital divide earlier in Chapter 4, so you might recognize the concept here also.

Negroponte was specifically interested in closing learning gaps between the world's wealthiest and poorest nations, and felt strongly that they could be closed by providing children with cheap access to a fun and innovative computers such as the bright-green and great OLPC XO. Dubbed the "$100 laptop" to match his vision for a cheap-yet-powerful computer for remote regions, the earliest machines used flash memory and USB ports for external memory, and included on-board microphones and camera technologies. They even have a novel wireless technology that allowed several computers to broadcast and share a single Internet connection, and newer models have touchscreen capability and other tablet features, similar to an iPad. The machines were also programmed to run off of a fraction of the energy of a standard laptop, and could be charged and powered using both solar energy and even a hand-operated crank. When asked how the OLPC machines compare to more expensive laptops, Negroponte responded that although the processing power and speed of his machines was much slower, "the XO's screen can be viewed as clearly as a newspaper in broad daylight, and the wireless range of the XO is several times longer than your average laptop. It's also more rugged, resilient and power efficient than most other laptops on the market."

According to OLPC, more than three million of their laptops have been shipped around the world. However, current pricing of their laptops (a floating price, but hovering around the $200 mark as of early 2016) has yet to break below Negroponte's visionary $100 cost.

You can read more about the One Laptop per Child movement at http://one.laptop.org/.

Digital Entertainment and Interactivity

These principles of compression, conversion, and convergence have had drastic influences on the entertainment industry. Perhaps, one of the most significant is that the digitization of media has allowed for a renewed focus on interactivity—being able to involve the user in the media content by allowing them to alter the form and content of the information itself.

Interactivity The degree to which a user can influence the form and content of on-screen content.

The role of interactivity in digital media cannot be overstated. As alluded to in the introduction of this chapter, a primary distinction between older and newer media is our ability to manipulate the form and content of the latter. Interactivity allows us a level of control over the content we consume, which is thought to lead to a more engaging experience. At the same time, increased interactivity can also place a higher level of task demand on the user in order to interact successfully with technology, which might turn some users off from trying new technologies that require skills they do not possess. For example, many people have a hard time enjoying the latest video game technologies for the same reason that many people enjoy them: the technologies allow the player to do whatever they want, but this freedom comes with the necessity of not just sitting back, relaxing, and being entertained. You have to actively take part in the entertainment experience when the medium is highly interactive. Moreover, these task demands are more than just skill challenges, as they can also place demands on the user's emotional or even social resources (see MC in Action: Video Games Demand Your Attention). This being said, interactive technologies are remarkably popular because they allow us to accomplish goals that we could not otherwise—at least one of your book's authors is particularly proud of his skateboarding ability in Tony Hawk Pro Skater while also willing to admit a much lower competency on a physical skateboard (with scars on his knees to corroborate this story).

Interactivity and Entertainment

In a similar vein, consider the manner in which we engage in entertainment narratives. Written narratives such as books, fables, and poems (even movie scripts and song lyrics) are often presented in a linear fashion wherein the reader's role is relegated to that of a spectator—the narrator takes the reader from introduction through climax to a narrative conclusion. In such settings, the audience member can take a passive role in consuming the narrative and trust that the narrator will guide them through the linear process.

However, imagine trying to passively use a video game. You boot up your video game console or computer system and launch your favorite game: for these authors, we will refer to the Konami classic side-scrolling platform shooter *Contra*. You dust off the cartridge and load it into your console and the start screen launches. A quick blurb about a war in the jungle leads to a start screen, and you are thrust into the role of a soldier of fortune—placed in control of the soldier's feet and trigger finger as the screen begins to scroll right. Inaction from the human player results in inaction on screen, as video games demand input from the user in order to progress the game screen and, relatedly, the story.

Why is this distinction important? It suggests a shift in the role of the individual from one of passivity to one of activity, of witnessing action to being the reason action happens. Interactive entertainment allows for users to co-create experiences with media producers, which is thought to result in a more engaging and individualized (albeit more cognitively demanding) experience. In fact, in newer video games it is the player rather than the producers who decide how each story will unfold (see MC in Action: Choosing My Own Adventure).

Research has tried to better understand the role of interactivity and entertainment. Although discussed in more detail in Chapter 13 in terms of media uses and effects, the notion of telepresence (Bracken & Skalski, 2009; see also Chapter 7) can be applied here. Giving users control over on-screen action helps them feel more involved in the actual environment by giving them a sense of nonmediation (Lombard & Ditton, 1997); that is, they feel closer to the on-screen action because

MC IN ACTION

VIDEO GAMES DEMAND YOUR ATTENTION

As an interactive technology, video games are among one of the most attentionally demanding media available to entertainment audiences. From solving puzzles to feeling puzzled while navigating perplexing control systems and ever more peculiar on-screen personae, Bowman (2016) explained four possible ways in which video games might be particularly demanding on users:

- Cognitive demand, which refers to the mental faculties that are required to understand and solve a game's challenges. Games such as *Super Mario Bros.* might be considered less mentally complex at earlier levels (and older versions).

- Emotional demand, which refers to the affective faculties associated with immersing oneself in and responding to a game's narrative. The emotional attachment that one has to their falling Tetris is rather low when compared to the main character of a role-playing game such as *The Legend of Zelda* or *Final Fantasy* (any one of them!).

- Physical demand, which refers to the physical faculties required to play a video game by way of different game controllers. While a computer mouse might have low physical demand, a *Guitar Hero* controller would be considerably more physically demanding.

- Social demand, which refers to the interpersonal and relational aspects of gaming. Many games either encourage the player to form a relationship with their on-screen avatar (again, similar to Banks' research from Chapter 6) or encourage gamers to connect with others.

Of course, not all games tax all four of these demand categories equally—Oliver and colleagues' research (2015) suggests that more enjoyable games might place greater focus on cognitive and physical demand, while more appreciated games might place greater focus on emotional and social demand. However, understanding the different types of demands stemming from interactive media might help both designers and researchers better understand the experiences players have while engaging them.

Can you think of any experiences playing video games that might fit well into one or more of these categories? Are there others that are not included in the list above? Share your thoughts and experiences with our official Facebook group at https://www.facebook.com/groups/234255823447372/, or with our many Twitter users, following the #MediaAsTools hashtag.

they forget that they are not actually in the virtual space. Of course, the user usually "knows" that they are playing a video game, but during the experience they are focused in the virtual environment presented on-screen rather than the physical environment in which they are sitting or standing. Although traditional media can also instill a sense of presence—anyone who has even found themselves lost in a book can attest to this—the interactivity afforded by digital technology is maybe better able to help players immerse their perceptual senses in an (albeit virtual) environment. Newer virtual reality technologies represent the pinnacle of

Virtual reality Technologies that simulate physical presence in virtual spaces.

MC IN ACTION

CHOOSING MY OWN ADVENTURE

Sandbox/sandbox video games A type of video game that allows players to progress through different points in the game environment in a nonlinear fashion and allows players to solve in-game challenges in a number of different ways.

Parkour/parkour gaming A type of video game play common to sandbox video games in which players walk around and travel in the virtual space of the video game without focusing on in-game goals and challenges.

Early video games placed the video game character on the left side of the screen and presented him or her with a series of challenges as they moved from left to right—usually avoiding enemy characters while jumping and ducking over different hazards. Perhaps best epitomized in the original *Super Mario Bros.* (Nintendo Entertainment System, 1984), most of us (at least, the three authors of this book) can remember running across eight different game worlds, stomping on turtle shells, and eventually finding Princess Toadstool was in another castle. While the player still had to navigate each world successfully in order to complete the game, there were few options: "A" was for jump and "B" was for run, and the only way to move was "to the right side of the screen."

Fast-forward to today's games, and players are given an enormous number of options in accomplishing in-game objectives or even creating their own objectives. This sandbox style of video game design was popularized by the controversial release of *Grand Theft Auto 3* (although earlier versions of the game also contained nonlinear storylines), which placed players in the role of Liberty City mobster Tommy Vercetti, assigned with achieving any number of tasks for the mob (among other unsavory individuals). Not only could players choose when and how to accomplish the game's numerous missions, but they could also choose their own in-game goals—such as finding different hidden game tokens and other hidden objects or just exploring the game's sprawling urban environment in a parkour style. On this latter point, some gamers even took to posting their in-game parkour videos on YouTube and other social media sites.

telepresence, as they wrap users in technologies such as headsets and hand controllers and sensors that allow us to see first-person perspectives while simulating the touch and feel of any number of virtual spaces. Imagine watching a Hitchcock film such as *The Birds* and having savage animals streaking toward you as you dive out of the way, perhaps "picking up" items such as a table to protect yourself or a shovel or rake to defend yourself (if you are near a garden shed)—certainly this represents very high levels of control over the form and content of on-screen actions. Additionally, this notion of something having to be "on-screen" might also be challenged, as recent developments such as Google Glass (see Chapter 1) have introduced the notion of augmented reality in which digital information and objects are overlaid in physical spaces, essentially turning your real world into one full of virtual objects.

Copyright Law in the Digital Age

As interactivity blurs the lines between media consumers and producers and makes you part of the creation of entertainment, there is an associated legal blurring of the rules and norms of content sharing – that is, media users sharing content to which they are not legally entitled. Web platforms such as the video hosting service YouTube find themselves conflicted. On the one hand, it encourages users to "Broadcast [Themselves]" by creating unique and personalized video footage for public consumption, but on the other hand it also must limit the usage and access to audio and video content owned by media companies. An example is: A teenager in Boston who is a fan of the popular animated serial *Family Guy* wants to put together a compilation video of his top 10 favorite jokes set to his favorite Justin Bieber song. So, who owns the video? Legal experts might suggest that FOX Broadcasting Company owns the *Family Guy* clips and Raymond Braun Media Group owns Justin Bieber's record catalog, and our Boston teenager is in danger of committing several copyright violations by distributing content that he does not own without acknowledging the original copyright holders. In fact, YouTube often will remove such videos at the request of copyright holders who feel that their content is being distributed without permission.

Perhaps, the most infamous example of issues of Internet copyright law comes from the file-sharing service LimeWire. Launched in 2000, LimeWire was a peer-to-peer file sharing service that allowed computer users around the globe to swap several types of computer files with one another through dedicated Web connections. The technology allowed computer users to share large files that could not be sent through e-mail, because any one user could download smaller bits of a file from several different other users—in this way "sharing" the file size and reconstructing it on any one individual's computer. Almost from its inception, many users found the peer-to-peer system of sharing particularly useful for distributing copies of songs and movies recorded from primary sources, such as one user burning the tracks from a CD or a DVD to their computer; as well, large and expensive computer programs could also be shared through these networks. Users of the network contended that they had already purchased the content from copyright holders and were free to distribute it as they wished, while media producers countered that purchasing a media product (such as a CD) only allowed for personal and private usage. Years of legal wrangling finally resulted in a court case pitting LimeWire against the Recording Industry Association of America, a group representing music copyright holders, who sought and eventually gained an injunction against LimeWire to disable the "searching, downloading, uploading, file trading and/or file distribution functionality" in October 2010. Questions of copyright and digital information have become an important legal issue in the information age, including the 2012 introduction of the heavily debated and eventually rejected Stop Online Piracy Act (see MC in Action: SOPA).

Burning In communication technology, creating data images on a physical storage device for later playback.

MC IN ACTION

SOPA

Responding to entertainment industry complaints about what was seen as widespread copyright infringement by Internet users, Lamar Smith (R-TX) introduced into the U.S. House of Representatives a bill that threatened to shut down access to Web pages that contained any copyrighted information without the permission of the copyright holder. For example, if your private Web page was streaming the complete *Iron Man 2* movie, access to your page would be blocked until you either removed the movie or got the permission of Marvel Entertainment (or the current copyright holder) to show the film for free.

Sounds fair, right?

An unforeseen problem with Rep. Smith's proposal was that it would hold Web pages such as YouTube, Wikipedia, and Facebook (among others) legally responsible for the content posted by their users, many of whom are anonymous. Let us consider Wikipedia for a moment. As discussed in Chapter 4, part of Wikipedia's strength is that the individual entries are written by multiple users—relying on crowdsourcing to get detailed and accurate write-ups of any number of topics.

Wikipedia as an organization does not edit or check any of the information posted to its more than 4.1 million articles (as of February 2013), and only a small handful of 1,400 administrative users actively monitor articles to protect from spamming and intentionally inflammatory edits that do not contribute to knowledge on a given topic (such as calling for the death of a president or celebrity). Because of the anonymous, open-source nature, Wikipedia (or rather, their parent Wikimedia Foundation) and other online companies argued that they would have to severely censor their pages or shut down their operations all together—after all, if only one of the 18 million Wikipedia users uploaded a single bit of information with a copyright claim, the entire Web site could be blocked. To demonstrate their point, on January 18, 2012, Wikipedia (along with other Web sites) staged a blackout of their site. SOPA was not passed by the U.S. House of Representatives, although a host of alternative bills have been proposed to find a balance between copyright protection and freedom of information— a critical issue that will continue to shape Internet law into the 21st century.

What about those comments, photos, and videos that you might share via social media . . . who exactly owns that content? As with many Facebook relationships, it's complicated. In writing for *The Telegraph*, Oliver (2013) explained that while many social media platforms such as Facebook, Instagram, and Twitter do generally allow users to retain the copyright to any content that they upload, many of these services retain the right to edit and use any user's content without paying any royalties, or even notifying the user about their intent to use the content. As explained to Oliver by intellectual property attorney Callum Sinclair, "With these terms companies are saying 'you own your content, but we can just use it however we want.'" In fact, some even argue that these usage rights might even apply to other users! (see MC in Action: My Instagram Made Over $90K . . . For Someone Else).

MC IN ACTION

MY INSTAGRAM MADE OVER $90K ... FOR SOMEONE ELSE

For many Instagram users, having others recognize and "like" one of your photos is a nice gesture, perhaps reminding us that we do really have a good eye for photography, or at least good taste in food or clothes. Having somebody offer you money for one of our Instragram photos could also be interesting (although that has yet to happen to any of your book's authors). Being offered $90,000 for a single print of an Instagram photo? That would put one well on the way to a career as a professional photographer.

Or, it would just be another payday for controversial painter and photographer Richard Prince. In reporting for *The Washington Post*, reporter Jessica Contrera reported on a May 2015 exhibit of Prince's at the Frieze Art Fair in New York, that consisted entirely of enlarged prints (not paintings) of a number of different Instagram photos, usually with a non-sequitur comment from @richardprince1234 contained in the comment feed of the photo (and also, in the enlarged print). The Frieze exhibition was an encore of a 2014 gallery showing called "New Portraits" which also contained a number of Instagram images, always other people's images and photos. The affair led Contrera to quip "Don't post anything you wouldn't want hanging in an art gallery."

You can read Jessica Contrera's article in *The Washington Post* at https://www.washingtonpost.com/news/arts-and-entertainment/wp/2015/05/25/a-reminder-that-your-instagram-photos-arent-really-yours-someone-else-can-sell-them-for-90000/

Mobile Entertainment— Entertainment on Demand

As digital technology continues to converge our many media offerings into one portable device, we see that individuals can have access to their entertainment on demand. This is compelling, as entertainment in the basic sense has traditionally been viewed as a means of escape and leisure to occupy or distract us from other more taxing pursuits.

But can it be more than this? Oliver and Raney (2011) argued that while the hedonic motivations of media usage are apparent, we can also use entertainment media for reflection and meaning. As well, as suggested in Chapter 6, we can learn from our entertainment media—and it is possible that this increased mobile access to media is helping us expand the spaces in which we can learn and grow.

One of these new spaces is our mobile space, that is, that time when we are moving from location to location. The widespread

©lzf/Shutterstock.com

adoption of the cellular phone in the 1990s expanded the space for human communication beyond restrictions of a terrestrial, or landline, telephone and allowed for us to be in connection anywhere a phone signal could be found. This freedom of communication spawned an expectation of connectivity on demand, and this expectation combined with technological advances in bandwidth allowed for us to share data as well as voice signals through our mobile devices. Indeed, the smartphone ushered in a modern era of interpersonal as well as mass information (and masspersonal information) on demand, and newer portable technologies have us entertaining ourselves on the go—giving us access to our music, movies, and television, and even our video games in spaces away from our living rooms (see MC in Action: Sony PlayStation Vita). Mobile technologies such as the PlayStation Vita perhaps best represent the notion of convergence on a functional level, and represent the continued blurring and merging of mediated communication channels.

Bandwidth For a given data signal, the capacity and rate at which it can transmit digital information.

Smartphone A cellular phone with computer-like functionality, such as a Web browser, internal data processor, and hard drive for data storage.

MC IN ACTION

Sony PlayStation Vita

The authors of this book remember fondly the Nintendo Game Boy. First released in 1989, the 3.5 inch by 5.8 inch by 1.3 inch "grey brick" gave video game fans an opportunity to carry their favorite video games anywhere—allowing them to play as Mario or Link (from *Legend of Zelda*) for as long as the four AA batteries would hold out. The graphics were in black and white, and the sound quality was not great, but if one of us could stretch our acid-washed jeans pocket large enough to fit a Game Boy, we could play video games almost anywhere. The system was an immediate and long-lasting success, selling nearly 120 million units worldwide and eventually introducing such technologies as color graphics, the ability to link Game Boys together to co-play video games, a "rumble pack" to simulate physical touch when playing some games (such as driving off-road in a racing game), and even a portable camera and printer to take photos and share them with friends. Of course, carrying around all of these attachments was cumbersome, yet remarkably popular. In many ways, the Game Boy represented an early converged entertainment technology:

a video game player, a communications device, and a portable camera, all usable on the go. Taking this further, rival Sega even developed a television antenna for their Game Gear portable system. Mobile entertainment might not have been born with the Game Boy, but its popularity was cemented.

Fast forward to 2012 and the release of Sony's PlayStation Vita. Meaning "life" in both Italian and Latin, Sony designed and marketed the device to represent a move to a singular mobile device capable of playing video games (the device has technical specifications on line with that of a PlayStation 3 console), high-definition television (it is capable of displaying over 17 million colors in high-definition resolution), smartphone browser (it has an onboard wireless Internet card that can receive and process enough data to run streaming video services), and communication devices (it has two onboard cameras and a built-in microphone for video calling). Certainly, the Vita represents an evolution from the original Sony Walkman—the wildly popular portable cassette player first released in the United States in 1979.

Key Terms

Hot media (pg 182)
Cool media (pg 182)
Media effect (pg 182)
Hedonic/hedonism (pg 182)
Enjoyment (pg 182)
Eudaimonic/eudaimonia (pg 183)
Appreciation (pg 183)
Voyeuristic/voyeurism (pg 184)
Digital Age (pg 186)
Analog (pg 186)
Digital (pg 188)
Ephemerality (pg 188)
Moore's law (pg 188)
Binary (pg 190)
Interactivity (pg 191)
Task demand (pg 192)
Virtual reality (pg 193)
Sandbox/sandbox video games (pg 194)
Parkour/parkour gaming (pg 194)
Burning (pg 195)
Bandwidth (pg 198)
Smartphone (pg 198)

References

Bowman, N. D. (2016). Video gaming as co-production. In R. Lind (Ed.), *Produsing 2.0: The intersection of audiences and production in a digital world* (Vol. 2, pp. 107–123). New York: Peter Lang Publishing.

Bryant, J., Thompson, S., & Finklea, B. W. (2012). *Fundamental of media effects* (2nd ed.). Long Grove, IL: Waveland Press.

Bracken, C. C., & Skalski, P. (2009). *Immersed in media: Telepresence in everyday life.* New York: Routledge.

Horton, D. & Wohl, R. R. (1956). Mass communication and para-social interaction: Observations on intimacy at a distance. *Psychiatry, 19*, 215–229.

Lombard, M., & Ditton, T. (1997). At the heart of it all: The concept of presence. *Journal of Computer-Mediated Communication, 3*(2), doi: 10.1111/j.1083-6101.tb00072.x

McLuhan, M. (1964). *Understanding media: The extensions of man.* New York: McGraw-Hill.

Oliver, M. B. (2006). Exploring the paradox of the enjoyment of sad films. *Human Communication Research, 19*(3), 315–342.

Oliver, M. B., Bowman, N. D., Woolley, J. K., Rogers, R., Sherrick, B., & Chung, M-Y. (2015). Video games as meaningful entertainment experiences. *Psychology of Popular Media and Culture*. doi: 10.1037/ppm0000066

Oliver, M. B., & Raney, A. A. (2011). Entertainment as pleasurable and meaningful: Identifying hedonic and eudaimonic motivations for entertainment consumption. *Journal of Communication, 61*(5), 984–1004.

Oliver, M. B., Weaver, J., & Sargent, S. L. (2000). An examination of factors related to sex differences in enjoyment of sad films. *Journal of Broadcasting and Electronic Media, 44* (2), 282–300.

Reinecke, L. (2009). Games and recovery: The use of video and computer games to recuperate from stress and strain. *Journal of Media Psychology, 21*(3), 126–142. doi: 10.1027/1864-1105.21.3.126

Sherry, J. L., Greenberg, B. S., Lucas, K., & Lachlan, K. (2006). Video game uses and gratification as predictors of use and game preference. In P. Vorderer and J. Bryant, (Eds.), *Playing video games: Motives, responses and consequences.* Mahwah, NJ: LEA.

Smith, O. (2013, January 4). Facebook terms and conditions: Why you don't own your online life. The (UK) Telegraph. Retrieved April 17, 2016 from http://www.telegraph.co.uk/technology/social-media/9780565/Facebook-terms-and-conditions-why-you-dont-own-your-online-life.html

Socha, T. & Pitts, M. J. (2012). *The positive side of interpersonal communication.* New York: Peter Lang Publishing.

Zillmann, D., & Vorderer, P. (2000). *Media entertainment: The psychology of its appeal.* Hillsdale, NJ: LEA.

CHAPTER 13

Uses and Effects of Digital Entertainment

In 2012, a pair of highly publicized mass murders brought into question perhaps one of the most widely debated questions in mass communication research: does violent media content result in violent actions? In July 2012, a man in Aurora, Colorado, was arrested after attacking the crowd at a midnight screening of *The Dark Knight Rises* (Warner Brothers Pictures, 2012)—storming a packed theatre armed with tear gas and assault weapons and murdering 12 members of the audience while injuring 58 others. Later that same year, a gunman attacked Sandy Hook Elementary School in Newtown, Connecticut, armed with assault weapons and fatally shot twenty children and six school staff members, before killing himself as first responders approached the scene. Speculation about the cause of both events was varied, but a common discussion in both events was the extent to which entertainment media might have played a role. In the Aurora shooting, the shooter was profiled by some as a major fan of the *Batman* character and franchise, and authorities found movie paraphernalia in his apartment when searching for clues about the murders. In the Sandy Hook shooting, many claimed that the perpetrator had spent a significant amount of time playing the first-person shooter video game *Call of Duty*.

Could violent entertainment media content have caused these tragedies? In Chapter 12, for example, we talked about how interactivity and presence might draw video game players further into the virtual spaces. Might this be resulting in players learning violence while playing video games? Is it possible that more interactive media such as video games would have a

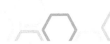

stronger impact on audiences than less interactive media such as movies? At the same time, if media can have a negative impact on its users, could it also have a positive impact? Programs such as *Sesame Street* and *Mister Rogers' Neighborhood* (see Chapter 6) have been used for decades to teach children scholastic and pro-social lessons. Could video games using the same lessons teach them better? If there is any effect, can the positive benefits outweigh the negative consequences? Indeed, there is and has been much debate about these questions, and this chapter will present the historical and current perspectives that help us consider answers to these questions.

Questions to consider when reading this chapter:

- How has the study of media effects evolved over the past 100 years?
- What are some of the leading theories about media's effect on users?
- How do we determine when material is obscene or not?
- How have newer media changed the way we study media effects?

History of Media Effects Research

The study of media's influence on our thoughts, feelings, and behaviors has gone through several different transformations since it was first taken up as an area of scholarly interest at the beginning of the 20ᵗʰ century. Indeed, when we consider the notion of how media affects individuals, we can often categorize the discussion into the scope and magnitude of the assumed effect being studied. Chronologically, we can understand these as an evolution from a universally powerful media influence, to a diminished influence, to a present-day perspective of powerful effects under limited conditions. Moreover, with newer forms of interactive and on-demand digital media, we might consider how newer technologies might change the ability of media to influence us—for better and for worse.

Of course, prior to the academic study of media uses and effects, history is full of examples of the fear that media messages may cause for individuals and society at large. For example, book burnings have been used as a way to prevent the spread of countercultural messages almost since the invention of writing. Historical accounts suggest that many early monarchs and religious authority figures ordered the banning and destruction of books—as well as the prosecution of their authors and printers—as far back as AD 300 and likely far preceding this. More recently, the late 1800s anti-obscenity crusades of U.S. Postal Inspector Anthony Comstock—a politician notorious for his conservative approach to morality—featured mass burnings of any printed materials that Comstock and his New York Society for the Suppression of Vice found lewd or of a sexual nature. Comstock and his group's political clout (he was able to secure a position as a special vice agent to the U.S. Postal Service, authorized to inspect mail for immoral content and authorized to carry a deadly weapon in the performance of his duty) were so successful in stirring up public concern about sexual deviancy and immorality that the Comstock Act was

Comstock Act Passed on March 3, 1873, this Act made it illegal to send "obscene, lewd, and/or lascivious" content through the U.S. Postal Service.
It was actually passed as an amendment to the original Post Office Act.

passed into law in 1873, which banned such materials being sent through the mail. Considering that there were few channels for distributing media content in the late 1800s, Comstock's crusade was considered a death knell to many content producers (including proponents of contraceptive education, labeled "lewd and lascivious content" under the Comstock Act and therefore made illegal to distribute). Even as recently as the 1990s and 2000s, parents groups have lobbied for schools to ban works of fiction such as the Harry Potter novel series for promoting witchcraft and even some versions of the *Merriam-Webster Dictionary* for containing definitions for "obscene" words such as "penis" and "vagina." Thus, while there has always been espoused public concern for media content (see MC in Action: "I Know It When I See It!"), the scientific study of media effects is relatively new.

The "Magic Bullet" Paradigm: 1900s to 1940s

The earliest studies on media effects suggested that media's influence on individuals was a powerful, universal, and direct one. This perspective was cultivated from reports of audiences showing extreme adverse reactions to the content of media at the time, including fright reactions and delinquent behaviors observed in children watching Hollywood films (the Payne Fund Studies of the 1930s), audience panic reactions to the infamous *War of the Worlds* radio broadcast by Orson Welles on October 30, 1938, and children's attributions of comic book content as a cause for their juvenile delinquency (Frederic Werthram's

© Everett Historical/Shutterstock.com

The Industrial Revolution changed the way people lived and worked in the United States.

Seduction of the Innocent studies of the 1950s). So, as entertaining and popular as much of this content was for its intended audiences, it was also found to have a very negative influence on them. For early scholars, evidence of children misbehaving and adults panicking in irrational fear of a Martian invasion were proof enough that the media acted as antisocial "symbolic bullets" (Lowery & DeFleur, 1995) striking the eyes and ears of individuals and impacting them in a uniform manner.

Looking back today, few believe the media can have such a strong effect. So then, how did the early scientists make this conclusion? A closer inspection of the role of media in society at the time explains why the Magic Bullet theory was a logical conclusion at the time. First, the concept of electronic mass media was relatively new to modern society, with film and radio enjoying widespread adoption in the first quarter of the 20th century, and radio broadcasting only coming into its infancy in the 1930s. Early society relied heavily on these devices for information and as result tended to believe the content they were reading or hearing without much criticism as there were few alternatives for information. Second, we can look at the manner in which society was organized at the time. As the United States progressed into the early 20th century, the country was squarely in the throes of the Industrial Revolution. This saw a marked change in the way

Industrial Revolution A period of time in the United States—generally the late 19th and early 20th century—when the country's economy shifted from a focus on agriculture to a focus on manufacturing. As part of this shift, many people began leaving smaller farming communities and migrating to larger urban spaces where factories were located.

MC IN ACTION

"I KNOW IT WHEN I SEE IT!"

While laws such as the Comstock Act have attempted to outlaw the production and distribution of obscene content, the definition of what makes something obscene or not has eluded society for generations. Historically, obscene material has been any material not seen as valuable by the authority figures or dominant political philosophy of any given society—an example of this being the persecution of Italian scientist Galileo Galilei at the hands of Catholic Pope Urban VIII as a heretic for the scholar's views on physics and astronomy. Yet, as rulers and philosophies change, so do standards of obscenity, which makes the crafting of a legal definition quite difficult. Indeed, writing his opinion for the obscenity case *Jacobellis v. Ohio* in 1964, Supreme Court Justice Potter Stevens included one of the most well-known definitions of pornography. He stated that hard-core pornography was hard to define, "But I know it when I see it."

In the United States, the Supreme Court set legal precedent in 1973 by developing the so-called Miller test during *Miller v. California*, a three-pronged test considered the first comprehensive definition of obscenity issued by the Court to date. In the case, pornographic film producer Marvin Miller was being prosecuted for sending brochures advertising his films to bookstores and restaurants in Newport Beach, California, that featured sexually explicit scenes from his films. He was initially found guilty of violating community standards of decency in sending his brochures without prior consent from those who received them, and he appealed his case to the U.S. Supreme Court.

He lost his appeal, but during the case the Court rendered perhaps one of the most important decisions surrounding media entertainment and content to date, as an official definition of obscenity that considered:

(a) Whether the average person, applying contemporary community standards, would find that work, taken as a whole, appeals to the prurient interest.

(b) Whether the work depicts or describes, in a patently offensive way, sexual conduct specifically defined by the applicable state law.

(c) Whether the work, taken as a whole, lacks serious literary, artistic, political, or scientific value.

Some critics have argued that the Miller test is still vague on what specific content is and is not obscene, but many argue that this in fact a great strength of the test as it allows for changing community standards to be reflected in changing thresholds of what might be considered obscene or not. For example, there is no known evidence of states banning literature on contraceptives in modern U.S. society, even though such materials were explicitly outlawed under the Comstock Act. Indeed, the third prong of the test is one of the hardest for opponents of questionable media content to successfully argue—as was the intention of the judges who heard *Miller v. California*.

Prurient Media content that has or encourages excessive interest in sexual matters, such as pornography.

Patently offensive Something that would be considered as being obvious; in this case, obviously offensive.

Miller test Also called the three-pronged test of obscenity, a U.S. Supreme Court test to determine whether or not content—usually sexual content—is considered pornography. The test is important because pornographic content is subject to different laws than regular media content.

people worked and lived—particularly in how they organized socially. As the economic focus of the United States shifted from farming to manufacturing, many families left smaller farming communities for the larger more urban areas where factories were located. According to German sociologist Ferdinand Tönnies, this population shift brought with it a change in how people organized—leaving the tight-knit *Gemeinschaften* (smaller communities marked in part by lots of social connections) and moving to more impersonal *Gesellschaften* (larger areas marked in part by very few social connections). Keep in mind that Darwinism was now widely applied to social reasoning too. Given this combination of factors—that we were fairly isolated, were heavily reliant on single information sources, and inclined to have instinctual responses to stimuli—it stood to reason to social scientists that our responses should be immediate, powerful and fairly uniform.

Why is the study of social organization relevant to understanding media effects? This social isolation led individuals to rely more on mass media as an information source than the relative strangers around them. Moreover, this increased reliance on mass sources of information likely further drove down conversations between individuals, preventing us from "fact-checking" our information with those around us and getting new bits of information. Together, these attributes of media along with early data suggesting large numbers of people showing aversive reactions to media led scientists of the time to conclude that magic "media bullets" were a force with which to be reckoned. An example often given of this Magic Bullet effect is the role of propaganda in the Nazi German regime of the 1930s. Here, Propaganda Minister Paul Joseph Goebbels was credited with harnessing mass media to convince an entire nation of people of the righteousness of the Nazi party platform, but this was found to only work in a media system such as Nazi Germany's in which the government controlled most of the mass media and individuals were discouraged from talking with one another for fear of punishment.

The "Paper Tiger" Paradigm: 1940s to 1960s

Continuing in the mid-20th century, the Magic Bullet perspective on media effects was a prominent way of thinking about media for the scientists of the time. However, problems began to arise with this perspective in reanalysis of data from older studies and the failure of scientists to replicate the results of earlier work. For instance, when scientists looked back at some of the data on fright reactions reported from the *War of the Worlds* broadcast, they found that the panic reactions reported by audience members were quite exaggerated—some audience members did overreact, but many more people did not; those who were more likely to believe in the supernatural, or those with lower emotional security seemed more likely to panic. In addition, attempts to reconstruct the supposed powerful influence of propaganda observed in Nazi Germany to other applications failed to produce similar effects. One of the more infamous examples of a failure to find strong propaganda effects was the U.S. Army's *Why We Fight* videos, a seven-part series of films commissioned by the military and directed by famed Hollywood film director Frank Capra designed to persuade Allied soldiers as well as the general U.S. public

to join the fight against Hitler's Axis powers. The films—inspired by Leni Riefenstahl's *Triumph des Willens* (*Triumph of the Will*, a German propaganda film commissioned by Goebbels)—were eagerly watched by both military and civilian audiences (as many as 58 million Americans were estimated to have seen the films), yet research on their effectiveness as propaganda tools proved inconclusive.

Moreover, looking at the content of entertainment and informational media of the mid-20th century revealed an interesting development in the sort of content being produced for audiences. In coverage of the Korean War and the Vietnam War, embedded journalists reported from active battle zones, beaming home images of war and conflict never before seen by modern media audiences. In contrast, coverage of World War II was often reliant on official military press releases that carefully controlled the information and images that made their way to the public eyes and ears. In addition, the 1950s saw increased political and social tensions in the United States as the civil rights movement intensified. Similar to coverage of Vietnam, newspapers and televisions stations intensely covered much of these events, showing the brutality and discrimination faced by African Americans and other minorities through a relatively unfiltered lens.

Embedded journalist Reporters who report on events by placing themselves in the actual event, such as a war correspondent traveling with a military division to report as part of the action.

From this, scholars began not only to question the existence of the supposed powerful effect of media on individuals, but they also began to propose that media content was in fact affected by society and not the other way around. Perhaps, media content was merely a mirror, reflecting back onto audiences the events of the day rather than shaping their opinions. From this perspective, mass media was seen as a paper tiger—a ferocious-looking beast that was ultimately harmless—and the research focus shifted to studying the media content itself rather than the negative effects of content.

Powerful, But Limited: 1960s to Today

Claims that such paper tiger media had little or no effect on individuals' thoughts, feelings, and behaviors seem shortsighted. For example, reanalysis of reported fright reactions from the *War of the Worlds* broadcast suggested that while the entire viewing audience was not of the belief that Martians were invading Earth, there were indeed pockets of individuals who did believe this to be the case. People who were more fatalist or who did not have much education found themselves duped by Welles' broadcast. As well, some people living in the town of Concrete, Washington, experienced a massive power outage during the broadcast, which for many residents was too much of a coincidence to be chance. And some people simply never heard Welles' disclaimers that the entire broadcast was fiction. And perhaps more telling, such fright reactions to media hoaxes continue to happen on occasion (see MC in Action: "That's Dihydrogen Monoxide in Your Faucet").

Fatalist/fatalism An individual who believes that they have little influence over their surroundings.

Moderating variables In statistics, a moderating variable is one that influences the association between a cause and an effect. For media effects, moderating variables change the nature of how media content influences individuals who consume it.

These different situations—fatalist personalities, education level, reinforcing coincidental events, and missing key broadcast messages—are what would be called by social scientist Wilbur Schramm as moderating variables. In statistics, a moderating variable is one that influences the relationship between two other variables. For example, we might see that sunlight is significantly related to the growth of a patch of flowers, but that flowers that are watered regularly grow far taller and more colorful than flowers that do not get watered regularly. In this case, sunlight seems to have a stronger impact on the growth of flowers when they are watered than when they are not, which makes sense given that watered flowers are able to more efficiently carry the food created by photosynthesis (transferring sunlight into food energy) throughout their root and cellular system. So, when we study media, we might think of moderating variables as conditions under which we might expect media to have a stronger or weaker effect on an individual. In this way, we understand media as a potentially powerful influence on our thoughts, actions, and behaviors, but we also consider the roles of the individual person and their social environment as being equally important. Indeed, some scholars wonder if the media message or channel itself or the individual using the message or channel are more important to consider when attempting to understand media effects.

MC IN ACTION

That's Dihydrogen Monoxide in Your Faucet

It is one thing when radio stations change their format or other crazy things they do. But you are messing with one of the big three, food, water, or shelter. They just went too far; I just knew I didn't like that.

~WWGR-FM General Manager Tony Renda

April 1 has become a bit of a bad day to trust new information, whether you hear it from a trusted friend or a mass media source. After all, April Fools' Day often brings with it a litany of practical jokes and hoaxes from unexpected (and often trusted) sources, causing most of us to be on guard throughout the day. Indeed, knowing that it is April 1 causes some people to not believe anything they hear, even if the information is not meant to be a joke—indeed, we might suggest "knowledge of the day as April 1" as a moderating variable in the link between novel information and trust in that information.

Yet, for many it seems that April Fools' Day is forgotten. Such must have been the case on April 1, 2013, when two morning radio DJs from a southwest Florida radio station WWGR-FM 101.9—known locally as "Gator Country 101.9"—went on air to announce a deadly situation involving the drinking water in the Lee County (Florida) water supply. Specifically, the DJs suggested that the water contained high levels of dihydrogen monoxide. Of course, a basic understanding of chemistry and molecular nomenclature reveals that "dihydrogen monoxide" is merely the molecular name for water when expressed in the common "H2O" format. However, there was enough public panic and concern over water safety that local utility boards were forced to release several statements ensuring residents that there was no problem with the water supply. The DJs were suspended, and some considered filing criminal charges against them for threating the safety of public water supplies—a felony in the state of Florida—before it was determined that they had broken no appreciable laws. After all, dihydrogen monoxide was indeed flowing out of everybody's faucets that day, just as it is today.

Antisocial Effects

Won't somebody please think of the children!

~Helen Lovejoy, of *The Simpsons*

The brunt of media effects research tends to focus on concerns over negative, or antisocial, effect on audiences and society at large. Such concerns are long-rooted in historical panic over media content such as the aforementioned book burnings of ancient (and not-so-ancient) rulers and government officials as well as general human concerns over obscene content. Many of us—the authors of this book included—can readily recall instances in which our parents would not allow us to watch movies or play video games that were overtly violent or sexual, for example. As well, many wonder as to the sort of judgments we might make about individuals whom we are exposed to in the media but with whom we never actually have real-world contact. As referenced in Chapter 6, many in the earlier days of television—including former FCC chairman Norman Minow—considered the popular form of entertainment to be a "vast wasteland" of "blood and thunder, mayhem, violence, sadism" and a veritable laundry list of other negative nouns.

Violence

Without providing a specific count, studies on media violence dominate the majority of publications in media psychology and mass communication research. As alluded to in the Aurora and Sandy Hook tragedies of 2012, there is widespread concern that the often violent content of popular entertainment media is cultivating an increased sense of aggression and violence in the people who view this content. In fact, so much research had been done on this topic that by 1972, then U.S. Surgeon General Jesse Steinfeld issued a statement suggesting that "the causal relationship between televised violence and antisocial behavior is sufficient to warrant appropriate and immediate remedial action." Many studies on the subject are careful case-controlled studies that manipulate levels of violent content in an experimental design before measuring individuals' levels of aggressive thoughts and feeling after exposure. However, the results of such studies are challenged by some and can be generally grouped into three areas of counterargument.

First, it is argued that increased aggression does not necessarily result in increased violent behavior and that using aggression as a measure of violence lacks face validity. For example, Bandura's social learning theory (see Chapter 6) and the updated social cognitive theory (see Chapter 9) suggest that for a behavioral effect to be realized, in this case a violent behavior, individuals would have to be exposed to the behavior as well as motivated to enact the behavior, and in many contemporary societies, individuals are routinely taught that violence is not an appropriate reaction to provocation. However, here researchers such as media psychologists Craig Anderson and Brad Bushman might counter-argue that anti-violence interpersonal lessons are counterbalanced by media diets that are heavy in violent content—claims backed by several content analyses of popular media entertainment such as the National Television Violence Studies of the 1990s (e.g., NTVS, 1996).

Experimental design A form of scientific research that attempts to isolate the effect of one variable on another by manipulating one variable and measuring changes in the other variable as a result of these manipulations.

Face validity In research, this is the degree to which a measured variable represents the concept it is supposed to measure.

Content analysis A research method that attempts to quantify, or count, the presence of a given variable of interest.

Second, some argue that the reported influence of violent media content on violent action is invalidated to some extent by declining violent (and even nonviolent) crime rates. For example, the 1990s were marked in later research as one of the least violent decades of the 20th century—with murder rates down nearly 50 percent and violent robberies down nearly 10 percent from the 1980s, both numbers dipping to 1960s levels—in spite of the fact that the 1990s also saw some of the greatest expansions in the media entertainment industry. Many in the industry pointed to these numbers to suggest that it was not possible for their product to be causing so many violent acts, because the violent acts simply were not happening at a rate that would be expected from theory. However, many scientists have cautioned about the potential for the relationship between decreased crime despite increased media entertainment options to be a spurious one, as fundamental changes in the criminal justice system might also be leading to a greater rate of prosecution and incarceration of violent offenders among other variables.

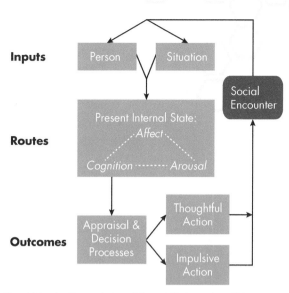

Republished with permission of Annual Reviews, from "Human Aggression" by Craig A. Anderson and Brad J. Bushman, Vol. 53, pp 27–51. Copyright © 2002; permission conveyed through Copyright Clearance Center.

Spurious In statistics, a relationship between two variables that does not actually exist in real life, but appears to be because of an unidentified common variable.

Finally, there is an argument that violent people are simply more likely to attend to violent media content and that nonviolent people simply do not desire or use such content. Proponents of this approach suggest that research should focus more on the motivations for one's attraction to violent content rather than the content's effect on those people. However, recent laboratory research (compare Whitaker, Melzer, Steffgen, & Bushman, 2013) has shown that inducing frustration can increase the appeal of violent content, which might start a reinforcing spiral by which the appeal of content results in the reinforcement of violence as an acceptable solution for one's frustration; indeed this logic is central to the general aggression model.

Violence and Interactivity

To this point, the discussion of violent media effects has not considered how interacting with the on-screen action might moderate effects. Consider the differences between watching a violent war movie and playing a violent first-person war simulation. In the movie version, the individual audience members are passive witnesses to the violent actions of their heroes—perhaps cheering as they shoot and kill their way through enemy lines and progress through the rest of the film's narrative. Contrast that with the video game version of the same war in which the player must actively commit each individual act of violence in order to progress the narrative from one battle scene to the next. In here, we see some of the principles of presence discussed in Chapter 12 playing a role. Violent video games require players to place themselves in violent environments and commit violent acts, and this requirement for action has been found in laboratory research to increase aggressive thoughts and feelings (compare Polman, de Castro, & van Aken, 2008).

This evidence suggests that video game players would be more likely to be negatively affected by violence than movie audiences because they are essentially closer to the action—the perpetrator rather than the witness. However, such an approach seems to minimize the influence of the individual in the experience, suggesting that they have no real control over their own decisions or the decisions that they make for their video game character. Yet, many video games such as the sandbox games discussed in Chapter 12 provide players with rather open virtual worlds in which there are no predetermined narrative conclusions. Returning to our war narrative example, watching the war film results in the same characters shooting and killing the same enemies each time the film is played. However, in the video game version, the player is placed in control of which enemies are killed, how they are killed, or whether or not they are even killed. That is, it is conceivable that an individual playing a war video game could choose a nonviolent path to narrative conclusion (to the extent that in-game goals did not specifically require players to kill other players). Research into video games and decision-making has shown that when players perceive a particular video game scenario as a moral one, they are significantly more likely to uphold rather than violate their own moral code when given the choice. In situations where a scenario was not perceived as a moral one, the decision to uphold or violate morality was almost completely random (Joeckel, Bowman, & Dogruel, 2012). Evidence such as this suggests that in virtual environments in which players place themselves in the gaming world, individuals use their real-world moral orientations to make virtual decisions—if they see an act as immoral in real life and the game does not require them to engage in it, they will not do it. Such a moral mechanic has in fact been incorporated into creating more meaningful video game experiences such as the controversial yet immensely popular 2012 war game *Spec Ops: The Line* (see MC in Action: Walker and the White Phosphorous).

Sex, Offline and Online

As discussed with the Comstock Act, there seems to have always been great public concern, at least in the United States, about sex in media. Similar to work on violence, many content analyses of sex in the media show it as a prevalent theme. Many children indicate that they learn a majority of their knowledge about sex from media portrayals of sexual acts (rating this as more influential than parents in a 1998 study conducted by CNN), and some children—particularly boys—report getting their information about sex from watching pornography. These are important findings because, at least in an entertainment context, the information is not meant to be necessarily accurate or educational, but rather, alluring and erotic and, well, entertaining. Moreover, when we consider sexually explicit materials such as pornography, these often contain portrayals of violent sexual media—often showing males engaging in aggressive and dominant sexual acts with female partners—as well as risky sexual behaviors, such as unprotected sexual intercourse (see MC in Action: Condoms Required in LA Porn). This sort of research concerns many media watchdogs because while many adults might be able to distinguish between sexual fantasy and reality, children often do not have the knowledge or experience to do the same.

Media watchdogs People and organizations, usually volunteers or concerned individuals without any legal authority, who tend to carefully monitor media content for the presence of antisocial content and share their concerns through public channels.

MC IN ACTION

WALKER AND THE WHITE PHOSPHOROUS

Lugo: You're f*cking kidding, right? That's white phosphorous!
Walker: Yeah I know what it is . . .
Lugo: You've seen what the shit does! You know we can't . . .
Adams: We might not have a choice Lugo . . .
Lugo: There's always a choice!

The preceding dialog takes place immediately before the infamous "White Phosphorous" scene from 2K Games' *Spec Ops: The Line*. The game is a third-person shooter in which the player assumes the role of Walker, the leader of a small but heavily armed reconnaissance team sent to Dubai to investigate a rogue Army commander named Konrad and his attempt to instill martial law in the Arab capital city following a natural disaster that forced the city's evacuation (all fictional accounts).

Shortly after their arrival in Dubai, the team learns that they are heavily outnumbered and outgunned by both insurgent forces (warring against Konrad) as well as Konrad's own guard, and they begin to explore the region covertly in order to learn more about the situation. Facing immense resistance from both factions, Walker orders his trio to fire a white phosphorous mortar into a crowd of insurgent forces

so as to eliminate them as a threat. Firing the mortar into the air neutralizes the insurgency but comes at an unexpected price: the collateral murder of dozens of women and children refugees who were being covertly protected by the insurgency. The player uncovers this chilling truth in dramatic fashion when walking through the freshly shelled city and stumbling across an image of a mother shielding her child from the phosphorous, both charred almost beyond recognition. Surrounding the woman and child are other fatally wounded children as well as a few soldiers, still clinging to life as they crawl along the ground asking the player "why?" Indeed, many players asked themselves the same question—which was precisely the goal of head writer Walt Williams: to create a video game in which the player is forced to judge themselves for the actions they have committed.

The complete gameplay scene from this can be viewed at: http://www.youtube.com/watch?v=-b7TaLjdXMc

Beyond the possibility of learning unhealthy sexual behaviors, media psychologist Richard Harris Jackson reviewed some of the more prevalent effects of viewing sexual content, which included increased arousal in participants and attitude shifts in support of the on-screen sexual activity (such as greater preference for violent sexual behaviors after watching pornography) as well as a decreased satisfaction with one's own lover after watching sexual media content. Perhaps, one of the more chilling studies was conducted by media researchers LeeAnn Kahlor and Dan Morrison (2007), who found a positive correlation between general television viewing and increased acceptance of rape myths—attributing this link to an increase in sexually themed content on television. Such research was argued to represent an extension from work done in the 1980s showing a similar link between the watching of violent porn and rape myths (compare Malamuth & Cheek, 1985).

Rape myth A belief that most rape accusations are false and that victims are at least partly responsible for their rape, often suggesting the victim to have been overly sexual or otherwise inviting the sexual act.

MC IN ACTION

CONDOMS REQUIRED IN LA PORN

The use of condoms is required for all acts of anal or vaginal sex during the production of adult films to protect performers from sexually transmitted infections.

~Measure B

In January 2012, the *Los Angeles Times* reported on a new health initiative in the city of LA requiring all pornography actors to wear condoms during film shoots. The measure passed with a 9-1 margin by the city council and paved the way for the successful adoption of The Safer Sex in the Adult Film Industry Act, known colloquially as Measure B, mandating all pornography filmed in LA County to require condom usage. The initiatives were hailed as victories for health advocacy groups such as the AIDS Healthcare Foundation. However, they were roundly decried by the pornography industry as an unnecessary restriction on free speech and expression protections.

Besides the public health debate over the transmission of disease, many wondered how this ordinance might influence those watching the films. For example, if we consider that many children and teenagers report using pornography to learn about sexual acts, we might wonder if seeing porn actors wear condoms during sex might encourage adolescents to do the same. Of course, as pornography is usually restricted for sale to minors, this was not likely a salient thought by those attempting to pass these laws. Yet, it begs an interesting (albeit highly controversial) question—can we use arousing, engaging, and popular content to teach pro-social lessons?

The complete text from this law can be found at: http://rrcc.lacounty.gov/VOTER/PDFS/ELECTION_RELATED/11062012_LACOUNTY_WIDE_MEASURE_B.pdf

---

Federal Communications Commission (FCC) In the United States, the federal office responsible for regulating communications technology, in particular wireless and broadcast systems, to make sure these channels are used in the public interest.

Age authenticator Programs, usually used by Web pages, that attempt to verify the age of a user before allowing access. Some programs require the user to create an online profile that they can use from one Web page to the next to determine their identity.

Sex and New Media

In part because of the negative social stigmas associated with sexual content as well as emerging scientific evidence that such content can have a rather strong influence on audiences, sexual content is regulated. As we saw in the Miller test, content that appeals only to prurient interests is restricted for viewing in many public places such as movie theatres and broadcast television. At the same time, it is not illegal to produce pornographic content, but rather it is the distribution of said content that is subject to regulation. For example, the Comstock Act made it illegal to mail such content, and the Federal Communications Commission (FCC) has the authority to bar the broadcast of said content by television stations. However, when we look at newer communication technologies, one of the prime areas of concern is the increased ease-of-access that media users today now have to this content. In 2010, research published by *Forbes Magazine* suggested that as much as 4 percent of the one million most trafficked Web sites on the Internet contained pornography, and as many as 13 percent of all Web searches were for erotic content. In total, some estimate that there are as many as 250 million different pornographic Web pages on the Internet—nearly one for every American based on 2000 U.S. Census population data. While many Web sites include age authenticators that are designed to restrict access by minors, these programs can be easily tricked by determined minors and have been criticized for being overly expensive. In 1996, U.S. President Bill Clinton signed into law the Communications Decency Act which made it a crime to knowingly transmit obscene material to minors, but there has been little research on the impact of CDA on access to pornography. In fact, the biggest impact of CDA in terms of legal precedent was the protection of Internet service providers from being prosecuted if users of their networks transmit legally obscene material.

Other Antisocial Media Effects

Another popular area of study in media effects is the manner in which society—and specifically, different individuals within society—are portrayed. George Gerbner's cultivation hypothesis suggested that (in a somewhat similar logic to the underpinnings of the Magic Bullet paradigm) television portrayals serve as a "great storyteller" for society, and as a result, television audiences are likely to believe what they see on screen. According to Gerbner, this suggests that television content is cultivating a view of the world that is more fantasy than reality. After all, things such as crime and violence are shown far more frequently on television than they are in the real world, and his research on the mean world effect suggested that heavy television viewers believed the world was a far more dangerous place than people who watched less television. Moreover, these crime portrayals tend to over-represent minority populations, such as news reports showing more African American criminals, which can impact how audiences view minorities. For example, research by former television writer and current media researcher Temple Northup finds that heavy news audiences tend to overestimate the guilt of African American over non-Black suspects. However, with more and more access to individuals and information than ever before through social and digital media, how might we expect these cultivation effects to hold up in the new media landscape? As far back as 1954, sociologist Gordon Allport found that one of the most effective ways of combatting racism was to expose individuals to people from other cultures and social groups. Allport's theories have since been evolved by media psychology and mass communication scholars into the parasocial contact hypothesis, which suggests that exposure to outgroups via mediated channels such as television content might work to combat potential cultivation effects (Schiappa, Gregg, & Hewes, 2005). Notably, modern entertainment media have become increasingly personalized and interactive. It is possible, for example, for audiences to interact with their favorite actors and characters via Twitter, Facebook, and other social media channels, providing more opportunities to interact with and contact these different people.

A final prominent antisocial media effect discussed here is that of the displacement hypothesis, which suggests that entertainment media usage is a socially isolating activity. Based on Robert Putnam's controversial text *Bowling Alone* (see Chapter 7), the argument here is that many modern forms of entertainment such as television, the Internet, and video games are inherently isolating—they require the user's complete attention and are often used alone—and that this was leading to a decline in social capital. Simply put, people were spending more time with media and as a result less time with each other. Yet, Putnam's work was criticized by

Communication Decency Act (CDA) Passed as part of the Telecommunications Act of 1996, CDA was one of the first attempts by the U.S. Congress to regulate obscene content—in particular, pornography—on the Internet.

Internet service providers Companies that control and manage access to the Internet by selling subscribers the necessary equipment and services.

Cultivation hypothesis The notion that through continual exposure we begin to believe that the social world has the same attributes and tendencies as that which we perceive in media.

Mean world effect A phenomenon by which individuals who watch a lot of crime and violence on television feel as if the real world is a violent and dangerous place; part of Gerbner's cultivation hypothesis.

Parasocial contact hypothesis A theory that explains that we can have contact with individuals from other cultures by seeing them portrayed in different media products, and this contact can influence how we understand a different culture.

Displacement hypothesis A theory that suggests that time spent using entertainment media might take away from our time spent with other people.

Social capital Economic value that comes from the information that we get from the people we know.

many scholars who in fact reported the opposite. Canadian sociologist Barry Wellman and his colleagues reported in 2001 (Wellman, Hasse, Witte, & Hampton, 2001) that communication technologies, specifically the Internet, were supplementing rather than damaging social interaction, and in fact people with Internet access reported being more involved in their surrounding communities—possibly as they are able to form more relationships online while being placed in more constant contact with their neighbors and the information and events relevant to their neighborhoods. Research on video games has reported similar results, arguing that many games encourage and even foster intricate social interactions between players by effectively functioning as "third places" of interaction (Steinkuehler & Williams, 2006). Given our focus in this book on regarding technology as a tool to foster human communication, these results should not be very surprising. In a similar fashion, entertainment technologies such as television and video games are often consumed in very social situations and tend to provide viewers (the former) or players (the latter) with common points of interest and conversation known to foster rather than hinder communication.

Pro-Social Effects

While many of the potential pro-social effects of media have been covered in other parts in this book—including counterargument for many antisocial media effects discussed in the preceding section—we might look at entertainment media as having the ability to teach us "good" as well as "bad." After all, it makes sense to suggest that if audiences could learn about violence, sex, and racist stereotypes from popular entertainment content, they could just as likely learn lessons about healthy living and bettering the human condition.

Health Influences

Edutainment A combination of education and entertainment, this notion refers to using entertainment content to teach different academic or social lessons.

While there is no conclusive documented history of the concept, examples of using entertaining media content to teach health messages, a form of edutainment in which educational (in this case, health information) is embedded within entertainment programs, can be found on a wide range of topics and channels. One prominent example is *Soul City*, an immensely popular radio and television serial broadcast in South Africa as a partnership with media producers, researchers, and physicians. Although the program attempts to address a much wider set of health and social issues, one of the more prominent ones is the portrayal of HIV/AIDS-infected characters—relevant in a nation in which nearly 12 percent of the population is estimated to have the disease according to a 2007 United Nations AIDS project (the highest such concentration of HIV/AIDS cases in the world). Specifically, the program was written to portray the disease as a manageable and preventable one rather than a social taboo and death knell, in spite of the fact that nearly one in two deaths in South Africa are related to the disease. In a 2009 interview with a doctor and researcher involved with *Soul City*, the World Health Organization estimated that the radio broadcast alone reached an estimated 80 percent of all South Africans. While research on the effectiveness of the program in managing the HIV/AIDS pandemic in South Africa is ongoing, recent reports suggest that prevalence of the disease in younger children is in decline.

For the Internet, there are numerous Web pages devoted to distributing health information from a variety of amateur and professional sources, from folk cures and personal blogs that champion the many different curative powers of petroleum jelly to official public health announcements from the U.S. Centers for Disease Control (www.cdc.gov). Perhaps, the most popular source for health information is WebMD (www.webmd.com, NYSE: WBMD), a Web site containing detailed and multimedia health information on a variety of different health-related topics from self-diagnostics to lifestyle news and information. Estimates in 2011 suggested the site to receive nearly 90 million unique visitors monthly, and Alexa.com rankings (a popular metric of Web site traffic) places WebMD as one of top 150 Web pages visited in the United States and one of the top 500 pages visited worldwide. While not an entertainment medium per se, WebMD has since branched out to include more edutainment-type information on their home page, including more lighthearted fare such as the "High School Reunion Diet" and interactive health-themed quizzes, games, and videos.

Video games have also been used to successfully teach health lessons. Similar to our discussion of video games in learning back in Chapter 6, designers have attempted to use the interactive nature of video games in the hope of communicating health information in a more engaging and entertaining way—particularly to children. Game designers and health communication researchers Debra Lieberman and Stephen Brown explain that the interactive, role-playing, and inherent learning elements of video games can be used to communicate not only basic and complex knowledge about diseases and health threats, but they can also be used to encourage and offer social support as well as improve self-concepts. These cognitive and affective influences are then thought to promote more healthy behavior outcomes (usually a focus on diets, exercise regimens, and self-care and maintenance) resulting in desired health outcomes. Research has generally supported the notion that video games can be used effectively to teach health information, and as result, there has been a sharp increase in funding to create such games for everything from promoting healthy eating habits to managing diabetes (see MC in Action: "Never Fear, Captain Novolin Is Here!"). There are even video games focused on teaching middle-school children about the harsh realities of teen pregnancy and sexually transmitted diseases.

Meaningful Media Experiences

While not an overt pro-social benefit of media, we can return to our discussion of meaningfulness from Chapter 12 to understand how media content can bring about a reflective state in its audiences. Recall from that discussion that movies such as *Schindler's List* and *The Boy in the Striped Pajamas* can be thought of as prominent examples of entertainment media designed for audiences to ponder rather than find pleasure. In both movies, audiences are introduced to vivid portrayals of the experiences of those detained, tortured, and often murdered in Nazi concentration camps during World War II—using dramatic narratives, dynamic film editing and perspectives, and almost deranged violent portrayals to communicate to audiences the extent of the atrocities committed by Hitler's forces. Of course, not all reflective content has to be negative, and there are numerous examples of

media designed to cheer us up or make us feel better—one of this author's favorites being *The Red Balloon* (Janus Films, 1956), a French short film that follows a little boy and his discovery of a red balloon floating in the schoolyard that takes on a life of its own.

MC IN ACTION

"Never Fear, Captain Novolin Is Here!"

Twelve-year-old Sarah Michael tells Wired magazine that Captain Novolin helps her know what foods she can eat and what foods she should avoid so she doesn't become ill because of elevated blood sugar. The game makes it quick to understand, whereas doctors just go on and on about what she should do.

According to the American Diabetes Association (www.diabetes.org), nearly one in every 400 children will develop some form of diabetes. One of the more devastating forms of the disease is called Type 1 diabetes—marked by the body's inability to produce its own insulin (insulin is the main vehicle by which the human body is able to convert food into the energy needed to sustain life). Type 1 diabetes is a particularly complicated disease when diagnosed in children because, while survivable, it requires constant monitoring and care. For example, children must learn how to read their own blood sugar levels and self-administer appropriate dosages of insulin shots, as well as adhere to strict dietary restrictions . . . all while living the normal, curious, chaotic, and developing life of a "normal" child.

To help communicate the complexities of diabetes to children, synthetic insulin manufacturer Novo Nordisk teamed up with video game developer Raya Systems to create a video game in which the main character was a superhero with the disease. From this partnership came the November 1992 launch of *Captain Novolin*, named after the synthetic insulin of the same name. In the game, players are asked to rescue a diabetic major who was kidnapped by evil aliens—engaging in otherwise normal superhero activity such as fighting the Cereal Killer and Larry Licorice in pursuit of the evil Blubberman. During gameplay, players have to carefully monitor Captain Novolin's insulin levels by helping him eat healthy foods, avoid junk food, and even match blood sugar readings to appropriate dosages of insulin injections—players are also presented with diabetes information quizzes during game play. Although the game itself features highly dramatized and fictionalized portrayals of diabetes, research on the game's effectiveness showed it to be successful in helping children talk about their disease with peers as well as remember the many different steps involved in managing it.

Diabetes-themed video games in particular have remained a particularly popular and successful method of teaching children how to manage the disease, with several published studies showing them to be an effective means of communicating knowledge about the disease, adhering to the often complex treatment regimens, and presenting actual health benefits (DeShazo, Harris, & Pratt, 2010).

The complete *Wired* magazine interview with Sarah Michelle is available at: http://www.wired.com/wired/archive/1.06/eword.html?pg=11

People have begun to use communication technologies to create meaningful entertainment experiences as well. Since late 2012, Internet users from around the world have been invited to upload quick "hug videos" to a Web page named The Nicest Place on the Internet (http://thenicestplaceontheinter.net, also see Chapter 7), and several social media campaigns on Facebook and Twitter feature users uploading and sharing inspirational messages, photos, and videos. January 2011 saw the release of the social media-based movie *Life in a Day* (National Geographic Films, 2011), a film produced by famed Hollywood director Ridley Scott that was created by splicing together over 80,000 different YouTube videos all shot by social media users on July 24, 2010. The film was designed to reflect on a single day in the history of humanity by essentially allowing us as humans to tell our own story and was met with largely critical acclaim for providing audiences with what film critic Helen O'Hara called a "moving and insightful" cinematic experience.

In fact, meaningful media experiences have even been reported with video game play—a medium not traditionally known for presenting somber or serious tones. Game designers have begun to realize that the interactive and immersive nature of video games might make them even more capable of bringing about feelings of meaningfulness than more traditional media for the same reasons that they are feared to have stronger antisocial effects: by their nature, video gaming requires the user's constant attention and active engagement in the on-screen action. Consider the *Spec Ops: The Line* example from earlier in this chapter (see MC in Action: Walker and the White Phosphorous), and we see a situation where the player not only has to consider the deadly consequences of chemical warfare but also has to cope with the fact that, at least in the virtual environment, they themselves were responsible for the destruction brought on by the white phosphorus mortar attack. Such internal contemplation, suggests game designer and scholar Ian Bogost, might be required for many people to truly process such abstract consequences by making them more concrete (MC in Action: Gaming and Guilt). In fact, emerging research suggests that while game play mechanics are more integral for understanding the more hedonically rooted enjoyment reactions to video games (called "pleasures of control"), mechanics of the interactive narratives are more strongly related to the eudaimonically rooted appreciation reactions to games (or "pleasures of cognition"). Indeed, many video game industry insiders predict emotional games to become increasingly commonplace, leading noted designer Jesse Schell to ask the audience of the 2013 Game Developers Conference in San Francisco (which included one of the authors of this text), "Are we going to have a Shakespeare of games? A game that was told so perfectly, and so well, that 200 years later people will insist we play it exactly as it was?" Judging from the audience's responses, the answer was less a debate as to whether or not Schell's vision was possible, and more an acknowledgement of a not-too-distant future of mediated entertainment. After all, just as Shakespeare used ink and quill—the technologies of his time—today's storytellers use pixels and computer processors to do the very same.

MC IN ACTION

GAMING AND GUILT

"What's relevant is that the level managed to make the player feel anything at all."

~Call of Duty game developer Mohammad Alvai, in an interview with Kokatu

For fans of *Call of Duty: Modern Warfare 2*, one of the most infamous levels in the game involved the player assuming the role of an undercover agent for a Russian terrorist cell. On the surface, such a role-play is commonplace among action and warfare games. The twist came in the form of the "No Russians" mission in which the player-as-undercover-terrorists burst into an airport full of innocentcivilians, before gunning them down as part of the mission objective.

Almost immediately after the game's release, players took to the Internet to discuss the "No Russians" mission—many as upset about the game's portrayal of terrorism as they were about their own actions during the level. After all, the player is not required to shoot any civilians in order to progress through the game . . . so why did so many players (a) fire on seemingly innocent civilians and (b) feel guilty afterwards?

Although not equipped to answer the first question, University of Buffalo media psychologist Matthew Grizzard and colleagues from Michigan State University found that committing violent atrocities in video games can actually spark feelings of guilt rather than enjoyment among video gamers. In a 2014 study in which his research team had players engage a first-person shooter as either United Nations soldiers (assumed to be on the side of good) or terrorists (assumed to be on the side of bad), his team found that players randomly assigned to the role of a terrorist experienced higher self-reported feelings of guilt (measured in terms of regret and being sorry for and disliking their in-game actions). Perhaps most importantly, however, is that those increased feelings of guilt also led players to be more sensitive towards moral issues related to care and fairness. Grizzard interpreted this data to suggest that not only do players feel guilty when they commit digital violence, but that committing these violent acts can actually make them more morally sensitive as a result. In a nutshell, it is possible that being bad in video games might actually be good for us!

Have you ever done something in a video game that made you feel guilty afterwards? Share your experiences with our Facebook group at https://www.facebook.com/groups/234255823447372/ or via Twitter, using the #MediaAsTools hashtag.

Alvai's complete interview with Kokatu can be read at http://kotaku.com/5931235/the-designer-of-call-of-dutys-no-russian-massacre-wanted-you-to-feel-something

Key Terms

Comstock Act (pg 202)
Industrial Revolution (pg 203)
Prurient (pg 204)
Patently offensive (pg 204)
Miller test (pg 204)
Embedded journalist (pg 206)
Fatalist/fatalism (pg 206)
Moderating variables (pg 206)
Experimental design (pg 208)
Face validity (pg 208)
Content analysis (pg 208)
Spurious (pg 209)
Media watchdogs (pg 210)
Rape myth (pg 211)
Federal Communications Commission (FCC) (pg 212)
Age authenticator (pg 212)
Communication Decency Act (CDA) (pg 213)
Internet service providers (pg 213)
Cultivation hypothesis (pg 213)
Mean world effect (pg 213)
Parasocial contact hypothesis (pg 213)
Displacement hypothesis (pg 214)
Social capital (pg 214)
Edutainment (pg 214)

References

Allport, G. (1954). *The nature of prejudice*. Cambridge, MA: Perseus Books.

Anderson, C. A., & Bushman, B. J. (2002a). The effects of media violence on society. *Science, 295*, 2377–2378.

Anderson, C. A., & Bushman, B. J. (2002b). Human aggression. *Annual Review of Psychology, 53*, 27–51.

Bandura, A. (2001). Social cognitive theory of mass communications. In J. Bryant & D. Zillman (Eds.). *Media effects: Advances in theory and research* (2nd ed., 121–153). Hillsdale, NJ: LEA.

Bogost, I. (2011). *How to do things with video games*. Minneapolis: University of Minnesota Press.

DeShazo, J., Harris, L., & Pratt, W. (2010). Effective intervention or child's play? A review of video games for diabetes education. *Diabetes Technology Therapy, 12*(10), 815–822.

Grizzard, M. Tamborini, R., Lewis, R. J., Wang, L., & Prabhu, S. (2014). Being bad in a video game can make us morally sensitive. *Cyberpsychology, Behavior, and Social Networking, 17*(8). 499–504. doi: 10.1089/cyber.2013.0658.

Jackson, R. H., & Barlett, C. P. (2009). Effects of sex in the media. In J. Bryant & M.B. Oliver (Eds.), (2009). *Media effects: Advances in theory and research* (3rd ed.). Hillsdale, NJ: LEA.

Joeckel, S., Bowman, N. D., & Dogruel, L. (2012). Gut or game: The influence of moral intuitions on decisions in virtual environments. *Media Psychology, 15*(4), 460–485.

Kahlor, L., & Morrison, D. (2007). Television viewing and rape myth acceptance among college women. *Sex Roles, 56*, 729–739.

Lieberman, D. A., & Brown, S. J. (1995). Designing interactive video games for children's health education. In R. M. Satava, K. Morgan, H. B. Sieburg, R. Mattheus, & J. P. Christensen (Eds.), *Interactive technology and the new paradigm for healthcare* (pp. 201–210). Amsterdam: IOS Press.

Lowery, S. A., & DeFleur, M. L. (1995). *Milestones in mass communication research: Media effects* (3rd edition). White Plains, NY: Longman Publishers USA.

Malamuth, N. M., & Check, J. V. P. (1985). The effects of aggressive pornography on beliefs in rape myths: Individual differences. Journal of Research in Personality, *19*, 299–320.

National Television Violence Study (1996). *National Television Violence Study: Scientific papers, 1994–1995.* Studio City, CA: Mediascope.

Northup, T. (2011). Is everyone a little bit racist? Exploring cultivation using implicit and explicit measures. *Southwestern Mass Communication Journal, 26*, 29–41.

Polman, H., de Castro, B. O., & van Aken, M. A., (2008). Experimental study of the differential effects of playing versus watching violent video games on children's aggressive behavior. *Aggressive Behavior, 34*(3), 256–264.

Putnam, R. (1995). Bowling alone: America's declining social capital. *Journal of Democracy, 6*(1), 65–78.

Schiappa, E., Gregg, P. B., & Hewes, D. E. (2005). The parasocial contact hypothesis. *Communication Monographs, 72*(1), 92–115.

Steinfeld, J. (1972). *Statement in hearings before Subcommittee on Communications of Committee on Commerce* (United States Senate, Serial #92–52, pp. 25–27). Washington, DC: U.S. Government Printing Office.

Steinkuehler, C. A., & Williams, D. (2006). Where everybody knows your (screen) name: Online games as "third places." *Journal of Computer-Mediated Communication, 11*(4), 885–909. doi: 10.1111/j.1083-6101.2006.00300.x

Wellman, B., Hasse, A. Q., Witte, J., & Hampton, K. (2001). Does the Internet increase, decrease, or supplement social capital? Social networks, participant, and community commitment. *American Behavioral Scientist, 45,* 436–455.

Whitaker, J. L., Melzer, A., Steffgen, G., & Bushman, B. J. (2013). The allure of the forbidden: Breaking taboos, frustration, and attraction to violent video games. *Psychological Science*. doi: 10.1177/0956797612457397.

The Future of Mediated Communication

Communication technologies continue to advance at an alarming pace. By that same notion, many technologies that are "can't miss" end up missing. For example, if this book had been published seven or eight years ago, discussion of the hot social network site would have likely focused on Myspace, with a limited (if any) discussion of Facebook. When Rupert Murdoch and News Corp bought Myspace in 2005, the price tag was $580 million. When it was sold to a group led by Justin Timberlake in 2011, the price tag had dropped to around $35 million. In less than six years, we saw a "hot new medium" sell for about 6 percent of its peak value! This cautionary tale of investing in communication technology also highlights one of the major points of this book: focusing on people and relevant characteristics of technology, rather than focusing solely on the "hot" new specific applications of a channel, will allow you to think about not only what we have currently, but will position you to respond to newer technologies as they come along. Channels change, but people and their goals largely do not. Google Glass is one technology that was mentioned as "coming" in the previous edition of this book. Since that time, it has already pretty much came and went.

So what does the future of mediated communication hold? If we could accurately predict this on a specific level, we would go out and invent the new Facebook and then retire on the revenues of that project without even updating a second edition of this textbook. We joke of course, but generally speaking, we have some ideas about what the future of MC will look like, and here we both summarize the major points of this book as well as make those predictions about the future.

From a functional perspective, we may assume that any communication technology that allows us to accomplish our goals "better" than previous technologies is more likely to take off. As we have discussed throughout this book, people want information, they want to build and manage relationships, they want to persuade others and sometimes be persuaded, and they want to be entertained. Thus, a technology that allows people to do any of these more quickly or more efficiently seems to have a better chance of becoming popular.

In terms of information, MC provides the possibility for a great increase in the amount of information that people can create, share, and consume. This has changed the gatekeeping role that media used to provide and has shifted the focus away from professional gatekeepers vetting information before publishing it and onto consumers of that information, in a sort of "buyer, beware" aspect. This allows the possibility for more and more complete information to exist about topics, but only if users are willing and able to contribute to the general pool of information available online. Thus, as the sheer amount of information continues to increase, it becomes essential for people to increase their media/information literacy.

MC can also be a powerful tool for relationships. Although many popular perspectives seem to suggest that relationships managed online are somehow weaker than or not as real as those managed face-to-face, we believe that the evidence paints a different picture. People can and do utilize various technologies to have very fulfilling and rewarding relationships, sometimes at a level higher than those that can occur face-to-face. For example, the ability to overcome space and time constraints means that people can communicate with each other more frequently and in more places, allowing for relationships to build more. In this way, relationships seem to be more about the effort put into managing them and the experience that one has within them that predicts the quality, rather than simply the channels used.

When thinking about the persuasive capabilities of MC, we can see how a classic understanding of persuasion in terms of message involvement might be even more important when we consider the interactive nature of new media technologies, as well as the wealth of information available to the average consumer (when considering advertising) or voter (when considering the election process). Advertisers and campaign managers now need to compete with a wealth of alternative information sources as well as other distractions in order to persuade today's media-savvy audience effectively. At the same time, social media users are sharing more and more of their personal information with advertisers—knowingly and unknowingly—which provides these organizations with enough detail to specifically target users with a nearly constant barrage of highly personalized sales pitches.

Finally, MC has provided vast increases for the consumption of entertainment, both in terms of content and mobility. Current technologies have given us the chance to consume almost any entertainment we want to (whether legally or illegally) and to do so on demand. This break from the characteristics of traditional mass communication has also provided users a greater possibility to become creators of content, rather than only being consumers. We can also look to entertainment as more than just a fun experience but also as one that has true meaning for the audience members—letting us feel both happy and sad and allowing us to better understand ourselves.

Given the notion of convergence, we also wonder if technologies that allow us to do some or all of these things might become even more popular—if we look at Facebook, for example, the platform has evolved somewhat from being just a social network of relationships into a place for reading the day's headlines (information), being targeted by advertisements and special interest groups (persuasion), and a space for listening to music, watching videos, and even playing embedded video games (entertainment). Such convergence is likely a major reason for the platform's continued success, as the constant ability for re-invention allows it to maintain continued usage and adoption. For health and campaign messages, this might be a good thing; for personal privacy concerns, we now see a debate as to how much information should and should not be available to those wishing to persuade us.

One final note for considering the future of MC: not all goals that people have are things we would consider "good." In fact, the same characteristics of MC can be used for both good and bad purposes. For example, anonymity can be used as a great thing as it allows somebody to search for health information about something they might feel embarrassed about. However, anonymity is not so good when it is used by a group of people to cyber-bully someone, using their computer to mask their identity while intentionally hurting another person without consequence. In this way, it is important to understand that MC channels themselves are not inherently good or bad, but they do facilitate in helping people to accomplish their goals, be they good or bad. **Technology allows people to be more human, yet it does not guarantee that people will be more humane.** We hope, after reading this book, you realize that because YOU are in charge of the Internet and the use of MC technologies, you also realize that YOU are ultimately in charge of how good or bad the Internet becomes. We hope that you accept that responsibility and use that power wisely.

Perhaps President Barack Obama said it best at his keynote speech delivered at South by Southwest 2016 (which one of the current authors was able to attend while another had to stay in the hotel room like an unlucky loser):

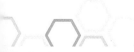

"We are at a moment in history where technology, globalization, our economy, is changing so fast . . . Those changes offer us enormous opportunities, but also are very disruptive and unsettling. They empower individuals to do things they could've never dreamed of before, but they also empower folks who are very dangerous to spread dangerous messages."

The full keynote conversation can be watched here: https://www.youtube.com/watch?v=wfsIZioIpdI. We would strongly encourage all readers to watch this video—perhaps in reflection of the lessons learned in our book—and reflect on the powerful role that mediated communication has, does, and will continue to play in society.

80–20 rule/Pareto principle A principle borrowed from economics that suggests that a majority 80 percent of capital tends to be controlled by a minority 20 percent of elite stakeholders. Pareto principle distributions have been widely applied to understand how land and wealth are distributed in several countries, as well as how Internet traffic can be understood.

Accuracy A dimension of critical thinking concerned with how correct information is.

Ad Council A nonprofit group that essentially founded social marketing, encouraging U.S. citizens to purchase war bonds during World War II and do other activities to help the war effort.

Advocacy newspapers Publications, either online or offline, that intentionally and openly adopt a subjective or editorial approach to journalism. Advocacy newspapers tend to actively align their editorial coverage in support or opposition of social issues.

Affective learning The feelings associated with the learning process.

Age authenticator Programs, usually used by Web pages, that attempt to verify the age of a user before allowing access. Some programs require the user to create an online profile that they can use from one Web page to the next to determine their identity.

Analog A storage medium that uses a physical device to store information for retrieval.

Appreciation An entertainment media effect characterized by eudaimonic reactions to content.

ARPAnet The Advanced Research Projects Agency Network, this system of networked computers was started in 1969 with funding and oversight from the U.S. military. The network was designed to allow researchers to share data quickly and confidentially across large spaces.

Asynchronous (communication) Communication that does not happen in "real time"—that is, communication that often takes place with some time delay. E-mail is a good example of an asynchronous communication channel.

Attention Focusing on a stimulus.

Audience-centered process Making sure to consider your receivers' goals, attitudes, knowledge, and so on when attempting to influence them through communication.

Augmented sociality Using technologies to access information from digital and social media programs, and working that information into face-to-face conversations.

Autotelic process A process or activity that is intrinsically motivated, having no external reward associated with its completion.

Avatar In video games, the on-screen character that represents the player's space in the video game. Mario and Sonic would be considered avatars, as well as any character that the player created themselves.

Bandwidth For a given data signal, the capacity and rate at which it can transmit digital information. The amount of capacity a channel has to carry a signal/information.

Base-rate Information concerning the typical incidence with which an event takes place in the social world.

Behavioral intentions Expressed desire to modify a behavior in the future.

Big 6 A six-stage model of information literacy designed by scholars to aid in the problem-solving process.

Big data A term that refers to the large quantities of information organizations can retrieve from Internet users regarding their usage patterns and preferences. The increasing focus on the electronic amalgamation of enormous amounts of consumer data in order to target consumers.

Binary code The language of computing technology; this is the storing of information in electrical circuits using a series of "1" and "0" commands to represent "on" or "off."

Breadth A dimension of critical thinking concerned with the overall coverage of the complexities of a given topic of discussion.

Bucket brigades A type of social network in which one person communicates or interacts with only one other person in a linear fashion, passing information from one to one.

Burning In communication technology, creating data images on a physical storage device for later playback.

Channel What a source uses to send a message through.

Chronemics Using a sense of time, such as response latency or pausing during a conversation, to communicate nonverbally.

Citizen journalism/citizen journalist An individual, usually an amateur, who reports on the events and stories around them using some sort of communication technology.

Clarity A dimension of critical thinking concerned with the vagueness of information; less vague information is usually considered more credible than more vague information.

Click-through rate A measure of the effectiveness of an online ad based on the number of hits it receives.

Code-switching A process by which a person switches their attention quickly from one task to another.

Cognitive dissonance A mismatch between one's beliefs and one's actions.

Cognitive learning The act of storing and understanding new information.

Communication Decency Act (CDA) Passed as part of the Telecommunications Act of 1996, CDA was one of the first attempts by the U.S. Congress to regulate obscene content—in particular, pornography—on the Internet.

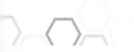

Communication There are many definitions of communication. McCroskey and Richmond (1996) defined it as the process by which we stimulate meaning in the minds of others using both verbal and nonverbal messages.

Comstock Act Passed on March 3, 1873, this Act made it illegal to send "obscene, lewd, and/or lascivious" content through the U.S. Postal Service. It was actually passed as an amendment to the original Post Office Act.

Consequence(s) A component of news that refers to the impact of a particular event on individuals or society.

Conservative In the context of politics and news, a conservative publication would be more likely to feature editorials and stories that support traditional social attitudes and values; the "status quo."

Content analysis A research method that attempts to quantify, or count, the presence of a given variable of interest.

Context collapse A situation, common to social networking sites, in which information created for a specific audience is shared with multiple audiences at the same time.

Cool media Those media that can be used without active engagement and attention.

Crowdsourcing Using larger groups of people—usually through social media technologies—in order to gather information on a given topic.

Cultivation hypothesis The notion that through continual exposure we begin to believe that the social world has the same attributes and tendencies as that which we perceive in media.

Cyborgs Short for cybernetic organisms; refers to the fact that people utilize technology to "extend" themselves.

Dating Web sites Web pages that are specifically designed to help users form and sustain romantic connections with other users.

Decentralized organization A company or organization in which there is no one main leader, president, or operating officer. Rather, the organization's leadership is broken up in several different parts of the organization itself.

Decoding A sort of reverse process to encoding; turning symbols back into meaning.

Depth A dimension of critical thinking concerned with the level of detail given to a current topic of discussion.

Diffusion (of innovation) A process by which inventions are adopted for use throughout society. These diffusion processes often follow a very predictable pattern of slow initial growth, followed by rapid adoption, and followed by another slower growth period.

Digital A storage medium that encodes information in binary code to be decoded upon request by a computer processor.

Digital Age An age of mass media characterized by using digital methods for message creation and transmission.

Digital divide An observation that there is a gap in technology access based on demographic and socioeconomic variables, creating digital "haves" and "have nots."

Digital natives Individuals born into a technological age who are experts at using and adapting to technology for a variety of end goals, including a preference for communicating through technological devices.

Digitization Converting information into binary code to be decoded upon request by a computer processor.

Displacement hypothesis A theory that suggests that time spent using entertainment media might take away from our time spent with other people. The notion that time spent engaging in one activity necessarily results in less time spent engaging in other activities.

E-mail A form of electronic communication in which users can send each other private messages to digital mailboxes, similar to sending a letter through a traditional mail service.

Economic divide One dimension of the digital divide concerned with financial barriers to technology access, such as the ability to purchase a computer.

Edutainment A combination of education and entertainment, this notion refers to using entertainment content to teach different academic or social lessons.

Egocentrism A logical fallacy in which individuals tend to process information in terms of their own viewpoints rather than reading the information on its own merits.

Elaboration likelihood model A model of human perception that states that we take in information in two separate ways: central, or factual arguments, and peripheral, or secondary stimuli.

Electromagnetic spectrum In telecommunications, the available range of frequencies—such as radio television waves—that can be used to transmit information.

Embedded journalist Reporters who report on events by placing themselves in the actual event, such as a war correspondent traveling with a military division to report as part of the action.

Emoticons Using combinations of keyboard symbols to represent facial expressions.

Empathy The ability to understand and share the feelings of others.

Empowerment divide One dimension of the digital divide concerned with understanding how to use technology to achieve specific goals.

Encoding A process of choosing the symbols to use to attempt to get a meaning across to another person; turning meaning into symbols.

Enjoyment An entertainment media effect characterized by hedonic reactions to content.

Ephemerality (ephemera) The concept of objects being transitory, or existing only briefly.

Equivocality Information that has more than one potential meaning or interpretation.

Ethos A core set of values used to extrapolate the details of a program.

Eudaimonic/eudaimonia A "pleasure of the mind" usually characterized by deliberation and insightfulness.

Exemplars Single observations that people make, and subsequently use to draw assumptions about people, places, and things they observe later.

Expectancy violation A situation in which our assumptions about anticipations of another's thoughts, actions, or behavior are not met.

Experimental design A form of scientific research that attempts to isolate the effect of one variable on another by manipulating one variable and measuring changes in the other variable as a result of these manipulations.

Exponential curves A term describing a pattern of technology adoption where the number of people using the technology suddenly spikes at a given historic moment.

Extended learning Educational endeavors (such as classes or workshops) that attempt to provide training to individuals across physical and temporal boundaries, similar to the concept of distributed learning.

Extended parallel process model A model of persuasion common in social marketing that suggests that fear can be a motivating factor to behavior change, especially when people feel they can do the behavior and it will work.

Face validity In research, this is the degree to which a measured variable represents the concept it is supposed to measure.

Fairness A dimension of critical thinking concerned with the objectivity given to different viewpoints regarding a given topic of discussion. Related to the news, discussing the elements of a story or events in such a way as that it is free from discrimination.

Fatalist/fatalism An individual who believes that they have little influence over their surroundings.

Fear appeals A campaign strategy that attempts to get people to change their behaviors by instilling fear regarding the behavior in question.

Federal Communications Commission (FCC) In the United States, the federal office responsible for regulating communications technology, in particular wireless and broadcast systems, to make sure these channels are used in the public interest.

Feedback Messages sent back to a source about the original message sent.

Functional approach The basic approach that this book takes to technology. It suggests that technology is best understood through the basic communication functions it helps people to accomplish.

Gatekeeper An individual such as a newspaper editor or television producer who is responsible for the selection of different stories over others.

Geo-positioning software Software programs that use satellite relay to determine the position of a person, place, or object on Earth.

Goldilocks effect A phenomenon that explains how having too few or too many friends or contacts can result in others making negative judgments about the social attractiveness of a SNS user.

Gossip Information related to ongoing events or stories, or the people involved in those stories, that has been neither confirmed nor rejected as accurate.

Handbills Short announcements or advertisements, typically printed on a single sheet, handed out in public areas.

Haptic communication Sending meaning through the use of nonverbal cues associated with touch.

Hedonic/hedonism A "pleasure of the flesh" usually characterized by immediate positive feelings.

Heuristics Cognitive shortcuts that we use to process information very quickly.

Heuristic systematic model A similar model to ELM, but one that argues we are more likely to use peripheral information if we cannot or do not want to expend energy on processing a message.

Homophily The extent to which two people (or two things) are similar to one another.

Hot media Those media that require our active engagement and attention in order to be used.

Human interest A component of news that refers to how a story might speak to the greater human experience.

Hyperpersonal relationships Relationships that develop online more than they would FtF.

Impression management The act of disclosing and concealing personal information in order to control the impressions that others form of you.

Industrial Revolution A period of time in the United States—generally the late 19th and early 20th century—when the country's economy shifted from a focus on agriculture to a focus on manufacturing. As part of this shift, many people began leaving smaller farming communities and migrating to larger urban spaces where factories were located.

Information literacy The ability of an individual to apply critical thinking skills to properly evaluate information.

Integrated marketing communication Using as many media channels as possible to promote a product.

Interactivity Having control of both the form and content of a media message. The degree to which a user can influence the form and content of on-screen content.

Internet As a common noun, a network of networks; as a proper noun, the global network of networks. It is a communication tool that is used for a variety of purposes.

Internet service providers Companies that control and manage access to the Internet by selling subscribers the necessary equipment and services.

Interpersonal communication Communication between a small number of people (usually, two individuals) who share some sort of relationship.

Inverted pyramid style A style of newswriting that presents the most important elements of a story in the first paragraph and adds more specific details in subsequent paragraphs.

Jacksonian Democracy A political belief that recognized the democratic authority of everyday citizens; a contrast with aristocratic politics of the early 19th century that focused primarily on issues dealing with the privileged class.

Jury theorem A mathematical proof that suggests that the probability of any group of individuals making a correct decision is based on the ability of the individuals within that group.

Learning management systems Computer programs that are often integrated with academic courses that allow for basic communication and instruction features to be delivered via the Internet. Systems often include online reading and lecture materials, as well as discussion boards and message systems to encourage student and teacher communication.

Liberal In the context of politics and news, a liberal publication would be more likely to feature editorials and stories that support emerging social attitudes and values.

Logic A dimension of critical thinking concerned with the internal consistency of the arguments being made during a given topic of discussion.

Marketplace of ideas A philosophy that suggests that ideas should be treated like free enterprise economic goods in that individuals should be able to read any number of ideas and decide for themselves those ideas that are useful and those that are not.

Mass communication Communication from a singular and impersonal source to a large and anonymous audience.

Masspersonal communication Patrick O'Sullivan's idea that technology makes the division between mass and interpersonal communication blurry, and thus we should look for more useful distinctions in communication.

Matthew effect In education, a process by which children who have early advantages—from greater reading and writing skills, to greater access to resources at home—tend to improve academically at faster rates than children without these advantages.

Mean world effect A phenomenon by which individuals who watch a lot of crime and violence on television feel as if the real world is a violent and dangerous place; part of Gerbner's cultivation hypothesis.

Media effect Something that happens as a result of using media. Effects can usually be understood as being cognitive (influencing our thoughts), affective (influencing our feelings), or behavioral (influencing our behaviors).

Media richness theory A theory in MC research that suggests that communication channels can be understood in terms of the number of social cues they provide the user, and there is an optimal matching of communication goal and communication channel based on which cues are desired.

Mediated communication Communication that relies on a technology channel in order to send a message between two entities.

Media watchdogs People and organizations, usually volunteers or concerned individuals without any legal authority, who tend to carefully monitor media content for the presence of antisocial content and share their concerns through public channels.

Message The actual symbols used in an attempt to share meaning.

Miller test Also called the three-pronged test of obscenity, a U.S. Supreme Court test to determine whether or not content—usually sexual content—is considered pornography. The test is important because pornographic content is subject to different laws than regular media content.

Modeling The process of learning a behavior by observing others.

Moderating variables In statistics, a moderating variable is one that influences the association between a cause and an effect. For media effects, moderating variables change the nature of how media content influences individuals who consume it.

Moore's law From computer science, a prediction that advances in technology allow for more and more digital information to be stored in smaller spaces.

Mortality salience The perception that one's behaviors may lead to death.

Motivation The perception of positive or negative outcomes that will follow a behavior.

Motor reproduction The ability of someone to reproduce a behavior they have observed and retained.

Multimodal learning Incorporating several different learning styles (i.e., visual learners, textual learners, etc.) into a single lesson plan or activity.

Multitasking A process by which a person tries to complete several different tasks at one time, usually resulting in poor overall performance from splitting one's attention to sub-optimal levels for each individual task.

Narbs Short for narrative bits; a term coined by Wake Forest University communication professor Ananda Mitra that refers to "an item of personal information posted online, particularly as it contributes, often unwittingly, to a personal narrative that individual is creating online."

Narrowcasting Transmitting information to smaller, less anonymous, and more well-defined audiences.

Netizen A notion that suggests all Internet users should consider themselves as residents of the Internet who are responsible for how the technology operates.

Networked Individualism A "social operating system" that suggests people operate and interact more as individuals connected to various groups rather than embedded members of groups.

News hole The space that is left for content once the advertising has been placed.

Node In social networking, it is the basic unit of analysis—usually any given person in a larger network of people.

Noise Something that impedes successful transmission of a message. This can be literal noise, but can be other things as well.

Normative theory/normative theorist Theories that offer suggestions or explanations as how a particular phenomenon ought to be.

Objectivity Related to the news, presenting a story or event in an impartial and unbiased manner. Objective news stories usually focus more on the facts and figures of a story or event, rather than the opinions of the person(s) delivering the news.

Opaque technologies Technologies that are still noticed during their use.

Opinion leaders People who influence others through word of mouth.

Para-social relationship A relationship that media viewers and users often form with on-screen characters that mirrors an authentic friendship or in-person relationship, but exists (by definition) only in the mind of the viewer or user.

Parasocial contact hypothesis A theory that explains that we can have contact with individuals from other cultures by seeing them portrayed in different media products, and this contact can influence how we understand a different culture.

Parkour/parkour gaming A type of video game play common to sandbox video games in which players walk around and travel in the virtual space of the video game without focusing on in-game goals and challenges.

Patently offensive Something that would be considered as being obvious; in this case, obviously offensive.

Penny press A term referring to cheap, mass-produced newspapers of the late 19th century that made their profits from ad sales rather than sales of the paper itself. Early newspapers that were printed during the late 19th and early 20th centuries that contained popular news and opinion articles and often cost only one penny. The penny press is considered the earliest form of the modern newspaper.

Plasticity The ability of the body, and the brain, to adapt and change.

Postel's law In communication technology, it suggests that a computing system should take a conservative approach in how it transmits data (being sure that it is standardized) but a liberal approach in how data are received (allowing any form of data so long as their meaning can be interpreted). This approach is often applied to management and organization, suggesting managers should be clear in their own instructions to others, but allow for a variety of different bits of information from those they manage.

Precision A dimension of critical thinking concerned with how specific information is.

Procrastination principle In social media computing, the notion that one should allow users to decide ways to correct broken aspects of a technology rather than imposing rules or regulations for dealing with errors. Such an approach is thought to allow for more innovative solutions.

Prominence A component of news that refers to how well-known the individuals in an event are.

Proximity A component of news that refers to how close an event is to its audience.

Prurient Media content that has or encourages excessive interest in sexual matters, such as pornography.

Quiz show scandal An event that took place during the 1950s, where advertisers were rigging popular quiz shows so that attractive contestants would be associated with their products.

Rape myth A belief that most rape accusations are false and that victims are at least partly responsible for their rape, often suggesting the victim to have been overly sexual or otherwise inviting the sexual act.

Reach The number of people exposed to an advertisement.

Receiver The target of a message; whose mind the source wants to stimulate meaning in.

Red herring A logical fallacy that employs extraneous or irrelevant information to an argument as an attempt to distract from the central issue of discussion.

Reinvention The degree to which an innovation is changed or modified by a user in the process of adoption and implementation.

Relevance A dimension of critical thinking concerned with information being related to the current topic of discussion.

Replacement hypothesis The notion that as new media are introduced they replace the time we spent with older media.

Retention Placing information in our memory for future use.

Salience Whether or not a particular thought or belief is on one's mind.

Sandbox/sandbox video games A type of video game that allows players to progress through different points in the game environment in a nonlinear fashion and allows players to solve in-game challenges in a number of different ways.

Scaffolding Tools that are used to bolster recall and manage relationships.

Script A cognitive shortcut that we rely on to understand how a sequence of events takes place in a given circumstance.

Self-efficacy Our beliefs in our ability to do something.

Serious games A specific category of video games that usually aims to teach a particular educational or social lesson.

Simulation A virtual environment that is meant to replicate an actual environment or situation.

Smartphone A cellular phone with computer-like functionality, such as a Web browser, internal data processor, and hard drive for data storage.

Social capital Economic value that comes from the information that we get from the people we know.

Social information processing theory A theory positing that humans use information to reduce uncertainty in order to forge relationships, and that the medium they use can subsequently impact how those relationships form. But they can and do form.

Social interactions Conversations between people central to the human communication process.

Social marketers Advertising and marketing professionals who use new media technologies, specifically social media, to attempt to influence audiences.

Social marketing The concept that behaviors can be promoted in the same ways as products and services.

Social media Communication technologies that allow users to create public profiles in order to connect and share content with other users, usually in a public fashion.

Social network sites (SNS) Internet-based computer programs that allow users to create profiles and share information with other users.

Social presence When using communication technology, a feeling that one is engaging another person in a nonmediated way.

Social shaping of technology A perspective that suggests that technology and society shape each other.

Source credibility Perceptions of the source of a bit of information as being a believable one.

Source The person/place/thing from which communication originates.

Sponsored links A type of advertising in which companies pay search engines to list their products or services first when certain key words are used in searches.

Spurious In statistics, a relationship between two variables that does not actually exist in real life, but appears to be because of an unidentified common variable.

Subjectivity Related to the news, presenting a story or event in a partial and biased manner. Subjective news stories usually focus more on the opinions a person(s) has(have) of a story or event, rather than facts and figures.

Task demand The amount of an individual's attention required by a given media channel for it to be used properly.

TCP/IP Transmission Control Protocol/Internet Protocol; this is a common method of formatting and sending data around the Internet. It is not a single protocol but rather represents a series of common protocols that standardize the way data are handled from all computers on a given internet.

Technological determinism A perspective that suggests that technology drives society and culture.

Telephone tree A type of social network in which one person is responsible for contacting a set number of people who in turn contact a set number of people "below" them.

Telepresence When using communication technology, a feeling that one is interacting in a mediated environment without consciously thinking about this mediation.

Television markets A designated metropolitan area in which network television may broadcast.

Terror management theory A theory suggesting that the induction of fear of death can lead to compliance with health messages.

Theory of media niche A theory of media that suggests that media channels rarely disappear but instead are repurposed to fit the evolving needs of audience members.

Theory of planned behavior A model similar to the theory of reasoned action, but with the added argument that self-efficacy moderates the process.

Theory of reasoned action A model of persuasion that offers that messages influence attitudes and subjective norms, which influence behavioral intentions, which then may or may not lead to behavior change.

Timing A component of news that refers to when a particular event happened.

Transparent technologies Technologies that have become so integrated, or seamless, into one's use that they are no longer noticed or recognized. An example of one for most people is the use of verbal language.

Trust your neighbor principle In social media computing, this notion suggests that we must trust the other users of the network to behave in the same ways as we do. Such a notion is key to the concept of netizenship.

Two-way symmetrical public relations An emerging perspective in public relations proposed by Dozier, Grunig, and Grunig that emphasizes the audience's role in actively discussing rather than passively receiving persuasive messages. In particular, this model requires organizations to engage in dialogue with their publics rather than simply distributing information to them.

Unique selling proposition A technique used by advertisers in which one characteristic of a product is promoted in order to distinguish it from other essentially identical products.

Usability divide One dimension of the digital divide concerned with educational barriers to technology access, such as the ability to operate a computer.

User-generated content Online content, both private and public, that is created by (usually) amateur media users, often without commercial influence. Sharing personal photos to Facebook or writing blog posts could both be considered forms of user-generated content.

Uses and gratifications theory An approach to the study of communication media that focuses on what people do with media, rather than what media does to people.

Vicarious experience The notion that humans can experience the world through observing others rather than through direct experience.

Virtual reality Technologies that simulate physical presence in virtual spaces.

Voyeuristic/voyeurism Watching intimate events between people from a distance.

Web 1.0 A term that refers to the earliest functions of the Internet as being a space for posting information, referred to colloquially as "read and retrieve."

Web 2.0 A term that reflects changes to a more collaborative Internet, referred to colloquially as "create and collaborate."

Web 3.0 A term that refers to the manner in which networked technologies can be programmed to analyze large trends in the massive amounts of data provided by their users, referred to colloquially as "the semantic Web."

You The most important thing for this book; used this way it refers to the idea that users are in charge of open systems like the Internet and thus have the freedom and responsibility for their success.

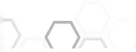

Index

Information effects, theories of, 78
   agenda setting theory, 79–81
   exemplification theory, 81–82
   framing theory, 82–83
Information literacy, 48
   "Big 6" model, 49, 50
   challenges associated with, 57
   conceptual models of, 49
   critical thinking, 59–62
   definition of, 49
   group decision-making, power of, 57
   Wikipedia and, 57–59
   in workplace, 52–54
Information resources
   identification of, 49, 50
Instagram, 197
Integrated marketing communication (IMC), 164–165
Interactivity, 12, 97
   in digital entertainment, 191–192
   entertainment and, 192–194
   violence and, 209–210
International Communication Association, 14
Internet
   audiences, 77
   as communication tool, 17
   creation of, 110–111
   as decentralized organization, 19
   definition of, 18–19
   features of
      generativity, 21–22
      no control of behavior, 22
      simplicity, 22–23
   as functional technology, 29
   functions of, 21
   social networking and, 129. *See also* Social networking
   as social space, 21–23
   usefulness of, 29
Internet-based media programs, 77
Internet service providers, 213

Internet technology, *Newsweek's* estimation of, 32, 33
Interpersonal channels, 12
Interpersonal communication, 7, 12
   and communication tool, 110
   vs. mediated communication, 7
Inverted pyramid style, news reporting in, 70, 71
iPad, 28, 190

J

Jacksonian democracy, 69–71
Jay and Silent Bob Strike Back (movie), 17
Journalism
   hybrid, 78
   traditional, 78
Jury theorem, 57

K

KDKA-AM, 72, 73
Kennedy, John F., 143
Khan Academy, 100
Kurzweil, Ray, 34

L

Law of accelerating returns, 32–33, 34
Law of decentralization, 19, 20
"Lean back" media. *See* Cool media
"Lean forward" media. *See* Hot media
Learning, 10
   affective, 92
   cognitive, 90–92
   distributed, 99–100
   extended, 105
   Facebook in classroom, 102–105

multimodal, 97
   social media and, 100–102
   social theory, 93–95
   through television, 88–89
   video games and, 95–98
Learning management systems, 99
Legend of Zelda, 96, 193
Les Miserables, 54
Lightweight technologies, harnessing, 28
Live news bulletin, 72
Live sporting event, 72
Logic, critical thinking, 62
Love and attachment, study of, 127

M

"Magic Bullet" paradigm on media effects, 203–205
Marketplace of ideas, 83
Maslow's hierarchy of needs, 42
"Mass amateurization of information," 78
Mass communication, 7
   channels of, 7
   vs. interpersonal communication, 7
   and message distribution, 9
Massive open online course (MOOC), 105
Mass media audience, 6
Mass media revolution, 65
Mass mediated communication, 6–7, 12–15
Masspersonal communication, 12, 14
Mass production, 6
"Matthew" effect, 91
Mean world effect, 213
Media, tool for communication, 31–44
Media as educators, 88
   affective learning, 92
   cognitive learning, 90–92
   distributed learning, 99–100

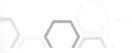